Tackling Single Parenting

From a Man's Point of View

by Steve Horner

BURGESS INTERNATIONAL GROUP INC
Minneapolis, Minnesota

Copyright © 1996 by Steve Horner

ISBN 0-9654086-0-4

Library of Congress Catalog Number: **96-96904**

All rights reserved. No part of this book may be reproduced in any form whatsoever, by photography or xerography or by any other means, by broadcast or transmission, by translation into any kind of language, nor by recording electronically or otherwise, without permission in writing from the publisher, except by a reviewer, who may quote brief passages in critical articles or reviews.

Printed in the United States of America.

J   I   H   G   F   E   D   C   B   A

BURGESS INTERNATIONAL GROUP, Inc.
7110 Ohms Lane
Edina, Minnesota 55439-2143

To Dedicated Parents Everywhere

Table of Contents

Acknowledgments . . . . *ix*
About the Author . . . . *xi*
Introduction . . . . *xiii*
Author's Note . . . . *xvii*

One DEDICATION COMES FIRST 1
In The Beginning 1
Tackling The Job 2
How Do You See Yourself As A Single Parent?. . . . 4
Dedication 5
Learning To Be Dedicated 8
Building Value Into Each Day 10
Getting Involved In The Community 11
Goal Setting 13
My Goal Of Independence 14
My Goal Of Getting My Children Involved 14
My Goal Of Teaching Love And Nurturing 15
Success Comes One Step At A Time. 17

Two EFFECTIVE COMMUNICATION. 19
Can We Talk?. 19
Putting The Techniques To Work 20
Effectively Handling Concerns. 21
Creating Open Dialogue 24
The Three Week Winning Call 26
Being Customer-Focused. 28
Back To The Three Week Winning Call. 29
Keeping The Communication Channels Open . . 31

Our Three Favorite Exploratory Questions..... 32
Defusing Anger........................ 33
Behavioral Styles...................... 38
Big Bear............................. 39
Party Animal......................... 39
Teacher............................. 40
Spock............................... 41
Practice, Practice, Practice.............. 45

Three COPING............................ 47
The Inevitable Struggle................ 47
The Power Of Prayer.................. 49
Finding The Inspiration To Move Forward..... 51
Surrendering To The Challenges
   Of Single Parenting................. 54
Support Is Essential................... 57
The Family Myth..................... 59
Support Groups...................... 64
Support Is Elusive.................... 68
Winning The Battle Of Stress Overload...... 71
The Obstacle Of Confusion.............. 76
Celebrate Success..................... 77

Four FAMILY FINANCES.................. 79
Money Can Be A Crippler.............. 79
Instilling A Sense Of Value Of Money
   In Children....................... 82
Keeping Your Money Out Of Other
   People's Pockets................... 85
The Damn Thing is Broken.............. 94
So, Let's Fix It....................... 96
I Don't Fall For The Guilt Trip Anymore...... 99
Advertising is Another Vacuum That
   Sucks Away Your Money............. 100
The Resulting Problem Is Debt........... 102
My In-House Management System......... 106
More In-House Management Tips.......... 111
Magic Formulas...................... 116

Five	CHILD CARE	117
	I Learned The Hard Way	117
	Hiring A Nanny	121
	How Not To Lose The Help Of A Family Member	123
	There Are Many Other Child Care Options Available	125
	More Options	128
	Change Is The Very Nature Of Child Care	130
Six	TEACHING DISCIPLINE: OBEDIENCE TO RULES	133
	Turn Out The Lights, The Party's Over	133
	The Four Elements Of Discipline	138
	Teaching Effective Discipline Begins At Home	141
	Building And Maintaining Discipline	143
	Consistency	144
	Firmness	145
	Anticipation	149
	Persuasion	153
	Punishment	155
	The Public Policies For Teaching Discipline Are Broken And Need To Be Fixed	158
	Corporal Punishment	159
	My Style Of Corporal Punishment	160
	The Problem Is Abuse	166
	Out Of Control Anger And Corporal Punishment Don't Mix	168
	Anger Control	171
	"Psychological Punishment"	173
	Fear	174
	Scorn	175
	Shame	178
	Fairness	181
	Convenience	186
Seven	BUILDING RESPONSIBILITY: BEING ACCOUNTABLE	193

TACKLING SINGLE PARENTING

I Heard It Through The Grapevine 193
The Problems Are Evident 194
A Higher Level Of Excellence 195
The Lessons Begin Early 200
Knowledge, Wisdom, And Sexuality 201
More About Gaining Knowledge And Wisdom . 208
Knowledge And Wisdom Build
   Reasoning Skills 212
Developing People Skills 215
Learning To Stand Tall 225
Integrity 226
Loyalty To Family 230
Loyalty To Friends 231
Loyalty To Country 231
Loyalty To God 231
Fairness 232
Honesty 235
Punctuality 238
Perseverance 241
Maintain Your Focus 247
In Conclusion 249

Eight   TIME TO EAT 251
I Made The Decision Not To Sentence My Kids
   To A Life Of Junk Food 251
Shopping For Groceries 252
Meal Preparation 254
Planning Ahead 256
What's On The Menu? 258

Nine   WHERE'S YOUR LEVEL OF HAPPINESS? . 265
The Best Things In Life Are Free, Aren't They? . 265
Beware Of Chicken Little 266
Where The Action Is 272
The Age Of Entitlement 277
Rise Up And Be Great 279
Where Did My Little Babies Go? 284
Where Wass Ya? 285

Acknowledgments

The author gratefully acknowledges those who provided candid, constructive feedback, editing, support and encouragement, and without whom this book wouldn't have been written: Gordy and Cel, Jack O., Paul, J.J., Joyce, Bill N., Jean, Dag, Steve S., Mike F., Patricia B., Mary T., Joan H., Tine, Steve C., Marc and Karen, Jules B., Ted S., Jack and Morrie.

About the Author

Steve Horner is a full-time, single parent of two teenage boys, their prime custodial parent since 1984. Horner was raised with five brothers in a traditional, two parent, Minneapolis family during the '50s and '60s. He served in the U.S. Army in Vietnam before attending college in Minnesota and California. He was in the broadcast industry for 15 years before starting his own marketing and communications business in 1986. Horner enjoys his work as an entrepreneur, writer, lecturer, and community volunteer, and participates in sports and outdoor activities. "My level of success isn't measured by the amount of money I make," Horner says, "but rather, the ability to pay my bills and take the time to do the things I enjoy most in life."

At the time of Horner's 1984 divorce less than 5 percent of all men involved in child custody suits were awarded physical custody; it's now closer to 20 percent. Horner is spending his single parent career in Apple Valley, Minnesota.

Introduction

Dear Reader...

Men are as different from women as one culture is from another. Communication experts, linguistic experts, and psychologists agree that these differences exist because of unique life experiences that are related to gender. Deborah Tannen, PH.D., the author of the best seller: *That's Not What I Meant,* said in her book, "culture is simply a network of habits and patterns gleaned from past experiences."

As young girls, many women played with dolls, playing "house" and "nurse." These socially interdependent roles encouraged nurturing and sensitivity to the feelings of others. As young boys, many men were encouraged to play with toy trucks, to build things, and to participate in competitive activities, such as "guns" and sports—games that are task and goal oriented, and that foster independence.

As men and women become parents they take their own, gender-unique experiences into parenthood with them. Both genders have specific behavioral styles, with their distinct parenting advantages and disadvantages. For example, many men are perceived as being too tough in the discipline department because of their task and goal orientation. On the other hand, many women are said to be too lax with discipline because of their sensitivity to the feelings of others. Men focus more on independence, while most women value interdependence. Most men are competitive in comparing themselves to others, whereas women typically care less about competition and more about cooperation.

TACKLING SINGLE PARENTING

John Gray, author of the best seller: *Men Are From Mars, Women Are From Venus,* said in his book, "Not only do men and women communicate differently but they think, feel, perceive, react, respond, love, need, and appreciate differently. They almost seem to be from different planets, speaking different languages and needing different nourishment."

Consequently, it would seem that the optimal child-rearing arrangement is for the parents of a two-parent family to understand each other's gender and behavioral style, and learn to maintain a "checks and balance" nurturing system. Unfortunately, in the nitty-gritty environment of single parenting, that's a difficult system to follow because of the absence of the opposite gender.

Contemporary teaching about single parenting has, for the most part, been unable to offer parents a gender-balanced, broad perspective of the parenting process. That's because most single parenting material has been written by women, offering readers the female perspective on the subject. There has also been material on single parenting written by male doctors and so-called male "experts" on the subject. In most cases, these authors haven't participated in the day in and day out challenges and difficulties to which only a full time single parent can relate. Many of their "expert" conclusions have been reached through textbook research and focus groups. It's similar to the battalion clerk telling the infantryman, "War is hell"—there's a lack of credibility. I bring the unique male perspective as one man who fully understands the meaning of being a full-time single parent.

Susan Reimer, a writer for the Baltimore News, wrote about the growing recognition of involving men in the parenting process in this excerpt from a December, 1995 story.

"There is an escalating demand for more involvement by men. It has gone beyond the "second shift" debate that insisted fathers share in the folding of the wash. We are now greeting these guys at the door and insisting that they nurture their children...and that they do it the right way. Our way.

"The cultural script for men is confusing," said Wade Horn, child psychologist and director of the National Fatherhood Initiative. "Studies that look at father and mother behavior show that men and women parent differently," Horn said.

"Fathers tend to be more physical, mothers more verbal. Fathers are more encouraging of independence and achievement, and mothers more encouraging of affiliation. Fathers tend to be strong disciplinarians, and mothers stronger nurturers. Knowing these differences we still say to men: Stop doing it differently and be more like mom."

Much of this message of, "Dear, you're doing it wrong," comes from a woman's need to control the child-rearing in the family. Though we want help, we want it done the way we have been doing it for generations.

The current welfare debate hinges on the notion that 30 years of the Great Society has rendered the father in our culture superfluous. We are finding out just how wrong we were. We mothers have to be willing to let them do it their way."

Tackling Single Parenting is not a cure-all to the thousands of difficulties and challenges involved with single parenting. It shows how one man, who has been a full-time single parent of two boys from their diaper days to their high school years, tackles the difficulties that affect his family. It's about bold, practical, thoughtful, and inspiring solutions from the front line trenches of single parenting. And as Jane Holleman, a writer for the Fort Worth Star-Telegram wrote in this July, 1995 excerpt, bold and practical solutions to the real problems of single parenting, seem to be rare.

"Oh, help! I'm laughing so hard that I think I might faint. The excerpt I'm reading from a new single parenting book on discipline is so funny. The excerpt isn't supposed to be hilarious. What makes it so funny is to picture yourself following even one of those parenting guidelines. For some of you out there...you direct descendants of Mary Poppins or Dale Evans...these virtuous notions might work. For most of us, however, the scenario is comedy writing at its best.

It offers some ideas on how to avoid having your kids spoil a trip to the grocery store. "If she gets out of control or embarrasses you, take her out of the store or to the restroom and talk to her quietly. Wait for her to calm down no matter how long it takes."

I'm confused. Is this discipline or quality time? Has rewarding your kid with your full attention replaced the good old time-out as a parenting method? Today you punish your kid by becoming her hostage in the bathroom? I thought parents owned the control. Guess I'm not an expert yet.

Parenting experts. I know they don't mean to be tongue-in-cheek. But down here in the mommy-daddy trenches, it sure sounds as if some of them are head-in-the-clouds."

Tackling Single Parenting is not a "head-in-the-clouds" guidebook. It's about solutions to the problems of single parenting that helped my family become more effective, productive, and content in today's complicated society. Some parents disagree with many of my parenting techniques. That's understandable. Parenting is as personal as your own name. Nevertheless, whether you agree or disagree with my parenting techniques and principles, they do provide viable options for all single parents to explore in their daily, individual efforts to tackle single parenting.

Author's Note

I don't pretend to have all the answers to raising children as a single parent, but I do know that my parenting techniques worked for me, and I'm convinced that you, too, can be successful using them.

For the most part, my parenting techniques are a departure from the invasive, ineffective parenting doctrines used and promoted in the world around us.

Steve Horner

Dedication Comes First

In The Beginning

I rushed through the front door of my home looking for my wife. Clothes and overcoats were scattered over the entryway floor next to the overturned hat tree. The mess was alarming because of the phone call I received from Joyce while at work about a half hour earlier. She and I had been married for nine years and had two sons: Paul was five, and J.J. (Joseph James) was two. I was the sales manager for an eight-station radio network in central and southern Minnesota. There were tears in Joyce's voice when she called the office. They were painful, angry, and frustrated tears. She told me that her divorce lawyer stopped by to tell her that I'd been granted physical custody of the boys. I asked her to try to stay calm and that I'd hurry right home.

I walked from the entryway, through the living room, and into the kitchen where there were thousands of bits and pieces of busted dishes on the floor and countertops. I called Joyce's name, and Paul answered from the upstairs bedroom. Joyce had a suitcase open on the bed and was throwing clothes in it. I greeted the boys and assured them that everything was going to be all right. I asked Joyce what was going on. "There's the court findings on the dresser. I'm packing my things and going to live with Kathy." Kathy and Bob were a young couple who had moved into the house next door, about eight months earlier. Now they, too, were divorcing. Bob had recently moved out and Kathy was living with her daughter, Paula, who was the same age as Paul. I opened the letter. "The Respondent shall have physical custody and residence which means routine daily care and control, and the resi-

TACKLING SINGLE PARENTING

dence of the children within the State. The Petitioner shall have liberal and reasonable visitation." It was the decision that I'd been fearful of not getting. But instead of celebrating, I stood there in disbelief that our marriage had come down to this. Ultimately, those words from the court have drastically changed my life, the life of my ex-wife, and that of our two boys.

Several months earlier, when Joyce first told me that she wanted a divorce, and after our subsequent conversations about the children, I said that I didn't intend to fight for custody. I had hoped we could agree to child support terms, and that Joyce would agree to stay in Minnesota with the kids, allowing the boys and me to see each other frequently.

That was not to be the case. Joyce soon demanded more money and told me she was going to take the kids to Arizona. The boys were born in Minnesota and had relatives here. I had a good job and didn't see the need to move. She was determined to leave the State with the kids, so I filed for custody, and won. As I've told people who asked: "We were both good parents. I was a good father, and she was a good mother, but I got the favorable decision. It was just how the wind was blowing that day." That was back in a time when less than 5 percent of the men who requested custody were actually granted it.

I looked up just as Joyce closed her suitcase. She walked to the front door, kissed the boys, and assured them that she'd be close by, and would see them soon. I was frantic. "What am I supposed to do with the kids? I'm expected back at work."

"That's your problem. You wanted the kids. Now you got 'em." And she walked out the door.

That was the first day of spring, March 21, 1984. It was also the first day of my new career as a single parent.

Tackling The Job

Most of us have heard people make statements like: "Today I'm going to tackle that messy garage," or, "I have to get busy and tackle that business proposal." The word "tackle" implies an undertaking that calls for determination. That's why it's a word that perfectly describes the attitude needed to successfully meet the challenges of single parenting in today's complicated and fast-paced society.

It doesn't matter whether single parenting results from an out-of-wedlock birth, from divorce, from adoption, or from death. The odds for success are stacked against most single parents right from the start. It's a tough job that holds very little glamour. It's also a job that can derail you, causing a collapse, because most people who try to tackle it have little or no training for the position, and not many people are there to help light the way.

Compare the training for parenthood to that for something relatively inconsequential, like professional baseball. Over the years, several neighborhood kids have told me, "I want to be a pro ball player when I grow up." If one of them really wants to be a pro, he'll soon find that talk is cheap, and hard work is what counts. If he progresses up through the ranks and makes it as a pro, he'll have learned many valuable lessons and skills that will allow him to fully appreciate his status. He'll do what's needed to maintain a professional level of excellence. Even then, with all his training and experience, he'll still be susceptible to drugs, crime, weariness, stress, illness, and any number of other problems. He can lose his focus, and take the big tumble.

Unlike the pro ball player, who had a predetermined goal, learned new skills, worked hard to reach his goal, and still had trouble maintaining his excellence, most parents have absolutely no problem reaching their goal of having a baby and becoming parents. Pregnancy can occur in a moment, and the parents may not have had a single hour of preparation for the challenging, life-long career they're about to undertake. The situation becomes even more cumbersome if only one of the parents is there to raise the child.

If the parent isn't prepared to tackle single parenting it can be a bad scene for the mother and her family, the father and his family, the child, and the whole society. In one way or another we're all impacted by the "big tumble."

I was not prepared for the challenges of single parenting. I've told friends that single parenting is more difficult than anything else with which I've had to deal. That includes a year as an infantryman in Vietnam. And it includes the murder of my best friend by two inner-city thugs while he was driving a taxi to earn spending money for Christmas. I've never experienced such loneliness while, at the same time, living such a hectic schedule.

TACKLING SINGLE PARENTING

How Do You See Yourself As A Single Parent?

One of the main reasons single parenting was such an uphill struggle for me at first was that I didn't fully comprehend what was involved, or what it meant to be a full-time parent. Wouldn't it be impossible to perform as a concert pianist or a major league ballplayer without understanding their functions? It's the same with parenting. It's a matter of self-image. When moms and dads don't have a mental image or understand what a full-time, nurturing parent is supposed to do and not do, then, it can be a difficult role to accept and ultimately be effective with the job.

Neil Tift, the director of the Father's Resource Center in Minneapolis, told me an eye-opening story about the time he addressed a group of 200 men and women who were gathered to discuss a subject other than parenting. He asked that they describe themselves with nouns, to use words like lawyer, little league coach, hard worker, thrifty investor, and so on. About 80 percent of the women included "mother" as a descriptor. About 85 percent of the women in attendance actually were mothers. The feedback from the men was quite a bit different. Only 6 percent of the men listed themselves as "fathers," even though close to 80 percent of them actually were.

The conclusion of this mini-survey seemed obvious. Many men who are fathers don't outwardly think of themselves as such. Maybe they don't think it's important, or maybe they don't take the job seriously. It's certainly not foremost on their minds. As a veteran, full-time single parent, I like to think that I'd have listed myself as a "father" had I participated in this survey, but I can't be sure. I do know that before I became a full-time single parent, the image I had of myself was much more as an athlete, cowboy, soldier, and businessman than as a father. While many of today's women were socialized as nurturer when they were young girls, many of today's dads—myself included—were brought up thinking that was women's work. We learned this from TV, movies, books, school, family, and peers. The girls took care of their younger siblings, and hired out as babysitters—things that most of us boys didn't do. It's because of such life experiences, that many more women than men can see themselves as parents.

When I tell another man that I'm a full-time single parent, and have been for several years, I hear, "Oh, good for you, that's really great." Then he quickly drops the subject. It's as if the job deserves praise, but, all-in-all, it's not very impressive work. It's similar to the guy who picks up trash along the highway. Most people are glad he's doing it, but don't heap a lot of respect on him for his efforts. However, when I and many other full-time single parents reveal our parenting status to a woman, the response is quite different. Most women respond with something like, "Oh, you poor thing," then they ask about the circumstances. Once again, due to life experiences, most women can relate to the difficult challenges of child rearing where most men can't.

Does the ability to relate to child rearing, by means of personal life experiences, automatically position women over men as more effective and productive single parents?

Certainly not! That would be the same as saying that most men are more effective and productive business professionals than women due to their personal life experiences. We know that's not true, evidenced by society's huge number of successful female professionals who are engaged in law-enforcement, politics, sales, administration, transportation, manufacturing, entertainment, medicine, engineering, education and just about any other profession you can imagine.

Many of today's high-powered female executives were encouraged to take on the role of nurturer as youngsters, and have had to work hard to learn the competitive nature of business to succeed. As a man who was raised with little or no emphasis on nurturing children, I've had to work hard to be an effective and productive parent to raise my children without a spouse. Even though I have many, trusty parental instincts, and strong management skills, my parenting proficiency has been mostly learned. It's the result of trial and error, research, personal observations, and, above all, dedication.

Dedication

The common denominator to achieving anything worthwhile is dedication. It means to give oneself up wholly to a person or to a goal.

TACKLING SINGLE PARENTING

It's like traveling cross-country in your car. As long as you stay on course, keep the car properly maintained, and have plenty of fuel, you'll be just fine. But the moment you miss your turn, ignore mechanical maintenance, or run out of gas, you have troubles.

For single parents, dedication calls for even greater strength, because unlike many two-parent families, the sole responsibility for income is up to just one person. There are the demands of raising children alone in a complicated society, and the grueling task of juggling home and work duties. Then, when everything else is taken care of, there isn't much time or energy left for your own social life.

There are all sorts of social barometers, such as the high juvenile crime rate, drug abuse, teen-age pregnancies, and serious discipline problems in schools to indicate that dedication to parenting, in general, isn't where it should be for a healthy society to exist. 1996 presidential candidate, Alan Keyes, didn't pull any punches in placing the blame squarely on single parents.

According to Republican party research, Keyes was the first African American in the nation's history to seek that party's endorsement. He was quite blunt with his audiences; "It turns out we don't have many problems in America. We have one problem that has many very expensive, very tragic consequences. The marriage-based, two-parent family is eroding and the result—single parenting—is a disaster for this entire society."

As the ratio of single parent families to two-parent families increases, and more blame for society's woes is directed at single parents, the need for dedication from single parents increases. But that's a hard story to sell.

In 1993 I was a candidate for my local school board, in Minnesota's fourth largest and fastest growing district. I told parents at the open forums that the problem in the schools was with the parents. "The parents aren't taking the necessary time to nurture the kids at home and are sending them off to school unprepared to learn." You might have guessed that this wasn't an award-winning platform on which to run, and that I lost the election. The parents rebuked me because they knew my policies would infringe on their time, and nobody seemed to care about the long-range benefits of my program. One woman stood up at one of the public forums and said angrily,

"Mr. Horner, as a single parent, I already have my hands full. How am I supposed to do any more than I already am?" I'd been allotted only one minute to respond. I told her I was simply reporting to the voters what I'd been hearing from the district superintendent and the local teacher unions: "The schools have to stop being babysitters. The parents have to start being more responsible and dedicated."

Have I been a perfect parent? No. Have I lacked dedication? Yes. I know there have been plenty of "what-ifs" and "wish-I-hads" with my single parenting. I, like most other people, have tried to learn from my mistakes.

One incident stands out as a memorable lesson in dedication. I was just a few months into my single parenting career, trying to sleep late on a Saturday morning. My five-year-old son, Paul, came charging into the bedroom. "Dad! J.J. has the messiest poop I've ever seen, and it's all over everything." I ran to the living room and became frantic when I saw the "poop" smeared on the carpet and all over my two-year-old. As I was cleaning up the mess that morning I realized how drastically my life had changed. To keep things running smoothly there wasn't going to be any more sleeping in. I needed to hit the ground running every day. I needed to be more dedicated if I was going to tackle the challenges of single parenting.

Dedication is one of those intangible qualities that you need to acquire on the road to excellence. If you want to put forth the effort, you'll get results. Unfortunately, we're all caught up in a society of quick turnaround and instant gratification. Dedication is one of those things where it takes time to see the results.

The results of your dedication can be richly rewarding, as J.J. discovered during the summer he was 13. He'd been playing soccer since kindergarten and up until that summer had been a mediocre player. It was frustrating for him because he loved the game. Finally, after yet another game without scoring a goal, I told him to ride his bike to the library and take out some books on soccer. Reluctantly, he rode off.

He returned two hours later with three books on soccer and a big smile. For the next couple of weeks, J.J. read the books, practiced kicking and passing techniques, and learned many new strategies to the game. Two games later, he scored his first goal. He scored his second goal on the last game of the season. The following spring J.J. practiced his drills every chance he had, and when the season began, he was ready. He scored at least once in each of his 14 games and twice had hat tricks of three goals each. J.J. was dedicated to improving his game and he was rewarded by better performance, which thrilled him and brought praise from his teammates. Both rewards returned extra value because they also helped him build his self-esteem, a crucial quality in anybody's life.

Learning To Be Dedicated

How does one acquire dedication? Is it something with which we are born, or something we learn? When I returned from Vietnam I thought I had trouble concentrating, so I went to an Army psychiatrist. He gave me some tests, and then chewed me out. "The problem," he said, "is that concentration takes hard work and lots of practice, and you haven't put forth the effort." Then he chased me out of his office and told me to work on it. At first, I was upset with this man, but then I took his advice and started to become much better at concentrating when I needed to accomplish a task. Dedication is like that. If you want to learn it, you need to practice. Not surprisingly, many people wonder if it's really that easy.

While discussing the topic of parental dedication with my friend, Jean, who's also a single parent, she said that she had learned a lot from me since we had known each other. She likes the way I'm able to pick myself up after both minor and major setbacks, and trudge on forward. She told me that she has learned from my child disciplining methods, and that she uses some of my money management techniques. However, there are a few things about me that frustrate her. "You always have a solution for everything" she said, "and life isn't that simple. There's the human element to single parenting. There's not a spouse for positive feedback, and there's not much appreciation shown for your efforts from your children, especially if they're young." She let me know in no uncertain terms: "Single parenting can be very scary and stressful when you realize there's nobody else to rely on for your family's well-being. Solutions aren't always as cut and dried as you make them out to be." This is an area of single parenting where gender, personalities, and life experiences come into play. I tend to be more "big picture" and results-oriented, and Jean focuses more on people and feelings. Neither one of us is wrong, we just have different approaches.

I told Jean that my approach to single parenting isn't about anguish and failure, blood and guts, drug abuse, hopelessness, heartache, crime, and conflicts, like a lot of the popular sentiment about the subject. Instead, it's about tackling the difficult problems and challenges of single parenting and, through a lot of hard work, finding ways to succeed. My approach is to find solutions to my single parenting problems; many of which have worked for my two boys and me. My procedures are not universal cure-alls. That's because each single parent's situation is different. Nevertheless, my solutions do offer every single parent some viable options worth exploring.

I understand what Jean said about single parenting being scary and stressful. I've lost a couple of jobs while I've been alone with my boys. There have been many months where I didn't know from where the mortgage payment was going to come. I was in my bathroom one morning, sitting on the stool with the flu so bad that I didn't know which end I'd explode from first. In the meantime, both my kids were vomiting in their bedrooms. I had pressing business demands and no groceries in the house. "I've felt so burdened with schedules, loneliness, and despair," I told Jean, "that one time, while on the way to a Cub Scout meeting with my son, I started choking up as if I was going to cry. I almost got downright emotional about the whole thing."

"Just once?" Jean shouted, "I have a good cry almost once a week."

That's the point I'm making. People are different and react differently to the challenges of single parenting. I have my good days, and I have my bad days. Either way, I just keep marching on. As far as I'm concerned, the alternative is to go backwards, or fall into a survivalist attitude. I decided a long time ago, right after my divorce, that I was going to be aggressive and keep progressing with my life. There are always the times when I have to take a couple of steps backward, but when that happens, I try to compensate by taking three steps forward. Some of the techniques that help me move forward I learned from my 25 years in business.

TACKLING SINGLE PARENTING

Building Value Into Each Day

I've noticed that the vast majority of highly successful business people with whom I've had dealings are upbeat, positive thinkers. I've tried to follow their lead. I've found that I perform at my best when I'm upbeat and positive. Most of those people have their own ways of maintaining their optimism. One method I learned from the owner and president of a hugely successful international company is something I practice every morning when I wake up. I thank God for another great day, and I tell myself that it's going to be the best day ever. This little morning ritual isn't always easy to do.

Sometimes it's easier to just lie in bed and feel sorry for myself. But once it's said, I'm off like a rocket to having another great day.

Here's one example that shows the importance of valuing each day. Say you're shopping from gallery to gallery for the "just right" painting for your living room wall; all of a sudden, something catches your eye. Unfortunately, the price tag discourages you. The gallery owner walks over and describes the marvelous history behind the artist of the painting. You're fascinated, and, instantly, your personal value of the painting soars, almost to the point where the price becomes irrelevant. Appreciating the value of each day is similar; if I can truly appreciate the value of each day, then I become a happier person and a more dedicated single parent. The question is: How can parents grow to more fully appreciate the value of each day? Highly successful business people do it by getting involved with their community. A business friend of mine provides a good example.

Doug is the president of a national association with over 300 member companies. Over the years, Doug and a group of other business people have organized an annual Christmas project where they pool funds, compile a shopping list, and distribute goods to families in need. One Christmas, when my kids were eight and eleven, Doug asked whether we wanted to get involved. I had done this kind of work when I was married, and it had always uplifted me. I saw this as an opportunity to open the eyes of my boys to the "real world," and help them feel the accomplishment and satisfaction that I've enjoyed.

We had a great night. It was cold and snowy, and I remember the look of determination the boys had on their faces as we pulled up to each address and unloaded the bags, bringing them up to the door. Most of our "customers" were single moms with young kids, and they all seemed really grateful. Each stop taught us the same lesson, which is still a part of our lives: no matter how bad we think we have it, we have a lot to be thankful for. It's an effective motto for building value into each and every day. This event not only turned into a Christmas present for the three of us, but it was also a terrific way of fending off the single parent blues and the "poor me" attitude that strikes so many single parents around the holiday season.

Teaching the power of community involvement is a popular lesson around our home. I tell my boys that community involvement helps people appreciate the value of each day so they can truly believe that each day is special. It's a philosophy which helps me stay upbeat about life.

Getting Involved In The Community

As a single parent, I especially need to be upbeat so that I can keep performing at my peak level. Being purposefully involved in one's community is an age-old activity that has served me well. "Unfortunately," I've told my boys, "it's generally seen as being on the decline." Our deacon clarified that idea before the congregation one Sunday. Deacon Chuck laid it on the line: "There are over 2,700 families registered at this church, and less than a third of them lend any financial support. Fewer still offer any time or effort to any of the dozens of ministries available, and even fewer get involved with the ministries that require long-term devotion, such as serving as religious education teachers. Yet, most of the 2,700 families demand that their church be there when they need it, and complain when it falls short."

I've pointed out to my sons that this is a popular attitude: "It's the same shortage of esprit de corps people show for their government, obvious by the growing hands-out mode of social programs, low caucus and voter turnout, and poor local government involvement by its citizens." It's the opposite of dedication.

Just think about it. How often do you hear people say they're much happier for not getting involved? Not often. On the other hand, I hear monthly at least one person say how fulfilled he or she is for being involved. During a business luncheon, I had a lengthy conversation with a 15-year veteran of active, community involvement. He told me that his work is rewarding for his system. "It gets me on cloud nine and lets me know I've struck a blow for freedom."

I'm trying to show my kids good examples of getting involved. Oftentimes, when I see people spout off in the editorial pages about government not doing enough for them, I try to get them on the phone to question them and ask what they do to help their community work out the kinks. Invariably, they have a hard time understanding what I'm talking about, so I clarify, "You know, stuff like helping your church, visiting the old folks, working with inner-city youth, coaching sports, cleaning up the parks, attending city and school board meetings, you know, stuff like that." Some of them hang up immediately. Some of them stumble around and ask: "Well, what do you do?" After I report my family's community involvement, then they, too, hang up. Others remain on the phone with me, and we exchange our goals, needs, and concerns in a productive manner. It's activities like this that might make some people say that I'm judgmental, and critical of others. I believe it's a way of staying involved, keeping a pulse on society, helping to change the social climate, and forming objective opinions. Even my kids think I get kind of wacky sometimes, but I believe they'll grow to see the merits of my efforts. I think my involvement makes me a more progressive and informed citizen, and that, in turn, helps to make me a more dedicated single parent.

Community involvement helps people become wiser, improving their judgment in the matters that affect them and their all-important families. That, I've told my children, is why wisdom is much more valuable than material wealth. It strengthens the family. Getting involved and gaining wisdom has helped me become a stronger, happier, more productive single parent. Here's how: have you ever been sitting around a group of people when everybody seems to be tuned into a particular subject, except you? How did it make you feel? It makes me feel awkward, dumb, and insecure. However, when I'm versed about a subject, I feel strong, smart, and confident.

After my best friend was murdered while driving a taxi, I decided that a positive approach towards self-healing was to get involved by attending cultural diversity meetings. I saw and heard first-hand what I perceived to be facts, myths, and theories about the major hurdles to reaching a peaceful, productive, multi-cultural coexistence in society. I heard the concerns of others, and I was able to voice my own concerns. I didn't have to rely on the biases of special interest groups, or the narrow-focus journalism of a media reporter to get the story. As a result of those meetings I formed objective opinions. Now, when the topic comes up, I can speak from experience and with the wisdom that confers authority and confidence, and that forms the cornerstone of a positive self-esteem. And, it's that self-esteem that helps me be a more dedicated single parent. Here's another way of being a strong and dedicated single parent.

Goal Setting

I've known a lot of single parents who lack inspiration. They don't get involved with community projects, they have few hobbies, and either they plant themselves in front of the TV or frequent a single's bar. They're unmotivated.

Motivation is an essential element of single parenting because it creates desire.

So, how do they get motivated?

Through my business and social dealings I've discovered that goal-setting helps build motivation. When I reach a goal, I benefit from the reward that the goal holds for me. The reward might be money, peace of mind, pride, or wisdom, among other returns. There are both long and short-term goals. Many runners, for instance, have long-term goals of running and finishing in a marathon, but once they're in it, they might have short-term goals of five miles, or so. The alcoholic person tries to stay dry one day at a time. By reaching their short-term goals the runner and alcoholic benefit from pride of achievement and therefore discover and reinforce the motivation and burning desire to reach their long-term goals. If they don't set up short-term goals, the long-term goals can seem overwhelming, and the whole project can get dumped.

Have you ever considered short and long-term goals for your single parenting? Let's face it, like a business, dedicated single parenting requires an enormous amount of time, energy, and money. It could serve you well to look at single parenting as an investment where you can expect positive returns for your efforts instead of "out the window" expenses, where you can't. Positive returns are rewards for reaching your goals—rewards that are motivational and that create desire. You might find that defining long-term goals and rewards of single parenting isn't as easy as it sounds—at least it wasn't for me. Over time, however, I've been able to pinpoint a few.

My Goal Of Independence

I want my kids to continue learning how to be independent. My reward is that after all these years of dedicated single parenting, I won't have them knocking on my door when they're 25, looking for a place to live. They'll be able to succeed on their own.

Just like the runner and the alcoholic strive to reach short term goals on the way to meeting their long term goals, dedicated single parents also have to reach short-term goals. If I want my kids to learn independence, it's up to me to give them the experiences that will foster independence. Even though it might be less of a hassle for the moment to simply spell out a word when my boy asks for homework help, it'll better serve my goal of teaching him independence if he looks it up in the dictionary. He doesn't always want to, and oftentimes I have to double-check that he has in fact made the effort to look it up. Nevertheless, reaching the long-term goal of my boy's independence is worth the extra time and persistence to make sure he's successful. Every time my kids and I overcome an obstacle to our long-term goals, we build pride in ourselves. Pride is a worthwhile and enjoyable reward to have earned.

My Goal Of Getting My Children Involved

A second long-term parenting goal of mine is for my boys to continue to learn about and enjoy business and community involvement. My reward is the pride I feel from their accomplishments and involvement.

Encouraging my kids to be active in school, community issues, and events, not only rewards me with pride, it also helps my boys build their own self-esteem and wisdom. By arming them with opinions, experience, and information, they can make better informed decisions, gain a sense of community pride, and prioritize their life pursuits by learning what's important to them and what isn't.

You might remember the single parent who stood up in the candidates' forum and sternly asked me where she was to find the time to get more involved with her children's schoolwork. I can't help but wonder whether her priorities were in order. How much time did her kids spend in front of the TV, and how late did they go to bed on school nights? I wonder how much time they spent at the mall hanging out rather than reading at home. I wonder how nutritious their meals were and how much time they spent as a family talking about each other's goals, needs, and concerns. I wonder what she found so important that it caused her to ignore short-term goals and, therefore, sacrifice the long-term goals.

Naturally, the suspicions I have about that person are based only on conjecture and national trends. She deserves a lot of credit for coming to the candidates' forum to learn about the issues. The point I'm making is that my boys and I have tried to keep our priorities in focus so we can reach our goals. A fancy paint job on a person's car won't get him or her anywhere if the tank is empty. Priorities have to make sense to successfully tackle this business of single parenting.

My Goal Of Teaching Love And Nurturing

A third long-term goal is for my children to continue growing to be loving and nurturing. My reward is the personal peace and happiness of knowing that my kids will be loving and nurturing to their own families, society, and me. J.J. is a natural in this department.

When J.J. was nine or ten, I asked him his secret for having so many friends. He told me, "It's because I respect them." Wow! What words to live by. Wouldn't it be a better world if we all followed that simple little rule? Respect other people by showing appreciation for their time, their talent, and their opinions. J.J.'s thoughtfulness rewarded him with lots of friends and rewarded me with compliments. There was the time I was in an office doing business: after I introduced myself, a woman stepped forward and asked if I were J.J.'s dad. She told me what a wonderful boy he was and how he always treated her "slow to learn" daughter so politely, while the other kids often made fun of her child. I thanked her and told her how proud that made me feel. That pride is a reward for reaching some of my short-term goals.

I can't rightfully claim credit for J.J.'s leadership qualities. I do know that my boys and I have always discussed feelings, good and bad, with no reservations. When J.J. was six years old, I saw him standing alone near a tree while several other children played actively around him. Later, I asked him what he had been thinking about. He wasn't quite sure, only that he "was just over there thinking." My first impulse was to tell him to get involved with the other kids. Instead, I made this a positive lesson for him. I told J.J., "A lot of kids are thinkers. They like to reflect on life and the things that go on around them. It's good to take time to do that." He felt comfortable with that image of himself and often, years later, I'd see J.J. climbing the tree in our back yard, leaning back on a limb and gazing at the sky in a very relaxed mood. If you ask me, that's an enviable state of mind. Helping my children feel good about themselves helps me reach my goal of raising loving and nurturing kids.

Another important ingredient to helping kids become loving and nurturing is sensitizing them to the feelings of others. When I first became a single parent in 1984, my 74-year-old mother told me that I had to be a "nurturer." I asked her what she meant by that, and I'm still not quite sure what her answer was. I think it had something to do with "being a woman and the love that only a mother has for her children." That gender stereotype bothered me. Finally, I looked up the word "nurture" in the dictionary. It means to give nourishment, to feed, rear, train. "What the hell do you think I've been doing?" I thought. "No news here."

Over the years I've come to realize that somewhere buried in the dictionary definition of the word "nurturing" is the word "sensitive." It means to be responsive to the senses—your own senses, and the senses of others. It has a lot to do with feelings. Being sensitive is an admirable quality, and I've tried to encourage my boys to be sensitive to the feelings of others. It begins by giving the child opportunities to be sensitive, and then complimenting him when he succeeds.

When Paul was just three or four, he enjoyed playing with dolls and stuffed animals. An older relative told him he was a sissy for playing with dolls. Later, I told that person not to say that to Paul because I had been encouraging him to play with his "guys" whenever he wanted. I told Paul that I thought it was cool that he did so. Even when Paul was ten or eleven, and getting ready for a sleepover at a friend's home, he would pack at least three of his "guys" to take along for company. I asked him if any of his friends made fun of him and he told me they didn't. Once again, I told him I thought it was cool.

When Paul was eight, his younger cousin went through a biting stage. Sometimes he would bite Paul so hard that it would make him cry. I'd get peeved because the mother never intervened. I asked Paul if he ever felt like hitting this kid to make him back off, and he said he had but that "he's much smaller than me." I told him, "I think you're quite a hero, have a lot of patience, and I'm proud of you."

We all know that there are plenty of opportunities to find fault with children, and my kids are no exception. However, accentuating the positive helps children define short-term goals of being loving and nurturing while they're on their way to meeting their long-term goals as loving and nurturing adults. Searching for opportunities to praise my boys' commendable behavior has helped them build positive standards from which to grow. It has created a reservoir of positive experiences that my children can reflect upon for strength and help them build strong self images.

Paul knew that I thought his association with his "guys" was not only acceptable, but admirable as well, because I told him so. I didn't leave it unspoken. He also knew that the patience he displayed with his biting cousin was admirable because I told him so. I didn't leave that unspoken, either. Those are ways that I use to meet my goal of helping my children learn to be loving and nurturing.

Success Comes One Step At A Time

I've had to learn to be dedicated to successfully tackle the challenges of single parenting. I've overcome the challenges one step at a time. When I first became a full-time single parent my youngest was still in diapers. People told me how much tougher life would get when they started school. I thought, "They must be crazy. I won't be changing diapers then." When they started school there were people who said, "Wait until they're in high school—then your troubles will start." I thought, "They must be crazy. I'll have much more freedom for myself then, instead of being confined to the house watching kids."

When interviewed on the radio about single parenting, I told the host that there are many times when I feel frazzled and at the end of my rope. There are many other times when I feel as though I'm semi-retired, enjoying life, and that single parenting keeps getting better and better.

Every day I try to stay dedicated and keep my priorities in order so I can reach my goals. When I'm strong and feel good about myself, then I can find the desire to help my children grow and develop in positive ways. When I feel strong, I can get involved with my children's schoolwork and extracurricular activities. By taking the time to get involved I can instill the values in my boys that will help them prosper through life—financially, mentally, spiritually, morally, and physically. When I stay on course, life is much more fulfilling and rewarding for my kids and me. When I stray off course, we don't do as well. Getting involved with my children is what successful single parenting is all about. Being dedicated helps me get the job done.

I know a lot of parents who have done an exceptionally fine job of raising their children. When I've complimented them for their efforts, many have humbly said, "I had nothing to do with it. I give all the credit to my kid." These parents are being much too modest by not accepting the child rearing honors that are due them. Dedicated parents deserve a huge amount of credit for the success of their children.

Professional golfing great Chi Chi Rodriguez, who was raised in grinding poverty in Puerto Rico, said something during an interview with which I agree and have not forgotten: "Behind every kid there's an adult." That includes the kids who do well, and the kids who don't. One of my long-term goals is to continue to be proud enough to say that I'm the adult behind my kids. Being dedicated to them is helping me reach that goal.

Effective Communication

Can We Talk?

The marvelous power to exchange thoughts with each other is a human characteristic that shapes national and international political policy, merges corporate giants, and develops profound theological theories. Yet, very few of us have had any formal one-on-one communication skills training. We've had years of language courses in school. Some of us have had sales classes, and others have studied debate and public speaking. But, when it comes to being able to express and understand each other's personal goals, needs and concerns, many of us still fall short.

Single parents need effective communication skills for many of the same reasons as anybody else: to effectively interact with friends, siblings, our own parents, ex-spouses, business acquaintances, and people with whom we deal daily. Oftentimes, however, the biggest communication problem single parents face comes with our own children. The traditional two-parent family consists of a man and a woman. Each one has particular gender-related experiences in life. They're treated differently by others, and they enjoy doing different things. It's as if men and women are from different cultures. The man in a traditional family portrays life to his offspring from his perspective. The woman in a traditional family portrays life to her offspring from her perspective. Therefore, their offspring get a look at life from both a man's and a woman's point of view.

How does a single parent, who can only perceive life from his or her own life experiences and unique behavioral patterns, be a well-rounded communicator within the family? For my family, the answer lies in utilizing communication skills that effective business people use on the job.

Single parents who learn to use effective communication skills with their children help each family member recognize the goals, needs, and concerns of the other members. They help to develop understanding, harmony, and satisfaction. Ineffective communication in a family blocks this knowledge and is like a house with a leaky roof. The slow decay might be out of sight for years, but eventually, the extent of the huge damage surfaces. Instead of rotten wood, families experience frustration, anger, and resentment.

W. Edwards Demming, who died at the age of 93 in 1993, was the man who embraced corporate "quality" before that concept was noteworthy. He was trained as a statistician and helped revolutionize Japanese manufacturing with his gospel of Quality Control—a philosophy that was virtually ignored in his native United States until the late 1970s. Demming and his teachings live on as the supreme truth of quality/management experts.

Demming taught that "quality is a philosophy, not a lesson." In business, quality is a way of performing. It organizes people with different backgrounds to achieve common goals. Improving quality mainly focuses on communication skills—effective communication is the common thread.

Putting The Techniques To Work

Throughout the work day, successful business people cross gender, economic, and age lines to learn the goals, needs, and concerns of others. They must know how to effectively handle objections and anger, find solutions, listen well, and motivate others to take action. These are challenges for the everyday business person as well as for the dedicated single parent. Learning a few professional skills and putting them to work in your family will make you more productive and effective in tackling single parenting.

Effectively Handling Concerns

Every now and then single parents need to help their children through periods of grief. Let me describe a solid communication technique that has carried me over the rough spots.

My boys have flown from Minneapolis to Phoenix and back again twice a year since J.J. was four and Paul, seven. They'd spend a few weeks in Arizona during the summer and a week to 10 days during the Christmas break. Flying there was always a super joyous occasion for them because they were understandably tired of me and looking forward to seeing their mom.

A particularly hard time for all of us was after they returned home from the Christmas visit. The first couple of nights back were the toughest. When I tucked them in at bedtime both the boys would sob so hard, longing for their mommy, that it would bring tears to my eyes. I felt really bad for them. This was a deep hurt that was real and wasn't going to go away by pretending it didn't exist. These boys were expressing their opposition to the situation—in the business world, you'd call that an objection. An objection is an expression of disapproval. It's not to be taken personally, but rather looked upon as an opportunity to discover the main cause for someone's concern.

The first step was to build a friendly rapport by assuring my boys that everything would turn out okay. I remember the power of positive assurance from my Army training. Even though the wound might be life-threatening, you want to tell the person that "everything will be okay." Even if you're not positive that you can deliver on your promise, the assurance will add confidence, which adds strength, and that's the tonic you seek.

Human Relations experts say the next step is to empathize with the person. Let them know you understand their disapproval. In this case I told the boys, "I know how sad you must feel not being with your mom. I know I would've felt bad if I had to leave my mom when I was your age." This allowed the boys to know they were not alone with their sadness. It's like the old saying, "misery loves company." It's true. It's a way of showing support and assuring them I'm on their side. This process opens doors and lets the communication continue and the healing begin.

Throughout the conversation, it's important to match the tone of your voice with that of the other person. If his voice tone is slight and soft, then yours should be the same. If his voice tone rises and gets louder, then so should yours. Matching voice tone helps build the comfort level and is another method of helping the words flow.

The objective is to build dialogue so the child can say in words what is hurting inside, a possibly difficult task for youngsters due to their limited vocabulary. Lead-in questions called "Teasers" help. "What did you and your mom talk about on the way to the airport?" Teasers help get the feelings out on the table and once they're out they don't seem so burdensome.

Another approach might be to focus on positive thoughts and ask questions like: "What did you and your mom do during your vacation that you thought was really special?" When you begin to get feedback, be a good listener and ask questions pertinent to what's being said. When my child tells a story, I ask him to pause so I can compliment him on his speaking. Questions and compliments encourage and help stimulate more dialogue. Even if I've heard the story before, I try to keep an interested look on my face and sit in a relaxed manner so I don't appear impatient. A loving arm upon his shoulders can be reassuring.

After some time and conversation, the true concern would surface. "It's just going to be so hard to wait seven months to see my mom again." That's it! That's the concern for which I was digging. Before the solutions start rolling out, it's a good idea to get agreement about the main concern.

"So, it's the long period of time between now and then that has you worried, huh?" If the answer is "yes," then you can start looking for solutions. If the answer is "no," then you need to ask more questions to uncover the main concern.

Now that we know the main cause of concern there needs to be a solution. A helpful solution to a case like this has two main ingredients: reassurance and security. "The time will go by really fast, and in the meantime you'll be talking to your mom on the phone. As a matter of fact, we'll call her tomorrow. How does that sound?" If you get an agreement that this solution will work, then you've gone about as far as you can for the time being. If you don't get agreement, then you'll have to try another solution, or take a step back to probe again for the cause of concern. Times like these can be pretty gloomy, but if you can keep the conversation flowing, and keep searching for a glimmer of hope, it's about all you can ask for. At least you'll know what the big tears and sadness are all about. In that particular case, my boys agreed that we had found a solution and were satisfied enough to kiss me goodnight, roll over, and go to sleep. The next day they were back to smiles and playing with their friends.

Effective communication means understanding that we often think we know a person's main cause of concern, when in fact we don't. The boys' concern could've been much more serious than loneliness. Maybe something happened during the break that has scared them, or maybe they don't want to live with me any longer. I've learned not to assume I know why my kids are concerned or worried until I have applied these communication steps:

1. *Seek a friendly rapport with the assurance that everything will work out okay*
2. *Show empathy*
3. *Probe for the cause of the concern, using teasers if needed*
4. *Get agreement about the main concern*
5. *Present a solution*
6. *Agree that the solution will work.*

These steps really worked for me and I continue to use them whenever I'm searching for a concern. Compare this step-by-step communication procedure to what's probably a more typical, quick-fix exchange:

Parent to sobbing child: "What's the matter, honey?"

Child: "Oh, nothing."

Parent, assuming that the problem is loneliness, but it goes unspoken: "Well, don't worry, everything will be all right. Now try to go to sleep."

Remember, an objection needs to be looked at as an opportunity to uncover concerns. In this quick-fix exchange, there was a huge opportunity to learn the concerns of the child and build a stronger base of communication for the future. Opportunity presented itself, but was ignored.

Creating Open Dialogue

Besides having a limited vocabulary to help express their innermost thoughts, young children are faced with another handicap. They simply haven't had enough different experiences in their lives for them to evaluate standards. Therefore, it's a good idea to create ways that help kids articulate their goals, needs, and concerns.

Since there weren't any books on divorce that were actually written by its young victims—the kids—my boys and I decided to try writing one, but it proved to be too challenging with my children so young. The book didn't get finished but I gained a huge amount of information from my boys while piecing together an outline.

Paul came up with the title. Actually, it was something he told me soon after the divorce, and it stuck with me: "I Wish Divorce Had Never Been Invented."

We laid out chapter titles and some subjects that could be covered. By asking questions, listening, and taking notes, I heard novel concerns from my children, that I, as an adult, had overlooked or couldn't relate to.

Here's the list of my boys' concerns regarding divorce.

1. *We miss our friends and relatives when we go away to visit my mom and then miss other friends and relatives when we come back again.*
2. *We have different rules to obey with dad than with mom.*
3. *"Why is this happening to me?"*
4. *Dealing with grandparents, stepparents, stepbrothers and sisters; confusing!*
5. *Comparing mom's cooking to dad's.*
6. *Sometimes it's kind of embarrassing telling my friends my parents are divorced.*
7. *It's impossible to have a pet at my dad's house because he's really busy. My mom has a dog that I love and I miss him a lot.*

8. My dad takes us to church and has gotten us involved at church. I think it has been good for us. Mom does not believe church is as important as dad does.
9. There are things we miss out on when we are at mom's and when we are at dad's: family get-togethers, family portraits, vacations. It makes me feel like I'm missing out.

I also heard some good stories that I hadn't heard before.

My kids told me about the time Paul had a nosebleed on the airplane while the two of them were on their way to visit their mom. First, the flight attendant gave him a cold compress and told him to lean his head back. Then the person sitting in front told him to pinch his nose tightly with his fingers. Then the person next to him said to use a warm compress and lean forward, while the person behind them suggested leaning back and tuck a wad of cloth under his upper lip. Obviously, these people were genuinely concerned for Paul's welfare but he said the situation got pretty funny with everyone falling over each other offering their own homespun cure, convinced that their's was the right one.

I love that story and it's especially meaningful because I used to get nosebleeds as a youngster. It's also a story, just like dozens of others, good and bad, sad and funny, that I might not have heard had it not been for the book and probing for material.

There are lots of other ways to facilitate communication besides writing a book: working on projects together, playing games, taking walks—and I'm always amazed at the revelations I hear around the supper table. I get updates on school, work, play, and life in general. It's tempting to "zone out" in front of the TV during supper because that doesn't take any effort; it also offers few rewards. Eating and talking together in the dining room is usually more fun, informative, and simply more productive. It takes more effort than zoning out, but it's worth it because you share each other's goals, needs, and concerns.

Eating supper together at home with the TV off is one of our priority functions toward building strong family bonds. I didn't realize how significant it was until Paul turned 16 and got a job at the local grocery store. He loved the work and the pay was good, but, unfortunately, the after-school hours meant sacrificing many suppers together as a family. I discovered that there were thoughts and discussions that went unspoken, so I tried to persuade him to cut back on his hours. I felt that the extra money and work experience that Paul would gain were no substitute for what we were missing as a family.

Here's another way to build communication skills that has been fun and rewarding for us. Do you remember hearing your voice on a tape recorder for the first time? You probably weren't very happy with it. That's because you weren't used to hearing your voice on a machine, and could've been embarrassed by what you heard.

I've taped my boys since the day they were born. I have their shrieks, first words, nursery rhymes, school songs, thoughts about issues, and so on. It's not only a thrill for us to listen to these old tapes years later, while sitting at home or traveling in the car, but it also gave my boys a chance to evaluate the things they said and how they said them. I often heard them correct the negative and accentuate the positive. It helped them improve their speech pattern—an important part of effective communication. Understandable speech helps my boys excel in day-to-day living, and in later years will help them succeed in business by being more articulate.

The Three Week Winning Call

Effective communication that helps us learn each other's goals, needs, and concerns comes in many forms. I used to work for Jack Lynch, a man who had a knack for spotting a grievance in an employee. Occasionally, I would be upset about an issue at work but would keep it to myself. Jack would spot my dissatisfaction and open with something like, "How's it going? Do you want to have lunch one of these days?" During lunch Jack would probe with teasers until I finally told him what was on my mind.

This was a terrific, proactive communication technique that encouraged Jack's employees to vent their concerns. Small grievances were addressed before they became big problems.

I know of a communications expert who works with front-line employees of several Fortune 500 companies. He has coined the term, THREE WEEK WINNING CALL , for a communication technique that serves customers similar to Jack's taking his employees to lunch. In business, the THREE WEEK WINNING CALL is a telephone call from the sales rep to the customer to determine whether the customer is satisfied with the product or service that was purchased. Three weeks is about the time required for people to realize what they like and don't like about something new.

I've translated the steps of the THREE WEEK WINNING CALL from a business scenario into a routine for the dedicated single parent. The process helps discover the positive and negative matters in the life of my boys. It helps me be proactive about the kids' goals, needs, and concerns, rather than reactive, saving us all a lot of time, grief, and energy. When I need an update in the life of my boys, I use the THREE WEEK WINNING CALL steps on a one-to-one basis.

The best way to begin is to establish a rapport that serves to promote communication. "Do you have a moment?" is a way of building rapport by establishing a convenient time frame. If the answer is "no," agree on a time that is convenient for the both of you. If the answer is "yes," it becomes an unsaid commitment from your child to take some time to talk to you.

Another way to build rapport is to match your child's voice tone. If he's talking loudly, then you, too, talk loudly. If he's talking softly, then you speak softly, too. Matching voice tone helps build the comfort level that promotes dialogue, and creating dialogue is the single most important ingredient to discovering goals, needs, and concerns. You build a dialogue by asking questions that provide clues. One helpful technique is to ask open-ended questions that can't be answered with a single word, and which are positive. "I've noticed you're working hard at math. What are some of the goals you're trying to reach?" It's a lot more effective than: "How's math going?" Answer: "Fine."

This method can be used for a variety of subjects: friends, sports, hobbies, other school subjects, work, and so on. Part of the key to success is opening the discussion with positive subjects. It's easier to talk about positive issues than negative ones, and it promotes dialogue.

At this point, if the dialogue is flowing, you have an opportunity to uncover hidden goals, needs, and concerns. Use the same open-ended style question that encourages dialogue. "I've noticed that you're not hanging around with "Jim" anymore. What are some things that are keeping you guys from being friends?" Now's the time to keep quiet and listen. Show your interest with facial expressions and ask questions that are relevant to the situation. The power of listening and asking pertinent questions can be boundless. Here's an example.

Being Customer-Focused

A business associate and I were at a business convention. There was one particular person who owned several companies with whom we wanted to visit. He appeared to be close-mouthed, though, and blunt to the other people with whom he talked. We gathered our courage and moved in. He was indeed curt with us at first, but we continued to ask him questions that showed interest in his goals, needs, and concerns, and then we listened to his responses. 40 minutes later, as the conversation was wrapping up, he smiled widely and told us how much he enjoyed talking with us. We thanked him, and, as we walked away, my associate recounted what had just happened. "He told us how much he enjoyed talking with us, yet he did 90 percent of the talking." We learned a lot about this man's business, and the experience was an invaluable lesson for me on how to be customer-focused.

In business, focusing on the goals, needs, and concerns of the customer is, simply termed, CUSTOMER-FOCUSED. Many business people say they're customer-focused but few really are. How about that phone solicitor who calls just as you're sitting down to supper: "Hello, Ms. Brown, this is Bob Johnson, and our carpet cleaning specialists will be in your neighborhood next week." Is this person really focusing on the customer's goals, needs and concerns? Hardly. This would be much better. "Hello, Ms. Brown, this is Bob Johnson, do you have a moment?" Now Mr. Johnson is focusing on Ms. Brown's immediate needs and concerns, and she will be more receptive to building a dialogue, now or later.

To genuinely focus on the goals, needs and concerns of someone else might be a difficult concept to understand. Maybe it's because we are more accustomed to acting on our own behalf. Another illustration will help. I saw the Clint Eastwood movie, *Firefox*. It was about a high-tech Russian jet that took instructions from the pilot via mental telepathy. The programmed language was Russian, therefore, the pilot had to think in Russian—a difficult task if you haven't learned the language. I realize that to help my kids communicate with me at the optimum level, I need to speak their language by focusing on and staying current with their goals, needs, and concerns. This way, we'll keep the "jet" flying in fine fashion.

Back To The THREE WEEK WINNING CALL

Now that you've built a dialogue between you and your child, the next step is to pay attention to the main cause of concern.

"Jim's been acting like a jerk lately. He's hanging around with a group of guys who think they're really cool."

Now that you're beginning to get to the main concern, keep probing. Ask pertinent questions to keep the dialogue flowing: "What do you mean he's been a jerk? Give me an example." It would've been easier to let the word "jerk" go uninvestigated and dissolve the conversation. However, by asking some key questions you'll learn a lot more.

"Some of the guys he's hanging around with smoke pot."

I asked 14-year-old Paul to pause so that I could thank him for being candid with me. I really welcome the opportunities to praise my kids, and I don't mean phony praise that isn't earned. I mean genuine praise for a job well done. It helps reinforce positive standards from which they'll grow.

I felt like I was getting close to the core of concern, so I repeated the cause of concern to see if I could get him to agree. "So, Jim is a jerk because he's hanging around with people who smoke pot. Is that why you aren't friends anymore?" If the answer is "yes," then it's time to explore solutions and close by getting a mutual agreement that the solution is a good one. That way you'll both be motivated to follow through. If the answer is "no," you'll want to go back and probe again for the main cause of concern.

The problem here isn't black and white. Neither is the solution. I figured that Paul was probably not going to say whether Jim smokes, but his answer would give me a clue about his feelings regarding pot, which I'm always interested in knowing. I asked, "Do you think you'll be seeing Jim again?"

"Not as long as he's hanging around with that group," he answered.

TACKLING SINGLE PARENTING

In business, the person making the THREE WEEK WINNING CALL to confirm customer satisfaction or concerns about a recently purchased product or service is bound to run into one of three types of consumers. The BELIEVER has only good things to say about the purchase. The IN-BETWEENER is a fence-leaner who has some concerns, and the NON-BELIEVER has nothing good to say about the product or service.

From early indications, Paul is a BELIEVER when it comes to being anti-drug. If his answer to my question: "Do you think you'll be seeing Jim again?" had been less emphatic and more like, "Oh, I don't know, maybe." He would then be described as an IN-BETWEENER or a NON-BELIEVER. Then, I would've needed to ask a few more questions to give me an idea about Paul's true feelings about drugs. An effective technique is to keep the questions open-ended and non-confrontational. The goal is to keep dialogue flowing, saying something like: "What do the kids who are smoking pot say about it?" Time now to listen for concerns and work towards solutions.

In business, BELIEVERS are anxious to tell you good things about the product and service. They're also open to hearing more good things about what the product or service has to offer. So, thinking that Paul is a BELIEVER, I asked him: "What do you think about smoking pot?"

"I think it's really stupid," he replied. At that point I took the opportunity to educate him some more about the negative effects of drug use. I was careful to teach, and not to preach. I didn't want to turn him off to my message.

I soon noticed that Paul was getting restless, so I wrapped up our meeting and thanked him for his time and attention. As he walked out I got a final agreement on our solution. "So you won't be seeing Jim as long as he's with that group of kids, right?"

"That's right," he answered walking out the door. We had arrived at a mutually agreed upon solution.

The communication techniques involved with the THREE WEEK WINNING CALL have really helped me stay focused on the goals, needs, and concerns of my boys. The steps are:

1. Establish a rapport by asking for convenience of time and matching your tone of voice to that of the other person
2. Ask open-ended questions that encourage dialogue
3. Ask open-ended questions that focus on goals, needs, and concerns as you probe for the main cause of concern
4. Get an agreement on the main cause of concern
5. Present a solution to the concern, and observe whether the person is acting like a BELIEVER, IN-BETWEENER, or NON-BELIEVER.
6. Get an agreement that the solution will work.

This, and the other communication techniques, may seem overly formal and mechanical. Remember, they're designed to be blended with your individual personality so that they become customized to the unique goals, needs, concerns, and communication style of your family.

With each step be a good listener, ask pertinent questions, and remain customer-focused.

Keeping The Communication Channels Open

There are a few other communication techniques that help me stay in touch with my boys' goals, needs, and concerns. For instance, a typical after school exchange might be "How did school go?" Answer: "Fine." "Anything new?" Answer: "No." I've told my kids that I expect to hear some news each day about school, and I've shared my reasons: It's because I'm interested in what they're doing, and kids, like adults, appreciate that you show an interest in them. This routine helps me monitor for sudden changes in comments and attitude that can signal a diversion, such as problems at school or with a friend, that needs quick investigation. Once again, it helps me be proactive about a potential problem instead of reactive to a full-blown crisis. Many times, I still get the "nuttin" response, so I get out the teasers again. I use open-ended questions that demand more than a one-word answer, and a topic that's positive. If a child has to grope for something to say it's easier for him if it's about something positive and upbeat. "What did your teacher say when you showed her your artwork?" This question demands more than a one-word answer, and it's a light-hearted subject. The goal is to build a dialogue so that you can hear more about your child's day. My boys know that I expect news after school, so a quick visit has become an after-school ritual. The problem is that I don't always have the time or patience to hear school talk. So, to keep the kids from feeling slighted, I'll be honest and tell them I'm interested in their day but that currently I'm busy. I'll make a point to visit with them later that day.

Our Three Favorite Exploratory Questions

My boys and I hear comments from teachers, politicians, businesses, parents, friends, and others whom we see daily. Much of what we hear is biased, non-factual, and incomplete. For example, many scholars portray Christopher Columbus as a villain, pillager, and rapist. This contrasts with the noble adventurer and hero whom I was raised to believe was Christopher Columbus. Which side is right and which side is wrong? Who knows. How can historians assess the character of a man who lived 500 years ago? Many of these same people can't decide whether someone as recent as Richard Nixon helped to end the war in Vietnam or intensified it, instead.

I've told my boys if they don't agree with, do not understand, or want to know more about something said to them, they should ask an exploratory question that leads to further dialogue through critical thinking. They'll be better equipped to evaluate the nature and validity of a subject—they can buy into it, or disregard it. These are the three exploratory questions that are absolutely essential to the success of my family's communication skills:

What do you mean?

Can you give me an example? and;

What do you think about this (or that)?

Here are some examples:
Last summer I stormed into the house and said, "Our neighbor sure is a nitwit." Instead of my boys being sucked into my anger they

asked, "What do you mean?" "For the last three Sundays," I told them, "he's been over there making racket with that damn power saw." Well, apparently, I was the only one bugged by the noise because J.J. said, "He probably works during the week and Sunday is his only day off." Thanks for the support, buddy! While at first I thought I'd been betrayed by my own son, I took a step back. I told him it was good that he questioned the reason for my anger and then made his own decision whether or not to join in.

The term: "Can you give me an example?" can be used the same way—to see if you agree with someone else's conclusions. Sometimes my ex-wife vindictively says nasty things about me to the boys. I've told them that what she says about me are her opinions, and that they can form their own opinion by asking her: "Can you give me an example?" There are times when I get angry at her and say spiteful things to which my kids ask me: "Can you give me an example?" Bravo! I know that I've taught them well when they catch me.

The question: "What do you think about this (or, that)?" is a customer-focus question that builds dialogue by showing that you value someone's opinion. If asked, most people feel flattered and will readily offer their opinion about an issue. For example, "What do you think about this terrific baseball game?" It's a technique that helps build dialogue to learn goals, needs, and concerns. It's a lot better than: "This game is really exciting isn't it?" Answer: "Yeah."

Every communication building technique is a two-way street. I've told my boys that they need to learn to understand my goals, needs, and concerns just as I want to know theirs. Some people think that I'm selfish in my request, but I think it's a generous gift to bestow. I believe that if my kids are able to use effective and productive communication skills in our own family, they'll be more skilled as communicators with their friends, business peers, future spouses, and children. Pretty valuable, if you ask me.

Defusing Anger

Parents with teenagers need to occasionally deal with their child's anger. Anger's like a stick of dynamite. Once lit, it needs to be quickly defused, or the situation can get much worse in a hurry. People who are angry have a need that is not being met, and their anger expresses their disapproval of the situation. I have a simplistic communication technique that works for me to settle down an angry teenager.

One summer I drove into the driveway and was met by 15-year-old Paul, dressed in his baseball uniform. "Hurry up!" He yelled. "Where have you been?" The first thing I did was to match his voice tone. His voice was loud so I raised my voice.

"What's your problem?" I shot back. Matching voice tone is important in finding the comfort level that creates a dialogue that uncovers the real concern. If I had spoken gently, "What's the matter, dear?" that might have irritated him more by making it appear I wasn't taking his objection seriously. Keep in mind that when coping with anger there's a delicate balance between matching voice tone and creating a disruptive shouting contest.

I thought that I knew what caused his anger, but I wasn't positive. That's why I asked him what his problem was so I could verify his concern. "You were supposed to be here ten minutes ago. I have to eat!" That's what I suspected. A typical, self-serving, impatient, teenage tantrum. If I had suspected that the problem was more serious, I would've probed until I found the main cause of concern, gotten an agreement as to the cause, presented a possible solution, and gotten an agreement that the solution would work.

Instead, because of the basis for his tirade and the fact that he wasn't listening to my explanation, I laid out the scenario as objectively as I could, then paraphrased what he was saying to me so that he could hear it for himself. "Wait a minute! Are you trying to tell me that after I've run around town as fast as I could, doing errands and grocery shopping, that you are mad at me because I'm a stinking ten minutes late in preparing your supper? Couldn't you have prepared a meal?" After hearing the situation from another perspective, Paul quickly quieted down and said he would take in the groceries. This "mirroring" technique defused Paul's impatience, helped him see the nature of his anger from another perspective, and helped him change course. I whipped up something for supper and everyone was happy.

When the situation is more serious, I use a communication technique that many professional family counselors use effectively for conflict resolution. I've dubbed it, "the notepad process." It's a method to help parent and child learn the goals, needs, and concerns of each other when there has been a total breakdown of communication, and accusations and name-calling start flying. "You always do this"; "No I don't"; "You're a dork"; "I want more respect from you"; "Shut up!"; "No, You shut up!" When Paul was 16 we got into a major dispute concerning rudeness and manners. I give credit to the notepad process for improving our relationship. Here's how it works.

During a major dispute, when things are totally out of control, it's best to take a "time out," leave the room and let tempers cool. Leaving the room, however, doesn't resolve the reason behind the dispute. After tempers are settled down, grab a notepad and pen and invite your child to sit at a table with you. You need to find the main cause of the dispute and then agree to a solution.

If your child is hesitant to join you, re-affirm your commitment by telling him that you love him and that you're concerned about the welfare of your relationship. You're trying to follow the same steps used to handle an objection. Start by building rapport. Match his voice tone and you'll help to build a comfort level that will get the communication started. Tell him that you intend to find out what's at the root of the problem. Words of love and concern help build a positive mood. Empathize with your child's anger and frustration. "I know that this is uncomfortable for you and that you're having all sorts of angry thoughts about me." Empathy helps your child feel that his objection is legitimate, and that you're taking it seriously, all of which helps to further dialogue. Assure him that his opinion is important to you.

After Paul and I were seated at the table with our notepad and pen, I asked him: "Why do you think we're having this disagreement?"

"Because you get angry all the time." I wrote Paul's answer on the notepad. My goal was to find the main cause of Paul's concern. "J.J. and I are always worried that you're going to yell at us for something." I kept writing. "You're the only parent I know who's like that. I wish I could live with a normal family."

I felt pretty defeated. It was as if I was hearing all of Paul's childhood frustrations that had been building up over the years. Problems that were caused by inferior parenting. Without the notepad, I might've interrupted Paul by then to argue. Instead, I stayed quiet and kept writing.

When Paul was finished I went back to my notes. "You said I get angry all the time. Does that mean every hour of every day and night?"

"I didn't say you get angry all the time," was Paul's response.

"Yes you did. I wrote it down right here," as I pointed to the notepad. The most valuable feature of the notepad process is that it keeps each person from conveniently retracting or denying something that was previously said. It whittles the accusations down to specific concerns that can then be properly dealt with. I asked, "If I don't get angry with you all the time, then when do I get angry with you?"

"It's like if we aren't perfect then you're yelling. You're always right and everybody else is always wrong." I wrote down Paul's comments and kept trying to get him to focus on specifics.

"I often admit to being wrong," I told Paul. Then I cited a recent example: "Just yesterday I made a mistake on a customer's contract that I recognized, and then apologized."

"You just don't understand," he responded.

"You're right. I don't understand." Probing for the main cause of concern can be a delicate process. The child can get frustrated and angry with this interrogation and feel as though he's painting himself into a corner. I told Paul that the emotion he's feeling is frustration and that we should both try to cope with it. I reminded him that our goal was to discover the reason for our dispute.

"Paul! Please help me understand the main cause for your anger. If I know what's bothering you then we can take steps to find a solution."

"You just keep talking all the time, dad. You never shut up." I kept taking notes. Then I got out the critical thinking, exploratory questions that I use to enhance dialogue.

"What do you mean by that? Can you give me an example?" My goal was to keep building dialogue so I could discover the central cause for Paul's concern. Most people, young and old, have a difficult time articulating the main cause for their anger. This communication process helped Paul be more precise about what bothered him. We were making progress. I felt that "You just keep talking all the time," is a lot less serious than "You get angry all the time."

"You just think you're right all the time," was Paul's answer.

"Paul!" I said pointedly, "I don't understand what you're saying. Obviously nobody can be right all the time. I like to think I'm a reasonable man. I realize that I'm not right all the time. So when you say that I think I'm right all the time, I don't understand what you're saying. I need you to give me an example so that I can get a better picture of what you mean." Now it was time for me to shut up, listen, and take notes.

"Like when we were watching Babe Ruth on TV the other night," he explained. "You just kept talking through the whole show. When they said he was a drunk and abused women you kept making comments about the program producers not knowing what they were talking about. It's the same when we take vacations. You always point out everything and tell us all about these things. Everything is just the way you say it is. You're right all the time. You always have an opinion. You need to loosen up and shut up."

Now I was getting a feel for what Paul was saying. He was shocked when I told him, "I understand what you're saying, and I agree with you. I can be overbearing at times." It seemed as though we had zeroed in on Paul's main cause of concern. Just to be sure, I needed to confirm our findings. I asked him, "For example, when we were at the baseball game and I pointed out some of the moves the relief pitcher was using in his wind-up, you got mad at me and told me to shut up."

"That's right, dad. I could see for myself what he was doing." That was the agreement I needed from Paul that we had indeed found the main cause of his concern and anger.

We had come to the root of the problem. Paul was now a young man and needed to exercise his independence. He didn't want dad to lead the way anymore. My constant chatter, which I thought was informative and helpful, was coming across to Paul as being arrogant, obnoxious, and a nuisance. This led to him acting disrespectful and sullen, which caused me to get angry at him. The solution to the problem was an easy one on which to agree. I told him that I'd keep more of my opinions to myself. Paul agreed to this solution. Two weeks later I asked him how I was doing and he said, "Much better." And I told him I was pleased with his upbeat attitude.

The notepad process is an effective way of probing and discovering an angry child's main cause of concern. It's a great method of eliminating the frustrations of "I didn't say that," or "What are you talking about?" The notepad process helps you trim off the generalities and zero in on the root of the problem. If you keep an open mind you might be surprised at what you discover. I started out thinking I was going to teach Paul a thing or two about respect. Instead, I learned a valuable lesson about myself.

Behavioral Styles

In the late 1980s, there was an independent research study that focused on salespeople. The study revealed that the most glaring difference between successful salespeople and those not as successful was the ability to recognize and effectively deal with different behavioral styles in the decision-making process. If understanding behavioral styles is so important in business, it must be just as important in family functioning. Understanding behavior can be especially significant in a single parent family, since the parent is often limited to understanding family concerns from a single viewpoint. Learning to understand different behavioral styles broadens one's perspective.

Carlson Learning Company in Minneapolis has defined four basic behavioral traits: *Dominance, Influence, Steadiness,* and *Conscientiousness.* Most people display prominent tendencies from one or two of these groups, but exhibit spillover tendencies from all four, depending on the circumstances. Each person is unique with hundreds, maybe thousands, of behavioral combinations, and shouldn't be typecast. The important thing to understand is that there are recognizable differences in each person. As my boys and I learn about each other's behavioral tendencies, preferences, and fears that are an inherent part of each type, we continue to improve our communication skills and further our capacity for being an effective, productive family, living in harmony.

Studies show that word association helps improve comprehension and memory. Therefore, I have renamed the basic behavioral styles to help you identify and remember each group. Following is a brief definition of the group and it's dominant tendencies, preferences, and fears. Determine which groups best fit the members of your family, and why.

BIG BEAR

Emphasis is on shaping the surroundings by overcoming opposition to accomplish results.

Tendencies:

Commanding - "Do that homework, and I mean right now!"

Results and task oriented - "Let's tear that old fence down today."

Quick thinker - "Makes sense to me; I'll do it."

Open to new ideas - "That's clever. I never thought of that. Let's try it."

Not into small talk - "I'm doing fine, thanks, but I'll talk to you later."

Preferences:

Wants to be in control - "You're not leaving until the work is done."

Enjoys lots of different activities - "Let's go camping this weekend."

Wants options instead of recommendations - "What else is going on this weekend?"

Wants direct answers - "I want to know why you're late."

Fears:

Doesn't want to lose control of the situation - "You tell her she's not the boss, I am!"

Doesn't want to be taken advantage of - "I'm letting you stay out until 11:00, but you had better not be late."

PARTY ANIMAL

Emphasis on shaping the surroundings by influencing or persuading others.

Tendencies:

> **Persuades instead of demands** – "Doing homework will help you get good grades."
>
> **Is expressive, and loves to socialize** – "I'm so excited! I can't wait for the homecoming party."
>
> **Places high importance on people** – "I wonder what my friends will think of my new jacket."
>
> **Places high importance on feelings** – "I think the poor woman feels insulted."

Preferences:

> **Needs recommendations instead of options** – "What do you think we should do this weekend?"
>
> **Enjoys enthusiastic and motivational settings** – "Let's get everybody together and plan Sue's surprise party."
>
> **Wants to feel like part of the group** – "I hope I'm invited to Bob's birthday party."
>
> **Likes to help people** – "Let's organize a fund-raiser for the needy."
>
> **Likes freedom from control** – "There're too many rules around this house."

Fears:

> **Social rejection** – "I'll die if I'm not invited to the party."
>
> **Lack of social recognition** – "I hope the newspaper article mentions the other awards I've won."

TEACHER

Emphasis is on cooperating with others to carry out the task.

Tendencies:

Loyal – "I'm proud to say I've worked at the same job for seven years."

Moves in an orderly and secure fashion – "First, we'll pool our money, then set a budget."

Patient and a good listener – "Let's sit and have a good long visit."

Has a high interest in data – "Our class is comprised of 55 percent female of which 85 percent have a 3.0 grade average or better."

Preferences:

Staying in one place – "I'm happy living right where we are."

Likes structure and organization – "First, let's form committees."

Developing specialized skills – "I enjoy the new product seminars."

Organized plan for change – "If we're going to adopt that procedure, we need to make a list of all the things that need considering."

Fears:

Loss of stability – "But I don't want to move. I like it here."

Not receiving credit for personal accomplishments – "I hope they realize it was my efforts that helped us win the award."

SPOCK

Emphasis is on working conscientiously within existing circumstances to ensure quality and accuracy.

Tendencies:

Motivated by logic – "That's not the way it was designed to work."

Introverted – "I'm quiet on the outside because I'm doing a lot of thinking on the inside."

No visible emotion – "So, they scored a touchdown. What's all the fuss about?"

Not much into small talk – "Please hurry and tell me the point of your story."

Critical of performance – "Bring your assignment home from school. I'd like to inspect it for myself."

Preferences:

Steady environment – "I like my work area just the way it is."

Working with a group – "Let's call and ask the committee chairs for their opinions."

Obeying laws and operating procedures – "You'll have fewer problems if you follow the manual."

Personal responsiveness to the efforts of others – "If it doesn't work come back and I'll take another look at it."

Fears:

Having personal efforts look bad – "Let's double-check our facts to make sure we don't make a crucial mistake."

Sudden changes – "I hope someone doesn't come along now and make last minute demands."

Understanding and effectively responding to different behavioral styles in people is just as valid and important as understanding the instincts of wild animals. We know that wolves are naturally territorial, and that deer run swiftly from danger. The main difference between the instinctive mannerisms of people and wild animals is that human beings can consciously alter their behavior. I learned about making those changes from Dag Knudsen.

Throughout my business career, I've been to at least a dozen business improvement seminars and have heard at least twice that number of speakers. None has impressed me as much as Dag Knudsen. Dag is a human relations specialist from Minneapolis with whom I worked for six years developing customized employee training programs. An integral part of Dag's employee training is not just understanding other people's behavioral styles, but more importantly your own.

Research demonstrates that the most effective people know themselves. That was news to me until I met Dag through a mutual business interest. I'd often heard that I could be loud, intimidating, and not a very good listener. Usually, I was offended by those statements because people habitually tell others what is bad about them, and not much about what is good. Always hearing about the bad side of your personality doesn't help motivate a person to improve.

Dag persuaded me to take a personal profile evaluation, available through Carlson Learning Company, which revealed that I was a BIG BEAR. I discovered that there were lots of personal tendencies of which I was proud, and a few that I needed to keep under control. For example, a couple of years ago I was jogging on the snow-covered trails through the woods near my home. When a cross-country skier approached I smiled and greeted him. He stopped abruptly and cussed me out for "Screwing up the tracks by running on them." I told him that I was staying off the ski tracks, but his mind was set, and he continued to cuss me out. I jogged on but was fuming. Being a BIG BEAR personality, it is my nature to want to be in control. I felt that this man was arrogant and rude to me on my own turf. "After all," I thought, "I run here everyday and I've never seen this guy before. How dare he boss me around." It was time to get even. As I circled the woods, I came to a junction that I knew he would have to ski through. Snickering to myself, I grabbed a medium sized fallen tree and placed it across the path, and walked away. As I approached my car, my pace became slower and slower. "Wait a minute!" I thought, "Here's the bad side of my BIG BEAR personality coming out. This man's thoughtless and rude remarks took me out of my daily routine—an inherent fear of the BIG BEAR—and I responded by acting deviously." I walked back to the woods, moved the tree off the trail, and felt a lot better about myself. I realized that my negative tendency had been at work, and so I made a conscious effort to correct it. No doubt my decision was a favorable one for the skier as well.

When single parents don't recognize behavioral patterns in themselves or their children there can be problems with communication which lead to frustration, anger, and hurt feelings. As my boys have grown, I see that J.J. displays more TEACHER qualities than me. Qualities such as patience and listening are not necessarily BIG BEAR hallmarks, so I have to consciously make adjustments to accommodate and encourage his steadiness by trying not to be impatient. Paul favors BIG BEAR like me; I have to give him slack so we don't clash over control.

Recognizing prominent behavioral styles in your child requires asking open-ended questions that demand more than a yes or no answer, and then listening carefully to the response. For instance, I was upset with President Clinton and politics in general, and angrily remarked at supper, "I think I should run for president and straighten things out. What do you think of that, J.J.?" The first thing that came to J.J.'s mind was a classic fear of the TEACHER behavioral style—Loss of stability.

"Aww, Dad! I don't want to have to move to Washington."

Conversely, when a job offer popped up out of the blue that required a move out West, I asked Paul for his opinion. He jumped at the opportunity for adventure.

"Let's do it, Dad! I want to see what it's like at another high school." Paul is definitely part BIG BEAR.

The blend of the four basic behavioral styles can vary significantly, and you can be vulnerable to typecasting people. However, by increasing your appreciation of the different behavioral tendencies, preferences, and fears of your child, you can anticipate and minimize potential conflicts. It can help you create a family environment that's conducive to effective communication, helping you keep in touch with your child's ever changing goals, needs, and concerns.

When the kids were much younger, and before I got professionally involved with behavioral styles, I had to rely on my instinct. I realized that my boys were getting a daily dose of my commanding nature, and I wanted to balance that by facilitating their association with people who placed more importance on people and feelings. For the most part, this has been the boys' grandmother, their mom, and female friends of mine. Those associations provided my boys with examples of behavioral styles that are not my strengths, and have positively influenced their growth. The four behavioral categories are interdependent, like a baseball team. Each group relies on the strengths of others for maximum effectiveness. Therefore, the same rationale would hold true if I exhibited prominent behavioral patterns from the PARTY ANIMAL, TEACHER, or SPOCK categories. Then, I would broaden my sons' horizons by getting them involved with strong, results and task-oriented BIG BEAR people.

Dedicated single parents can gain insight into their own minds, and into the minds of their children, by learning to understand behavioral styles. Understanding these styles improves communication skills by helping to recognize and deal with each other's goals, needs, and concerns.

Practice, Practice, Practice

Open and effective communication is the make-it or break-it factor for single parents and their children. However, just like the skilled surgeon, pianist, or ballplayer, effective communication takes practice and diligence to acquire. It's hard work. You can't read this chapter just once and expect to effectively use new and improved life skills. Research shows that a lesson should be read seven times for maximum understanding and retention. Share the lessons with your children so they can learn to understand your behavioral style as well as their own, then practice, practice, practice, to make the new skills become a natural and automatic part of your daily living.

When you include effective and productive communication skills in your family's lifestyle, you'll quickly discover that it's an invaluable support system for building strength and harmony within your family, helping you tackle the difficult challenges of single parenting.

Coping

The Inevitable Struggle

A couple of months after my divorce was final, I went out partying with a group of buddies. We ended up at a swinging new nightclub in downtown Minneapolis where I met a woman with whom I enjoyed dancing. While the band took a break, I bought a couple of beers for us, and we visited. I told her I was recently divorced. She said she had been divorced 12 years previously and hadn't remarried. She told me a little more about her life as a single parent, and then we finished our beers and danced until the band stopped playing. We didn't exchange phone numbers, so when we said good night to each other, that was the last I saw of her.

As I drove home I thought, "That poor woman. I can't imagine being unmarried 12 years from now. I can't imagine being unmarried two or three years from now. God, that's really pathetic. Being alone all those nights without a spouse to sleep with. I really feel sorry for her." Now, many years later, here I am in a similar situation. I'm still single, sleeping alone, and raising kids alone. I certainly have a much better understanding and appreciation for what that woman was experiencing that night I met her, years ago.

You can't understand all the pitfalls of single parenting unless you encounter them yourself. It's the same concept when women tell me I can't understand the agony of childbirth. They're right, just as they can't understand the anxiety of combat under fire. Some things you just have to experience to comprehend the emotions involved, and single parenting is one of them.

TACKLING SINGLE PARENTING

A few years after the encounter at the night club, a long-time acquaintance and I were discussing single parenting. Even though she had been married for over 20 years, and had never been a single parent, she seemed to have all the answers. "I suppose it's tough being a single parent. At least I have someone I can throw my frustrations at."

I'm afraid that the burden of single parenting is a little heavier than mere frustration. It's learning to be successful at working through the challenges of depression, stress, anger, loneliness, guilt, fear, anxiety, self-pity, despair, disappointment, grief, weariness, and confusion.

You need to cope.

The dictionary defines coping as: "to successfully contend with something." You need to learn to cope with the weight of single parenthood, because you're the leader of your family. You're in charge. As you go, so goes your family. Your kids need your constant love, support, and strength. Even though it often seems impossible, you have to do your best to come out the winner. It's like competing in sports.

When an athlete prepares to compete, he or she carefully studies the opponent or challenge. She analyzes her opponent's strengths and weaknesses, devises mental strategies that will help her win, and prepares herself physically.

In the case of the dedicated single parent, the real opponent is the overall state of single parenting. The opponent is not your children. They're on your side. The opponent is dealing with and overcoming the problems of being a single parent in a complicated and demanding society. Just as the athlete prepares for an important contest, the dedicated single parent needs to prepare and stay in condition for the inevitable struggle. Before I stepped into the role of single parenting, I had no idea about the enormity of the struggle that awaited.

I'm the kind of guy whom most people would classify as an optimist. I enjoy life and, for the most part, I'm eager to begin each day. While I was still married, Aurora, a friend of Joyce, asked me what I did to get myself up when I was down. I told her I wasn't quite sure. Even though I had "down" days, I couldn't remember any one, specifically. It's like looking out from the splendor of the mountain top and forgetting what the dark and cool shadows of the valley feel like.

Those memories flashed back to me as I lay in bed, staring at the ceiling, shortly after my divorce—I couldn't move. It was as if someone had kicked a hole through my chest. I searched long and hard, but for the first time in my life, I couldn't get through the despair to find the inspiration to get out of bed.

An hour earlier, my mind had been racing so fast from one issue and event to another that I began to get dizzy. I thought about the past. Things I might've done differently to keep the marriage intact. I thought about the present, about my job, and about the bills that needed to be paid. I thought about the future.

How am I going to get through this with the least possible damage to my boys and me?

My mind went from fast forward, to reverse, to stop. My body could hardly move. My thoughts turned to a blur.

What's next? Total meltdown?

And then it occurred to me that I should call Aurora and tell her that I thought I was having a bad day. That made me laugh, and got me out of bed that morning.

The Power Of Prayer

Depression and hopelessness are horrible afflictions. The funny thought about Aurora got me out of bed, but what was next? I was in my car on a business trip later that day, still feeling crippled. I spoke right out loud and told God, "I need help." I held out my hand and asked God to take hold of it, and to comfort me.

I was raised to honor and trust in God. I believe God is real, and that He will help us through our grief, if we only ask. So there I was, confronted with my mortality and human limitations, and surrendering to a higher power to ask for strength, hope, peace, and wisdom. My prayer was genuine, and my pleas were solemn. Nevertheless, I still hoped that an angel like Clarence, from the movie *It's a Wonderful Life,* would appear in the front seat and counsel me, and give me a clear direction for the future. It would've been impressive but Clarence didn't appear. Instead, I thought of a strategy to resolve a problem at work. That thought calmed me, knowing I was going to hurdle at least one known obstacle in my life. That too was impressive, and I thanked God for the fresh insight.

TACKLING SINGLE PARENTING

Let's face it; we're all human, with human frailties, and life can be terribly burdensome at times. Prayer helps relieve that burden for me. I truly believe in the power of prayer, because my success and happiness are the direct result of it. Prayer gives me hope, and I can COPE WITH HOPE. In fact, I'm quite sure I couldn't handle the job of dedicated single parenting without the inspiration and motivation that I receive from hope.

Prayer also helps me in other ways. I find peace by praying during a church service. I've met many people who say that organized religion is hypocritical, and that they praise God simply by walking through a quiet forest. I agree. Organized religion isn't perfect. That's because it's made up of imperfect people, just like you and me. I also agree that God is everywhere that we look for Him, including the forest. It's the community aspect of religion that gives me strength and wisdom. While at a church service I'm likely to hear stories about other people living through difficult times. I hear stories of how others overcame their personal burdens, and those stories help me. At other times, I feel that I contribute to the welfare of my church community by the good example of being present, and also by the gift of a handshake and smile that I can extend to another person. It helps me forget my own problems while helping someone else feel good.

The most valuable gift I've received as an adult has been a prayer. Soon after my divorce, my mother gave me a small, wallet-sized card with Psalm 23, a psalm of David, the greatest of the kings of Israel. It describes the connection between a shepherd and his flock that he guides, comforts, and protects.

1. *The Lord is my shepherd, I shall not want.*
2. *He makes me lie down in green pastures; He leads me beside still waters.*
3. *He restores my soul. He leads me in right paths for His name's sake.*
4. *Even though I walk through the darkest valley, I fear no evil; for You are with me; Your rod and Your staff, they comfort me.*
5. *You prepare a table before me in the presence of my enemies; You anoint my head with oil; my cup overflows.*

6. Surely goodness and mercy shall follow me all the days of my life, and I shall dwell in the house of the Lord all the days of my life.

I kept this prayer in the door compartment of my car and read it aloud many times every day. Sometimes I read it fast. Other times I read it very slowly, pondering each phrase. Whenever I read it, I felt a renewed purpose in life—stronger, and more peaceful. After several weeks, I had memorized Psalm 23. I felt comfortable saying it aloud without reading from the card. One day, I looked for the card and discovered it had dropped out of the car and was lost. I missed it at first, because I had planned to save it as a souvenir of my tough days. Then, I had a hunch that someone who needed it more than I had found it and that my mother's gift, Psalm 23, would continue to be useful to someone.

Finding The Inspiration To Move Forward

It has been said that God helps those who help themselves. The problem becomes one of helping yourself when you're in the dire straits of early post-divorce, coupled with the daily demands of single parenthood. One moment I'd be up, and the next I'd be down. I'd be angry, then I'd need to resolve the anger. I struggled with low self-confidence, that I was convinced stemmed from a wife of nine years who suddenly wanted out of the marriage. Adding to this jumble, I was fired from my job because my performance had slipped in the midst of all the turmoil. All combined, it was as if a tornado had blasted though my life and savagely scattered the pieces about for miles. I tried desperately to find a direction. I felt lost. I needed goals.

I took lots of walks in the woods near my home. No music cassettes, no radio—just my own thoughts. As I walked, I focused on setting priorities. What was going to be my next step to piece my life back together? I needed to sort things out. With each walk, a new thought occurred that gave me hope, and inspired me. Maybe it was a subject that I needed to read up on from the library. Maybe it was a job interview that I should arrange. Maybe a shot at self-employment. Perhaps a method to stretch my budget. Even a way to improve my love life.

TACKLING SINGLE PARENTING

Every time I took a walk, a new idea occurred to me that gave me hope for the future.

Those ideas were a step-by-step program for recovery. Those walks helped me build a road map with goals along the way so that when I woke up each morning, I could focus on a purpose and get inspired enough to get out of bed, newly enthused to work on my new found goal. Years later, I have since talked to dozens of dedicated single parents who found recovery through the same method of taking walks, where they were alone in the fresh air, without music or interference, allowing new thoughts to surface as stepping stones for the future.

The hard part about getting new ideas is putting them into action. That's where most people lose their footing. Ideas need to be followed up on so that your stepping stones for the future are arranged. It takes work, but as was said earlier, God helps those who help themselves.

An old German proverb on adversity says: "If it doesn't kill you, it'll probably make you stronger." When a friend told me that, I added, "I'll bet the author was a single parent." I like to think that this job of dedicated single parenting has made me much wiser and stronger. However, from the very beginning, there has never been any guarantee of success. Every day, dedicated single parents must seek and find the inspiration they need to carry on.

Inspiration is different from motivation. Inspiration is like the gas in your car that gives it the power to move. If the purpose of driving to New York City is to see the Statue of Liberty, then that is your motivation. Inspiration is power. Motivation is purpose. Finding your own inspiration to get a job done takes practice and experience. Unfortunately, not everyone comes through when they need to.

When my paper copier finally gave out after years of loyal service, I went shopping for a rebuilt one. The office machine sales manager was Dave Osborn, a well known running back for the Minnesota Vikings football team during the '60s and '70s. Dave loves to talk football, so the conversation easily moved to his old coach, Bud Grant, who was elected to the Football Hall of Fame in 1994. I asked Dave what Grant would tell his players to fire them up for a game. "Bud never used hype," Dave told me. "The players were expected to get themselves pumped up for a game because that's what they were getting paid for. If they couldn't do it they would soon be out of a job."

That's how it is with dedicated single parenting; you either come up with your own methods of personal inspiration, and move forward in life, or stay uninspired and spiral downwards.

There are many ways to build daily inspiration. My friend Jean depends on inspirational readings that she picks up at bookstores, rummage sales, and the library. She loaned one of these books to me—it's about people loving each other. Jean usually wakes up early, before her kids, and reads in bed before she has to get up. When she runs into an excerpt that she feels has an extra inspirational lift to it, she'll copy it down and tape it to a kitchen cabinet or to her refrigerator. Here's a typical excerpt that she has underlined from *Loving Each Other* by Leo Buscaglia: "The happiest people in the world would probably still be happy if deprived of everything except life." Here's another: "He who has the courage to laugh is almost as much a master of the world as he who is ready to die." These are typical of the inspirational thoughts that Jean uses to kick-start each day.

Some people read the Bible in the morning as their means of inspiration. Others read poetry, or work on arts and crafts. Some even find inspiration in doing housework before they head off to their daily jobs. My son Paul is a chatterbox in the morning. Even though he drives J.J. crazy at the breakfast table, Paul says it's what he does to get himself "pumped" for the day.

Many people get their day's first dosage of inspiration from TV news and variety programs. Millions of people enjoy listening to the radio to find their morning inspiration; some like the talk and humor, others want the music. When I was driving across town to work each morning, I would often pop in my "Best of Sam and Dave" cassette to get myself primed; rockin' and rollin' on the freeways worked for me.

Exercise is another terrific inspiration builder that works wonders. When the weather permits, I'll hustle down to the park and do about a half hour of calisthenics on the basketball court. I have a program that consists of stretching, push-ups, sit-ups, and jumping jacks. When we have inclement weather, I'll exercise in my living room. Sometimes I crank up my stereo and find fun and relaxation by "conducting the orchestra." My workouts give me an opportunity to shake out my frustrations, vent my hostilities, and they're also terrific inspiration builders.

TACKLING SINGLE PARENTING

While I'm working out, useful ideas or revelations may occur to me. I'll pause, write 'em down, and resume bouncing.

I have another source of inspiration but it's apparently not available to everyone. I have an outspoken behavioral style that allows me to publicly express my opinions on issues. My sometimes loud and unreserved style is seen by some as a negative trait, but I regard it as a positive, productive tool as long as I keep my emotions in check.

Several times a week I'll call the author of a slanted newspaper article, or a legislator who's sponsoring a controversial bill, to express my thoughts. It's not that I'm angry, it's just that I don't agree with what's often promoted out there. I'm glad that I'm passionate enough to defend my convictions and make my views known. My phone calls usually lead to constructive debate. Other times, the person on the other end doesn't appreciate my critique and hangs up, which is O.K., too. Either way, I almost always learn something new.

I'm certainly not the first person to use this feisty behavioral style to my advantage. When Bobby Kennedy, the slain president's younger brother, first started his run for the presidency, he unsuccessfully tried to come across as the cool, collected, Jack Kennedy. It wasn't until a campaign advisor suggested that Bobby let his true, feisty nature shine through that his popularity started to rise. Bobby was later quoted as saying, "Some people are comfortable in repose, I seem to be comfortable in conflict." Getting my social juices flowing serves as inspiration and helps me get my day into high gear. Give it a try.

Surrendering To The Challenges Of Single Parenting

Inspiration helps dedicated single parents be effective and productive in the challenging job of single parenting. However, there are days when there doesn't seem to be enough inspiration in the well to help me charge ahead. I was talking to a single mom who lamented, "Wouldn't it be great if we could just sign out for a couple of days with no kids and no responsibilities? It just seems so unrelenting. Sometimes I feel like the whole world is closing in on me."

Single parenting is a demanding position to hold, and there are many complications. When the kids were much younger, there were times when I felt as though I had shackles on my ankles. I couldn't leave the house for 10 minutes to get a gallon of milk without getting the boys ready to take along. There was a steady barrage of interruptions when the kids were young. I was the only adult available to answer their questions and to monitor their activities. I soon discovered that personal projects that demanded long stretches of concentration were difficult, and frustrated by endless interruptions. They were best left until after the kids had gone to bed.

Feeling exhausted and defeated are common ailments of dedicated single parenting that I've fallen prey to many times. I told the single mom that it was a good thing that there're plenty of rewards. I was referring to the smiles, hugs, kisses, the joy of singing a new song together, and the giggles when we're playing. I love the enthusiasm on their faces during the season's first snowfall, and the startling effect of a thunder clash during a rain storm. There was the look of pride I experienced by watching my sons tie their shoelaces for the first time, and the nervous hesitation of calling a girl on the phone. Much about raising children is going back to familiar places, but this time with a friend who has never been there. I can't imagine what this job would be like without the payoffs. Still, the challenges can be wearisome, and sometimes seem over-bearing, and endless.

It was difficult to build an outside love relationship when the kids were young. If the woman didn't have kids of her own, she wouldn't understand why I couldn't get out more often, or, didn't have much energy or money left when we finally got together. If she also had young children, then we were both short of time, energy, and money on our dates. I wondered if I would ever fall in love again. Neil Diamond's *Play Me* said it perfectly: "For I've been lonely in need of someone, as though I've done someone wrong somewhere." I was the solitary man longer than I'd like to admit.

There's another extremely difficult part of dedicated single parenting for some people. It's not being able to afford the nice clothes, trips, cars, homes, and gifts that they see their siblings and friends enjoy. It's a jealousy thing. It can be disheartening and can bring on a feeling of missing out.

I was one of those people who felt that he was missing out, until I made some adjustments to my thinking.

Joyce finally moved all her belongings out of the house after we had been divorced for several months. I remember my stunned face in the bedroom mirror. I told myself, eye-to-eye, that I was going to succeed at being a dedicated single parent. I concluded that afternoon that I was going to have to make do with less money. Making money takes time, and that's time away from my kids. Making money takes energy and patience, and that's energy and patience away from my kids.

After my awareness meeting with myself I started to make the transition from part-time baby-sitter to full-time dad. Surrendering to the challenges of my new position seemed to make my days and future brighter.

I spent a lot of time with my kids when they were young. I packed picnics for the beach, we hiked through the woods, made tree forts and slid down snowy hills. Sometimes we would hop a bus and ride downtown to explore the city, or to visit museums.

One summer I organized the neighborhood kids and produced *Peter Pan* in our garage. It was great fun for the kids and the audience, comprised mostly of parents.

Those projects never cost much money. Best of all, they helped my boys and me build strong community bonds in our family. Those bonds benefited us by helping to create and maintain the love, trust, respect, understanding, acceptance, and support that we have for one another. And I reaped another huge benefit from my boys expending their physical energy on outdoor projects —when it was time to come in for the night, they were more apt to sit down and read a book or go to bed early, instead of driving me mad by bouncing off the walls like a couple of wild kangaroos. I was able to enjoy much needed peace and quiet.

Even today we spend lots of time together, but it's different because the boys are much more involved with their own friends and activities. I still try to build on the bonds that we have created by occasionally initiating pick-up sports games, and staying involved with their school work and other interests.

Spending less time concerned about money and more time developing family bonds have made me more effective and productive in coping with single parenting. I have discovered, however, that some of the activities I try NOT to do are just as important. Over-indulgence is one of those things I try NOT to do.

I have occasionally felt that I'd been restricted to a wearisome task of single parenting for overly-long stretches of time; making me want to get out and party. There were a few nights over the past single parent years that I've had a couple of beers more than I should've. I felt miserable with a hangover the next day, was edgy with the kids, and was hardly inspired to do the things I should've been doing as a dedicated single parent. When I had questions and concerns about my drinking, I went to the library to read A. A.'s 87 page booklet, "Living Sober". It gave me valuable insight into the complexities and pitfalls of alcohol abuse, and has helped me make better choices for a healthier lifestyle. I finally learned that the price is too high for REVENGE INDULGENCE. That is, to overly gratify my desires because I feel it's deserved for being "confined" to the task of single parenting. Besides, I have a better time out on the town when I keep to my limit than when I don't. I'm also a much better dad to my kids the next day.

Support Is Essential

Another big problem in single parent coping is not getting the support you need and expect from others. What level of support have you received with your single parenting? Has it strengthened you? Support is essential to the success of dedicated single parents. Most parents realize how instrumental support is to the success of a mission because they have personally witnessed the positive results of supporting their own children.

When my boys were just starting to walk, their mother and I would kneel three or four feet apart with open arms, smiles, prompting gestures and words—all of which encouraged those first wobbly steps. When the child fell, we reassured him that he would eventually succeed, and when he did succeed, we praised him. That kind of support is invaluable in helping us mere mortals achieve our goals.

Have you ever watched how actively athletes support each other? A baseball player stands up to the plate in a clutch situation. All his teammates are cheering for him from the dugout, building his confidence, and encouraging him to succeed. The windup, the pitch, SMACK! A home run! His teammates go crazy as they all "high-five" their hero as he approaches home plate. They pat him on the butt and say "way to go," as he trots towards the dugout.

Who's there to serve up this kind of butt-patting, "way to go" support for dedicated single parents? Who's there to accentuate the positive, and help eliminate the negative? I wish I had received more support for my single parenting efforts. I wish there had been more people around me to buoy my spirits when I wasn't doing so well, and to be my cheering section when I did succeed.

I remember going out with my buddies for a couple of beers and talking to them about some of the challenges which I faced as a single parent. I kept their attention for about two minutes before someone would bring up women, business, or sports, and leave me hanging. Of course, that's not unusual. How often have you seen a group of guys drinking beer and chatting about the trials of raising kids? Maybe once? Maybe never? It's not a "guy" thing to talk about with other guys.

One of my brothers was in town from out of state. He spent a night or two with my parents, who live close by. I made several attempts to get over and visit with him, but it was not to be. Both of my kids came down with the flu. When I finally talked to my brother and told him what had been going on, he matter-of-factly said, "Well, Steve, that's what happens when you have kids." As if my eyes needed to be opened to the realities of parenthood. Thanks for the comforting words, pal.

Another brother popped in on me on a Saturday morning while I was trying to keep the kids busy with their weekly household chores. This was his first visit to my home in over two years, and I had yet to hear anything positive from him about my child rearing. He caught me at my worse moment. His first words were, "Steve, I don't think you should be yelling at your kids like that." I felt hurt and angry at his insensitive comment. Years later, Jackson Browne still reminds me of my brother's visit: "Don't confront me with my failings, I had not forgotten them." I could've used a little more understanding that morning, and less criticism.

All things considered, I can understand my buddies' and my brothers' lack of understanding for the challenges of full-time child-rearing, especially the wide-ranging challenges of dedicated single parenting.

They've never had to be concerned with this issue first-hand, and they can't comprehend what's involved. After all these years, I've finally come to learn that if it's support and understanding I'm looking for, I'm never going to receive it from these guys, or from most other guys. As a matter of fact, to save on personal frustration and anger, there have been a few times when I was late for a business meeting with another man because of a child related cause such as illness. I didn't bring up the child issue as an excuse. Instead, I blamed my tardiness on something that he could understand and relate to, such as car trouble, or last-moment business complications.

My rationale was, "Why bore him with an experience that he can't relate to?" It's much like trying to sell the merits of Christmas to Ebenezer Scrooge, or teaching an elephant to dance. The goal may be attainable but reaching it can be very exhausting. I felt sure, however, that I could rely on my sisters-in-law for at least a small amount of "way-to-go" support because of their years of "front-line" service in full-time child care. Certainly they would understand what I was going through.

I was wrong.

The Family Myth

There was a family get together about the time my boys were in early elementary grades. We were all gathered around a big dining room table, snacking and chatting. My brother's wife told us about her sister and husband's new baby. She spoke of how tough it was for her sister to continue her job while juggling the extra demands of the new family member. The more I listened, the hotter I got under the collar. I kept thinking, "Here's my brother's wife, who doesn't work outside the home, has a husband whose income ranks in the upper 3 percent nationally, has a maid come in once a week, and has never given me a single encouraging word about my single parenting. Now she has the audacity to ramble on in my presence about how tough her sister's life is as a new mother while she's working in the same profession as me, selling air time for a radio station." It was maddening. "At least she has a husband who can pick up the slack." I told her. "I'm responsible for all my family's needs from A to Z."

This infuriated her. Instead of receiving a little acknowledgment from my family for my single parenting, I was ridiculed. "The reason you do well as a single parent, Steve," snapped my sister-in-law, "is because you're a white guy in a white-guy society. Women have it a lot tougher." This comment came straight from a person who would have a hell of a hard time convincing me that being a woman had handicapped her in society. In fact, it has probably been to her advantage. "Ohhh," I remarked sarcastically. "That's why this job of single parenting has been so fun and easy for my kids and me. It's because I'm a white guy. My hard work and dedication has nothing to do with it. Thanks. Now I know."

My sister-in-law's remarks are typical of what I call "the family myth." The ones from whom you expect support with your single parenting efforts are sometimes the very ones who rear up to bite you with insensitivity and a lack of love.

During that time, I was dating Linda, who was also a single parent. When I told her my sister-in-law story, she said she was in a similar situation recently, but instead of being chastised she was made out to be the hero. "After my sister-in-law told her story," Linda said, "she turned to me with a look of amazement, "How in the world do you manage so well as a single parent?" I told Linda, "That's the lovely bit of support I had desperately needed from my family, but didn't get, again."

A friend suggested that I try to find out why I wasn't getting the kind of support from my family that I expected. He recommended a group counseling session. "Good idea," I said. So, I arranged a session that consisted of three brothers, two sisters-in-law, a facilitator, and myself.

It was a disaster.

During the session, I stated that I felt I wasn't getting the kind of support and understanding I had hoped for from my family. That touched off an explosive barrage of finger pointing, "you said, he said, she said, I said" dialogue that only served to frustrate the situation for all of us. Two main points of controversy that I did hear were, "Steve, we didn't know you needed help." To which I answered, "I tried to make it clear with phone calls and letters." Then they qualified their support for me by saying they offered to loan me money, to which I replied, "It wasn't money that I needed." I needed the kind of stuff that money can't buy: love, acceptance, and understanding.

I had always thought that I'd be able to depend on my family if I needed to, but that was a myth of mine. I found out differently when I was down and out.

All single parents need to be on guard for the "family myth" so they'll recognize it if it strikes. If I had to list the single most difficult challenge of coping with single parenting, it would be trying to cope with that myth. It's easy to dismiss the lack of devotion from scoundrels, but when it comes from the ones you love, it becomes a real test of your character.

Over the years, I discovered that not only did my family lag in support of my parenting efforts, society, in general, watched blindly as I floundered. When J.J. was five and Paul, eight, we were in a department store shopping for snow pants. I must admit, it was stupid of me to put the pants on J.J. backwards as we were checking out sizes, but I certainly didn't expect the kind of wounding rudeness that I received from a prim and properly dressed woman in her early fifties as she walked by. "Oh, that's perfect, dad, I can tell who usually dresses your kids." I was stunned, but it was only temporary.

"Lady! For your information, I dress these kids every day of the week, and I have been for a couple of years, and mind your own damn business."

This lady could've made my day a bright one had she come over to lend a hand and a word of encouragement. Instead, she seized the opportunity to ridicule my efforts.

It was also about that time that the three of us were doing the weekly grocery shopping when I did another lame brain thing. I let J.J. ride under the grocery cart as we cruised the aisles. As I approached the meat and produce section, I heard J.J. let out an ear-piercing shriek. I immediately grabbed him up in my arms—he had pinched his hand between the wheel and the cart, and his little fingers were bleeding. We were making quite a commotion, and I was sure that someone, either a shopper or an employee, would offer some help, at least direct us to the bathroom. Nothing. The store was full of shoppers but nobody, not one, paid any attention to us. Finally, I yelled right out loud, "Does anybody know where the bathroom is?" Someone nodded in the general direction so I grabbed Paul, left the cart, and attended to J.J.

The most outrageous example of society's spindly support for me as a dedicated single parent took place about a year and a half earlier at a friend's lakeshore cabin. The three of us were enjoying free run of the cabin on a warm, summer-like, Saturday morning. I was doing the breakfast dishes and telling the kids to stop horsing around on the outside deck. Then I heard a scream. The boys had fallen off the foot and a half high deck with Paul's weight on top of three year old J.J., while J.J.'s little arms were outstretched for support against the ground. The weight had been too great. When I came running out, I saw that J.J.'s forearm was completely broken in two. Not just fractured, but the two bones in his forearm were broken in half, and his forearm was dangling at a ninety-degree angle. I popped the arm back in place and asked the guys next door, who were on the roof shingling, to call an ambulance, or give me a hand. They didn't take me seriously, and not one of them got off the roof to help. There were several women in the house, and when they heard the excitement, they came running over. As it turned out, the hospital was 20 miles away and it would be quicker to put the kids in the car rather than wait for an ambulance. J.J. rode in the back seat with his wobbly arm propped up on the arm rest. Paul sat next to him comforting him while feeling horrible about the accident. Do you know that I couldn't get one of those adults to ride with me? I couldn't believe it.

These few examples of the non-support I've experienced as a single parent are not intended to make people feel sorry for me, or to whine about life not treating me fairly. It's just that I've always been the kind of guy to stop along the highway to help travelers who have car trouble, and I go out of my way to do favors for my neighbors. So, these non-support situations don't feel good. It's as if society was saying, "Hey buddy! You wanted custody of these kids, now find out what it's like to have them full time."

My experience suggests that the non-support situations I've encountered would've been different if those involved had been dealing with a woman instead of a man. Instead of my beer drinking buddies giving me just a few moments of their time while I bent their ear about single parenting, I wonder if their interest would've risen had a woman been telling the same story. Instead of my five brothers showing little or no interest in my single parenting, I wonder if their level of support would've been higher had they been dealing with an only sister, instead of another brother. How about the sisters-in-law? Would they have expressed more love and concern for another sister-in-law single parent, than they have for the white-guy brother-in-law? Would the brazen woman in the department store have acted differently had she seen another woman struggling with two youngsters, instead of a man having problems. Can you imagine a woman being panic-stricken in a grocery store because her young son is hurt and crying and not have anyone help her? And how about the roof shinglers? How long do you think it would've taken for the first man to scurry off the roof to come to the aid of a woman whose young son had just broken his arm in half?

I suspect that much of the frustration, anger, and loneliness of non-support that I, as a man, experience with single parenting is similar to what many women in business experience by being meticulously scrutinized, held to different standards, and thwarted by the "glass ceiling."

Almost every day we can read stories like the resignation of Dee Dee Myers, former press secretary to President Clinton. Ms. Myers was angry about her non-support, "Women have made a lot of headway in Washington over the past few years but this is still a man's town."

Some of the weak-kneed, non-support episodes I've experienced as a male, single parent, have proved to me that single parenting is still very much of a woman's town. Nevertheless, I have tried not to let a little discrimination get me down. My kids and I have burst through that "glass ceiling." Yet, I still feel the pain of people not caring or reaching out to me in my single parent struggles.

Maybe you've heard that wise, old African proverb about families: "It takes the whole village to raise a child." My non-support experiences have brought the full meaning of that proverb closer to home. They've made me much more sensitive to the needs and concerns of other single parents and their children in our "village" in which we all live.

It was during this period that the local news media focused on Kathleen Morris, a local county attorney, who was being mocked and accused of botching a high profile criminal case that generated a great amount of public fervor. I remember an interview with Morris, and how I identified with her feelings when she quoted Sigmund Freud: "I am as isolated as you could wish me to be. The word has been given out to abandon me and a void is forming around me." I was comforted knowing that my grief had company, but the inspiration from a newspaper article doesn't last long. I needed support groups.

Support Groups

People in need, such as dedicated single parents who face challenging responsibilities, might find support groups helpful. Support groups consist of people who understand the challenges with which others are confronted because many of them have experienced similar challenges. Support group members learn from each other's strengths and weaknesses. In many cases, simply having the comfort of other people listening to your troubles, and offering a fresh perspective, is all a distressed person needs to feel better.

Support groups help build self-confidence, lend encouragement, and give praise to dedicated single parents who need to find the strength to keep going when times are hard.

The first support group I built involved my mom and dad. They raised six sons, so they have a pretty good idea of the difficulties that come with parenting. Even though there have been some rough spots, our relationship has remained beneficial—for them, for me, and for my children.

My parents are from the "old school," and that's how I was raised. They emphasized spiritual, moral, and work ethics, financial conservatism, and loyalty in marriage. My parents grew to have a deep love for Joyce, and they felt a great loss when our marriage broke apart.

Two years after the divorce, and finally getting back on my feet, I began to house shop. My parents had been empty nesters for about 15 years, and had moved to the suburbs 10 years before my divorce. After weeks of real estate hunting it occurred to me that the most logical place to move was near to my parents. Since my boys could not be near their mother, it made sense for them to live near their grandparents for family bonding purposes.

When the boys were much younger, my mother read to them, played games, and romped with them in the nearby park. The kids felt loved from the grandmotherly attention, and my mom often told me, "Trying to stay up with those boys is helping me stay young."

In later years, the boys have been able to occasionally stop in and visit with their grandma and grandpa on their way home from school. They sit in the dining room, talk about school, discuss life in general, and eat cookies. We have shared dozens of birthdays, anniversaries, and holidays together, and because of my parent's age, I have enjoyed helping them with heavy maintenance tasks around their home.

Many times my mother has lifted my spirits by praising my housekeeping and making positive comments about how clean and fresh the boys' clothes look and about the nutritious meals I serve. My dad has not been as vocal, but the message was loud and clear in an unsolicited "letter to the editor" he sent to the newspaper when I ran for the school board. He said that I provided my children with love and care and "under Steve's guidance, his boys, Paul and J.J., rank high academically." Comments like those make me feel good and inspire me to keep up the good work.

I really believe that each member of our support group has added to the welfare of the other members. It has also added to the strength of character of my boys and greatly contributed to their stability.

One summer evening when the three of us were riding our bicycles home after a visit with my parents, Paul said, "I sure love my grandma and grandpa. I hope it's a long time before they die, because I will sure be sad when they do." My parents and I love each other, but life isn't always rosy between us. There are times when I could use a little more understanding from them.

I've been with my parents when I was totally exhausted from the responsibilities of work, home, and kids. If I were to yawn or otherwise express my weariness, my dad would hastily inquire in an interrogatory manner: "What's the matter?" If I answered by saying that I'm beat from all the running around, he would reply "Oh," as if my reason for being tired was groundless, and as long as it wasn't life threatening, then everything would be all right. I bristle when I get the ol' half-hearted treatment and wish that just once he would say, "I bet that is a hard job, Steve. Tell me what you did today that has made you so tired."

When J.J. broke his arm at the cabin, my folks were angry at me, which quickly turned to sullenness, because I didn't report the news. They felt they deserved "the courtesy of a call," but with the tension surrounding the accident, calling my parents was the last thing on my mind. Anyway, I caught hell for it.

Another time, when my boys were away visiting their mom, I met up with my folks at church. My mom asked how I was doing and I told her I'd been feeling lonely. I didn't expect it when she said, "Well, you have brought this on yourself." I felt that comment was insensitive and it didn't sit well with me.

I've heard my parents' ill-founded criticism of my child-raising capabilities: "Paul is so miserable without his mother"; "Steve, you need to be a better nurturer"; "The boys aren't doing as well in school as they used to." I disagree with those comments. They're frustrating and maddening. There are times when I really appreciate my parent's support and involvement, but it's hard to take their criticism whenever I don't take their advice.

I discovered I'm not the only single parent with this problem.

I consulted four different family therapists who specialize in blended families. I told them about the concerns I had with my parents, and listened to their professional opinions. Here are some of the conclusions I've drawn from those meetings. Maybe you can relate to them.

Conflicts over the welfare of the children between the single parent and the grandparents is a common problem, which the therapists said they see frequently. When a spouse leaves the scene, a new struggle for family leadership emerges, to the point where the grandparents might question: "Who's in charge of the children, them or the parent?" In most cases, the grandparents mean well. They see their child, who is the struggling single parent, as needy, so they want to come to the rescue. They also have a vested interest in their grandchildren. If the grandparents begin to assume too much power and authority over the children, the single parent becomes resentful, resulting in heated arguments among the adults. A couple therapists said that simply being more assertive might help to ease the tension. Telling the grandparents that, "I'm a capable parent and we're doing fine," helps to reassure them.

My parents and I have many of the same opinionated behavioral traits; we're assertive people by nature. In the past, when I've asserted myself by telling them that I'm a capable parent in charge of my family, they've usually construed that stand as a hostile act, from which they would feel dejected.

Doctor Cheryl Leitschuh, a licensed psychologist who works with children and families in St. Paul, said that each situation depends on the particular dynamics of the family.

"Sometimes the people involved need to step outside their immediate system for outside opinions. It might be other family members, friends, relatives or professional therapists who are needed to point out to the single parent: 'Maybe your parents are right, you do need some help' or, 'I agree with you, your parents are stepping over their bounds.'"

Over time I've learned to simply step back from tit-for-tat arguments with my parents. Instead, when they hurl angry generalities at me, such as, "Steve, you need to be a nurture," I reply with one of my family's three favorite critical thinking, communication questions: "What do you mean?"; "Can you give me an example?"; or, "What do you think about this? (or, that?)."

Those three questions are powerful tools that help me learn the specific cause of concern from the parent making the angry accusation. If, however, I continue hearing the same objection over and over, then I know there isn't much substance to it. For example, "Steve, you need to be a nurturer." Answer: "What do you mean?" or "Give me an example of where I'm falling short." If the reply is simply an angry generality like: "You know what I mean," and doesn't focus on specifics, then without being confrontational, I tell my parent that I need specific examples, and not generalities. Most of the time, those questions help me disarm angry generalities from my parents that could otherwise cause hurt feelings and foster bitter arguments. If tempers become flared, the notepad process★ can be effective in straighten-

---

★ from the Communication Chapter

ing out the differences. Nasty arguments could jeopardize the relationship I have with my support team, which, in spite of a few shortcomings, is a valuable reinforcement to my single parenting efforts. Learning communication techniques that keep the dialogue flowing and boil angry generalities down to specific concerns were milestones on my road to success. You might want to give them a try. They work.

Since my divorce, several people have told me how lucky I am to have had supportive parents in a time of crisis—there's a lot of truth to that assessment. I think I am lucky.

As human beings we all had our beginnings as just two tiny reproductive cells and the conditions under which each of us was born vary infinitely. While I didn't have anything to say about to whom or where I was to be born, I'm smart enough to realize that I got a pretty good shake in life, and I appreciate it. I'm also smart enough to see many other people, who also had a pretty good shake at birth, needlessly break off their parental relationships because of angry disputes caused by the volatility of divorce. So, when people say that I'm lucky to have supportive parents, I agree with them. However, I want them to know that a parent/adult offspring relationship, like any human relationship, takes more than mere luck to work, especially during emotionally stressful times that a divorce triggers. It takes understanding, forgiveness, lots of patience, and a willingness to reach out to each other. My parents, my kids, and I have all hung in there pretty well through the trying times. We've worked hard to make our support group benefit each member.

Support Is Elusive

Anyone who's needed a support group can tell you that support rarely comes knocking on your door unexpectedly and wraps its warm, gentle arms around your grief to comfort you. Support is much more elusive. Dedicated single parents who find the support they need push themselves out the door or pick up the phone and hunt for it.

Since I'm basically a lively and outgoing type of person, being tied down at home with young kids night after night, made me crave meaningful, inspiring, adult conversation.

The first place I looked was my church.

I asked the church office about a singles group. When I discovered one didn't exist, I created one. I wasn't the only single parent needing adult interaction away from the kids. The office ran a small ad in the Sunday bulletin announcing the formation of a single parent group. The following Monday we had over 30 people show up for the first get-together. I was a member for about a year. We enjoyed plenty of good times together through group discussions and other outings, like family picnics. I left the group when I developed other interests, but I still delight in greeting group members at church services, and have remained friends with several of them over the years.

Many single parents claim that the largest concentration of other single parents looking for both support and fun can be found at single's dances. I attended several different club dances until I found the crowd with which I felt the most comfortable. I was looking for a generally up-beat group, one that drew an equal number of men and women, and which fell into my age range.

There's one important feature of a single's dance that I feel is an advantage over the bar scene for meeting people. Almost everyone at a dance, simply by being there, has made an implied statement that they're reaching out to others. Making conversation is easier because it's expected and welcome, unlike a bar, where you never know the kind of response a greeting will bring.

Networking can also be effective. Spread the word that you want to meet other people to family members and your matchmaker friends. A happy, long-term relationship can be just an introduction away.

Team sports like volleyball, softball, and even some non-team sports like skiing and bicycling, generate friendships through common interests. Many people who aren't athletes get involved by cheering from the sidelines. There are other types of clubs looking for members too, such as bridge groups and those that engage in different dining or travel experiences.

"Eligibles" sections in the newspaper seem to be a growing business; probably because it's an effective way of bringing people together. I've placed eligible ads several times, and most have resulted with positive experiences. My "connection" and I might not get past the initial phone conversation, a walk through the park, or a brief luncheon date, but I've become a wiser person from most encounters. Each person has his or her own tale to tell; I usually hear something new with each person I meet. I've learned about effective child rearing techniques, heard personal success stories, and listened to interesting business ideas. There's untapped treasure in every human being. It just takes time and attention to discover it.

I met Jean through an eligibles ad, and we've been seeing each other for about two years. We enjoy each other's companionship, which adds extra bounce and anticipation to our social calendars, and it helps maintain our positive attitudes. We also add support to each other's single parenting.

Jean is a single parent of two daughters, who are about the same age as my boys. She understands many of the same challenges of single parenting that confront me. We comfortably discuss common ground child issues like discipline, school, homework, and even meals. We know we can't fix each other's problems, but we try to understand each other's issues by asking relevant questions and showing concern. Just having an ear on which to unload and a hand to hold for comfort is, many times, all either needs, to help lift the other's spirits when we're down.

It's important for single parents to have support. Support helps build confidence and strength through encouragement. With the increasing numbers of single parent families, there are new support options popping up regularly. I recently learned about a Lutheran Social Service program, Families Home Together. It's a program that pairs single parent families to share housing and encouragement with each other. It's another example of the support that's available for single parents and their families. But it remains up to you to find the kind of support that's beneficial for you and your children. Just remember, support doesn't come knocking on your door—you have to hunt for it.

Sometimes, knowing that you're not alone in your struggle can help you cope while you're searching for an understanding friend. This poem, written by Tine Thevenin, helped me cope with my loneliness before I realized that it was support for my single parenting that I needed most of all. Perhaps you'll find comfort in it as well.

"It is strange, how quiet everything gets, when a human being has confessed to being in despair, to being lost, to being lonesome. It is as if the whole world draws back and looks on helplessly. The sobbing echoes then for the whole world to hear. One lonely person in the multitude of the universe, pressing itself around him yet leaving him in a void, exposed, afraid, wondering why? Wondering, where is everybody?"

J.J. told me once that action hero G.I. Joe has a motto: "Knowing is half the battle." If you come to realize that support is missing from your life as a single parent, I hope you begin your search for a supportive person or group right away. It can help make your job of single parenting a lot more satisfying and productive for you and your children.

Winning The Battle Of Stress Overload

Have you ever thought, "When does this job of single parenting get easier?" There are many days—too many for that matter—when the hectic schedule and the challenges of juggling home, work, and kids are overbearing. The job becomes excessively stressful and wearisome, taking a toll by making me angry and impatient with my children and other people. I learned a memorable lesson on stress overload while visiting my brother in California.

Joyce and I had been having marriage problems. We agreed that it would be a good idea for me to get away for a couple of days. I flew out to visit my brother Phil, who was opening up a new bar and restaurant in Ventura. His grand opening was set for a Friday night. I volunteered to have advertising flyers printed and then I distributed them around the area.

While on the beach, I approached a man and a woman in their thirties; his body language and angry expression suggested that he didn't want anything to do with me. I kept walking towards him, holding up my bundle of flyers.

"I don't care what the hell you're selling I don't want to see it," he yelled. "I can't consider one more issue in my life because if I do I think I'll explode."

This man, I thought, has a giant case of stress-overload. So, I said in a comforting tone of voice, "Don't despair brother, Jesus loves you." My comment surprised him, and got a chuckle out of him. He could probably tell from my cutoffs and T-shirt that my mission was not as an evangelist. As he reached for one of my flyers he said: "What do you have here?" The three of us chatted and I learned that he was taking a doctor's prescribed breakaway from the tension of the computer business in California's Silicon Valley. He was relying on the salty, ocean breezes to unknot his muddled brain. We talked some about the complicated society in which we live. He told me that he was coming to the same conclusion that some of his friends had: "Faster is better, but slower is more humane." I told him those are well-advised words we should all live by. I offered to buy them a pitcher of beer at the bar later but they didn't show up. I'll always remember our conversation.

"Faster is better but slower is more humane."

Many dedicated single parents get into the rut of trying to accomplish too much in too little time with the end result of stress overload. Here's a lesson I learned from business.

I'm the only employee of the Steve Horner Corporation. I'm the sole person responsible for running a successful company. I canvass for new clients, devise and implement advertising and marketing strategies for my clients, create new ads, and do all my company's billing and book work. As I go, so goes the Steve Horner Corporation. For now, my family and I are happy keeping the business at its present size.

Being a one-man show though, limits how much money I can make. If I bring in lots of new business and, all of a sudden, all my clients simultaneously decide to have me work on their projects, I'll get swamped, get behind, and irritate them all. To be a good manager, I must limit how many customers I can effectively handle at one time. I make less, but I keep my customers satisfied and my life under control.

Being a dedicated single parent also requires being a good manager because, you too, are a one-person show. To be effective it's wise to keep the demands placed on you at a manageable level.

A good manager makes tough decisions and holds to them. Years ago when Paul was about to turn 13, I made plans for him and 20 of his friends to celebrate with a hay ride at a horse ranch. I needed to buy food, shop for a gift, and coordinate travel plans with the parents. The hay ride was planned for noon on a Saturday.

In the meantime, I'd been running wild with a very demanding customer who had also planned a big event for that Saturday. I was scheduled to be done with my business work Friday afternoon. On Saturday morning, my customer called and wanted me to do some extra work on her project that morning. When I told her that I couldn't because of my boy's birthday party I could feel the resentment sizzle through the phone lines. I said I was sorry, but there was nothing I could do. Had I acted and worked really, really, really fast, maybe I could've taken care of my customer's concern, but that wasn't the humane thing to do. I didn't want to jeopardize my son's special day by losing the patience and energy I needed to personally cope with it effectively. The hay ride and party was a big success but I stopped getting new business from my client, forfeiting thousands of future dollars.

That's the way it sometimes goes with dedicated single parenting. I've recognized that my business can't make as much money as I'd like because making money interferes with the needs of my children. I've told my boys that they also have to do their part and not expect to have the goodies that some of their friends might, and in the meantime, be content with what they do have.

To be an effective and productive single parent, I have to stay focused on keeping my schedule at a humane pace. That often requires a delicate balancing act between business and family demands. I need to keep paying attention to the importance of making wise management decisions. That's a fundamental principle to reduce the strain of single parenting in my life. There are other stress reduction methods that also work for me.

Daily exercise helps me vent my frustrations and build a feeling of well-being. Books, music, movies, concerts, stage plays, and community involvement also help me control stress by compelling me to slow down and relax and focus on issues outside of myself. Some people rely on hobbies, like playing an instrument, or team sports, like volleyball and softball, or individual sports, like hunting and fishing.

I was jogging one day in the woods near my home when I spotted a man fishing on the shore of the lake. "Catching anything?" I yelled as I ran past. "Yeah! Quiet time," was his answer.

We're constantly bombarded with noise nowadays, and quiet time has become an important way to reduce stress. I like to stretch out on my living room floor, or maybe on a park bench, close my eyes, and take a short, rejuvenating break from the noisy, busy world by shutting

TACKLING SINGLE PARENTING

it out. I instruct my mind and every cell in my body to slow down and relax. It's a quick switch from high gear, to low gear. It feels good. In addition to quiet time, I rely on plenty of rest, a balanced diet, hot showers in the winter, cool showers in the summer, and lots of laughs. For years, experts have claimed success at linking humor and laughter to helping relieve heart and muscle ailments, improving brain functions, and even to helping cure debilitating illnesses like cancer. It's a fact that humor eases the tension of stress.

I was in Vietnam when humor helped reduce the stress of a freaked out infantry point man. It was another hot, muggy evening during the spring of 1968. My friend, Mike Coltrin, and I had enjoyed a few cold beers at the N.C.O. Club at Camp Enari, the 4th Infantry Division Headquarters near Pleiku in the Central Highlands. During our walk back to company headquarters we started marching down the middle of the muddy road singing the Battle Hymn of the Republic. As we approached the company area, somebody yelled to us, "Hey, you jackasses. Get down!" Coltrin and I huddled up with a group of guys near a bunker. The power generator had been shut off, so the compound was eerily quiet, and dark. "Burchette has gone crazy and has been scattering rifle fire around the area," came the hushed explanation.

Al Burchette was an all right guy from Ohio, and had been the point man for our company in the boonies. Coltrin and I thought that the name "Burchette" sounded a lot like "birdshit," so that's what we called him:

"Hey, Birdshit! If you're pissed off, why don't you take it out on the idiot second lieutenant instead of us pee-ons? Coltrin and I will steal a deuce and a half, pick you up, and the three of us will get the hell out of here. What d'ya say?"

Burchette hurled back some expletives and then tossed his rifle to the ground. Our ripe humor had eased an explosive situation caused by a really stressed out dude.

I often rely on humor to curb my stress. It might not be your type of humor, but it works for me. Like the time I stood in the checkout line at the grocery store. It had been a long business day, and I was trying to rush through my domestic chores. I felt burned out. Suddenly, I grabbed one of the weekly news tabloids off the rack and held it up.

"Oh my God!" I blurted out loud. "Here's proof that there's life on other planets." "Ahhhhhhhh phooey," the older woman in front of me said disgustedly. "You can't believe everything you read in there." The check-out lady could hardly contain her laughter. I loved it.

On another day, I was frantically trying to juggle kids, business, and everything else I needed to get done. During the noon hour, I rushed into a Denny's restaurant for a quick bowl of soup. The tables were full so I went to the counter. Just as I sat down, a tall, burly black man wearing sun glasses sat down next to me. The waitress was right there and asked if we were together. I responded by putting my arm around this guy's shoulders and said, "Together? Hell, can't you see we're twins?" Being an average size, 40-something, balding white guy, my comment brought a big laugh from all three of us.

The management of the Minneapolis Public Works Department bowed to the disgruntled whims of one angry woman who had been whistled at by a public construction worker. Their new policy stated that workers on the job could not "ogle" at women for more than nine seconds without being reprimanded. I, and thousands of other people in the Twin Cities, thought that was going a little too far with the gender sensitivity issue.

So, I took action.

I bought a bright yellow construction helmet and wrote "I love to ogle" in bold black letters on the front and back, and replaced "love" with shiny red hearts. I bought googly eye glasses at a novelty store, packed up my binoculars and commercial size broom, donned my jeans, work boots, leather gloves, and sunglasses, took off my shirt, and went downtown.

I found a busy corner, adjacent to a public crew working on the street and I began to ogle. The reaction was hilarious. The crew loved it. Cops and bus drivers gave me "thumbs up." A few women who walked by didn't appreciate my antics, but most did. One woman jumped out of her car and came running with a camera.

"This is great," she laughed, as she asked a bystander to take a picture of us together.

The brief but humorous episodes at Denny's, the grocery store, and going downtown to protest the ogling policy, might seem outrageous to many people, especially where I live in stoic Minnesota, but who cares? As Waylon Jennings avows: "I've always been crazy but it's kept me from going insane." These whimsical impulses make me laugh, feel carefree, and put the thoughts of my hectic schedule on the back burner for awhile, giving me time and space to relax. It's a break from the seriousness of life, and the endless demands of others. Acting "crazy" is one of my many anecdotes for curing the blues and making myself happy. I recognized a long time ago, that with each passing day, I'm as happy as I set my mind to be.

The Obstacle Of Confusion

We all realize that life is full of roadblocks that we must either go around, or climb over. We know from experience that we're bound to run into obstacles in our quest for happiness. Early in my divorce, I ran into one of those obstacles—It was called confusion.

Communication with my ex-wife had completely broken down before the divorce, so I never got a clear-cut answer why she divorced me other than, "I don't love you anymore." I wondered what I could have done differently. What could she have done differently? I was confused. Then came the confusion of trying to keep my children supported up on the frayed edges of what was once our family's solid home front. I found an unexpected friend in my journal.

For several years prior to my divorce, I had kept a daily journal that mostly detailed weather patterns, lighthearted personal thoughts, family, and business events. I kept adding new material, and very rarely flipped back to read prior entries. During the turmoil of the divorce and for years after, I discovered that I found great comfort in my journal. My new entries helped define my thoughts, and organize the confusion in my life. Sorting out, and then recording my problems on paper helped me piece together a road map for the future. My philosophy now is that you can't know where you're going until you know where you are and where you've been.

I've spoken to other single parents who've been advised by psychotherapists to write down their thoughts when they're confused. One single parent told me, "I went to a therapist and told her that I'm so confused, but I don't know exactly why. I just know I'm miserable."

Her therapist suggested that she write down her thoughts to help clarify her predicament. Her recording helped her understand her mixed-up, post-divorce situation, and gave her some peace. As G.I. Joe says, "Knowing is half the battle."

Celebrate Success

Dedicated single parenting is full of trial and error. When you get through a particularly challenging episode, do yourself a favor, and take time to reward yourself. Give yourself and your children a chance to celebrate success together. While I was going through my post-divorce challenges of learning how to be a dedicated single parent, moving to a new home, and settling into my own business, my boys and I took the time to commemorate each accomplishment. We paused to reflect when we met a goal, such as good school grades, or a new business account. We didn't need much fanfare. Maybe a picnic at the lake, a bowl of ice cream, or supper at a sit-down restaurant. At those times, I would tell my boys about our progress, and how proud I was of all of us for making our single parent home a success, in spite of the hardships. Reaping rewards for a job well done helps us cope, as a family, with the challenges of single parenting.

Striving to cope with the difficulties of single parenting is needed to succeed at tackling this job. Coping can be a real struggle, and I've fallen down on the job many times. Like the time I took the boys to church services at a different church than we normally attend. We left the house in plenty of time. I should've taken Paul's advice on the quickest route to the church, but I was intent on taking a shortcut. My "shortcut" took an extra 20 minutes, because the road was under repair and we had to double back. I was furious at myself. I was cussing and yelling, and the more I cussed the madder I got, because I felt childish and hypocritical for acting like this on the way to church. I finally settled down and accepted that we were going to be 20 minutes late.

I tried to come to grips with having blown my cool, no doubt from the stress brought on by the ever-present demands of single parenting. I could only apologize to the boys, assure them that I was mad at myself, not them, and tell them that my behavior was improper and not to be imitated.

TACKLING SINGLE PARENTING

There was another, unexpected turn of events. My two-year relationship with Jean broke up. The blame can't be pinned on either one of us, specifically. The break-up was a culmination of disputes over issues that many busy, dedicated single parents would find familiar—time, energy, understanding, values, and kids. We loved each other, so breaking up was hard to do.

I miss my friend, sweetheart, and support.

My break-up with Jean is another example of the many challenges with which single parents have to cope. Those unfortunate incidents remind single parents that we're not perfect, nor are we alone. Many of the pressures of single parenting are universal, and they take their toll on each of us. Learning to cope has helped me keep the negative experiences to a minimum, and to effectively deal with the hardships. Coping helps my boys and me continue moving forward with our single parenting efforts.

Family Finances

Money Can Be A Crippler

I'm certain that if I had begun my single parenting as a wealthy man I wouldn't be the satisfied, successful business owner that I am today. I wouldn't know half as much as I do about anything, and I doubt that my boys would be doing as well as they are, in school or out of it.

Not having money was a blessing rather than a curse. Nothing encourages creative thinking quite like being destitute. Wealth would've allowed me to take a comfortable, unencumbered sight-seeing tour through single parenting. It could've been the most destructive path for my family. Having money would've provided the convenience of ever-present child care and self-indulgent personal entertainment, rather than the opportunity and need to better myself and my boys.

In the years following the divorce, my boys and I spent most evenings at home enjoying our time together by preparing meals, playing games, reading, and getting smarter. Reading books never interested me much before. After the divorce, however, I decided to make the most of my single parenting years and reading became a way to make progress with my life. Not much fiction; mostly about famous people, issues, and events. I read often to my kids, benefitting all three of us. Our reading sessions broadened my boys' horizons with new knowledge, improved their vocabularies, and gave us plenty of cozy, quiet time together.

Having money might've caused me to miss the gnawing, gut-wrenching fears that accompany an uncertain future. Those fears forced me to explore every option for providing my family with security, and eventually starting my own business. Wealth would've eliminated my need to learn to be thrifty, wise, strong, and creative. With money I would've missed the feeling of pride that comes with achieving success on your own. Money might've acted as an enabler and, as I teach my children, enablers can prevent people from moving ahead when they must.

The word "enable" means to furnish with power—something many of us need a boost of now and then during our lives. It's short-sighted, however, to furnish people with lifetime crutches.

Enablers come in many shapes and sizes. Local and federal governments become enablers when their social programs stunt personal initiative and ambition. I think charities often engender many of the social problems caused by enabling activity. In early 1995, *The St. Paul Pioneer Press* published my views about enabling and its negative impact on people:

> "I'm confused about Mary Jo Copeland and her Minneapolis charitable organization, Sharing and Caring Hands. Copeland has addressed the congregation at my church in Burnsville each year for about the last three years. With each visit she has made a plea for support by quoting huge increases in the number of people she serves every month. The last number was 12,000, up 2,000 from the year before.
>
> "I wonder why her numbers are increasing. An inner-city church that our congregation serves with a monthly 'Loaves and Fishes' program used to attract over 500 hungry souls. Now that number is down to a third of that. Minnesota's unemployment rate is the lowest it has been since 1978 and a full two percentage points below the national average. Inflation is hardly noticeable. A December 25 front page photo in *The Pioneer Press* showed a long line of people standing outside Sharing and Caring Hands waiting for free food, entertainment and gifts. The people standing in line appeared to be young, able-bodied people wearing designer jackets. Some were listening to head phones. This candid photo was in sharp contrast to the recent onslaught of paid newspaper ads asking

for money and featuring Copeland huddled in a group of stark-eyed, refugee-looking youngsters of several races.

"The question I have for her: Is the $4 million she is raising annually being used to help eliminate an existing problem of poverty in the Twin Cities or is her 'guiding light' simply drawing flies from a wider area? I think her organization should be more appropriately named, Sharing, Caring and Enabling Hands."

You'd think that if Sharing and Caring Hands played such an essential role in society that at least a few people would be up in arms over my lambasting letter. I received only one phone call concerning the article and that was from my friend, Tom. Tom and I had met during a long distance bicycle ride two summers earlier while my kids were in Arizona with their mom. He jokingly yelled, "Horner! You're an insurrectionist! My wife and I gave money to that group this past Christmas." As it turned out, he and his wife agreed with the article's conclusion. He paraphrased the old saw, "Why limit your charity to giving a person a couple of fish when you can do him a much bigger favor by teaching him how to fish?" I agreed wholeheartedly. Abraham Lincoln said it best, "You cannot help men permanently by doing for them what they could and should do for themselves." I told Tom the story of my being on the U.S.S. Sanctuary hospital ship in February, 1968 after being wounded in action in Vietnam. The wounds I incurred to my neck, shoulder and leg weren't life threatening, but they kept me confined to bed for several weeks. I also suffered from an infection and malaria, so I felt pretty miserable.

While I was mending, a Navy corpsman, Boone, had been assigned to help make me comfortable. Boone would bring me my mail, magazines, sodas, breakfast, lunch, and supper. Whenever I needed anything, I only had to call on Boone.

One morning I called Boone and asked him why he hadn't brought my breakfast yet. He said, "Get it yourself." I cursed at him. I felt abandoned. "Boone! I'm weak as hell. My leg is still killing me. Please get my breakfast for me!" Boone simply said, "Get it yourself." I stumbled out of bed, put on a robe, and I cussed out Boone with every slight, dizzying step I took on the way to the mess hall.

TACKLING SINGLE PARENTING

I didn't see Boone for about three days after my first solo journey to breakfast. By then I was out of bed, except to sleep at night. Most of my time was spent on deck, soaking up the warm sun of the South China Sea. "Ahhh, this is the life," I thought to myself as I closed my eyes and leaned back on my deck lounger.

"Was it worth the effort to get your own breakfast last week?"

I opened my eyes, and there was Boone, standing between the sun and me. We both laughed and had a good-natured visit. I told him how mad I'd been at him, and how quickly that anger turned to gratitude for making me get out of bed and work for myself. He said, "I knew you were mad but it was what your body needed to heal." We remained good friends until I left the ship. Boone had taught me a valuable, lifelong lesson on enabling.

Tom's response to my hospital ship story was, "You betcha! Enabling is definitely a big part of the larger problem."

Enabling can be a disabling crutch to which I try to prevent my family from falling prey. Sometimes we need the crutches kicked out from under us so that we can resolve the difficult situations as they arise at home, school, work, play. We need them kicked out from under us so we can ultimately better ourselves.

Instilling A Sense Of Value Of Money In Children

I avoid being an enabling parent by not handing over piles of money to my sons on demand. When Paul was 14, he knew students who received as much as $50 a week in allowance. I wouldn't be surprised if some kids got twice that amount. My boys earned $1 a week from the time they could handle a dust rag and vacuum cleaner. Paul maxed out at $4 per week at 15. He stopped receiving an allowance when he began working regular hours at an outside job, but even then he was still required to do his household chores. At 13, I increased J.J.'s allowance to $4 per week.

$4 a week isn't a lot of money, but I made it seem like a lot. When both boys were receiving allowances, I only paid them every four to six weeks. After Saturday morning chores were finished, I would boldly announce, "PAYDAY!" My boys would hustle into the kitchen where we counted off the number of weeks due from our special allowance calendar. $24 seemed like a lot of money to a fella J.J.'s age, especially when I slowly counted out four, crisp, five dollar bills followed by four, crisp, one dollar bills, laying them one by one on his eagerly outstretched hand. Payday was always accompanied by a big hug, a kiss, handshake, and a hearty "thank you" from me for a job well done. The proud answer I enjoyed hearing most was "you're welcome!"

After payday, both boys realized that they had a sizable wad of money in hand; they also knew that three to five dollars had to go into savings, and the balance needed to last for another month, or longer. The boys have been stashing away a portion of their allowance, gifts, and outside work money since they started receiving allowances. J.J. has close to $4,000 and Paul has about $5,600. That's a nice start to buying a house or setting up a business when they're ready.

Paul realized that if he wanted to join his friends for a first run movie, the hefty ticket price would cut a huge swath through his budget. When J.J. wanted to play video machines, he knew that two or three dollars was a big chunk to pay for a few minutes of entertainment. The way I see it, the small allowance didn't discourage my boys from seeing every first run movie that came along or spending long hours with expensive video machines. Rather, it encouraged them to think about alternative activities where money didn't play a part. Lots of money only serves as an enabling crutch to a youngster. With limited funds, my boys matured by learning thrift and by coming to understand that money doesn't buy happiness—two fundamental principles I use to teach about financial affairs.

The kids have handled their money pretty well over the years. If they ran short during the month, they could borrow a couple of bucks from me until payday. My goal was to leave it up to them to volunteer to pay me back. Sometimes, however, it required a few reminders. Paying debts on time is another important principle of financial affairs. That's how a person establishes good credit and more importantly, a good name in the business world.

Like a lot of parents, I, too, can be a pushover. When the kids were out of money—and I knew they hadn't been wasting it—I'd flip them a couple of bucks just to keep them in spending cash; "it's a reward for being a good guy." If they wanted an extra $10 or $20 however, to make up the difference in cost for a name brand pair of shoes or clothing item that I thought extravagant, then they had to get out and work for it. It's an amazing phenomenon to see how a "must have" item can quickly lose its importance as soon as a son or daughter realizes that he or she must fork over part of the cost. Sometimes, however, a "must have" item creates determination.

I remember the first time I told Paul to go out and look for work. He was nine or ten and had been bugging me to buy him an entire set of TOPPS baseball cards. "I'm happy you're interested in your hobby," I told him, "and I'll gladly contribute some money to your set, but you have to pick up the bulk of the cost." He became frustrated and teary-eyed with me and asked, "How am I supposed to make money? Nobody will hire me until I'm older." I told him to go around the neighborhood, knock on doors and ask for odd jobs. He came back in about an hour with his young face full of excitement. "Dad! I have two jobs." He told me that one job required him to pick up apples from under an old apple tree in a person's back yard, and that somebody else wanted him to help with garden work. He told me that he was just checking in so I'd know where he was going to be, and then off he flew. A few hours later he came back with two, five dollar bills and a big grin.

Both kids have been industrious over the years. J.J. has made as much as $20 on a hot afternoon selling lemonade, and Paul made $41 one day trading and selling baseball cards at a homemade stand near a busy intersection close to home. Business wasn't always so brisk every time they set up shop, but experiencing the ups and downs is part of learning about business. Both boys have had money stolen from their stands, an unfortunate lesson that's also part of business. They have learned to appreciate the effort that goes into earning an honest day's wages.

Keeping the boys in business required extra time and patience for me when they were younger. I taught them how to make change for customers, and the difference between expense and profit. I helped J.J. make pitcher after pitcher of lemonade, and helped Paul lug his card stand to the corner. It wasn't long, however, before the finer points of making money got through to them. J.J. learned to take his own seed money and bike to several stores to find the cheapest price on lemonade. He learned that the more he saved on overhead, the more he could put in his pocket. I reminded J.J. not to compromise on the quality of his product telling him that a lousy product today would mean fewer customers tomorrow.

A short time later both boys organized and operated a garage and driveway rummage sale, completely on their own. They sorted and priced old, usable clothes, toys, books and other knick-knacks that I was happy to get rid of. They set it up each morning and tore it down in the afternoon for two consecutive weekends. They netted close to $100. I was really proud of their effort and success, and not once did they need to involve me in the project.

When Paul was 15, I encouraged him to look for a regular job. He rode his bike to ten stores applying for work, until he was finally hired by a lawn and garden store. For the rest of the summer, he diligently rode his bike to and from that store, a distance of just over two miles each way, and was never late. He told me, "I like working hard. It really wakes me up and gets me going." I told him that's the attitude that bosses like to see in their employees, it leads to raises and promotions.

Proper fiscal management is a learned process. When I was growing up, it was not popular for parents to share family expenses with their children. The topic of money was "hush, hush." I didn't benefit from that philosophy of privacy as a child. It handicapped my understanding the monetary value of big ticket expenditures, like business, real estate, and automobiles. I've taken the approach of sharing information about expenses, taxes, and income with my kids. It creates a benchmark from which to judge value. If my kids know how much I make, and how much I pay out in expenses, then they learn how much money it takes to live comfortably, as we now do.

The long hours I've worked with Paul and J.J on financial affairs, without serving as an enabler, has rewarded all three of us handsomely with the pride and hard-earned money that comes from a job well done.

Keeping Your Money Out Of Other People's Pockets

Have you ever thought about your philosophy toward money? What's your general attitude about the almighty dollar? Throughout history, many people have expressed their feelings on the subject. A business acquaintance told me, "Money is the gauge I use to judge the success or failure of my business." Henry Ford once said, "Money is like an arm or a leg; use it or lose it." Timothy, in the New Testament, says, "For the love of money is the root of all evil." Then there's the admonishing, old New England saying, "If you want to know what God thinks of money, look at the people he gives it to." Out of all the philosophies about money, the one I most closely follow is that of former U.S. Supreme Court Justice, Oliver Wendell Homes, who was known as the "Great Dissenter" because of the brilliance of his dissenting opinions: "Put not your trust in money, but put your money in trust." When I say, put your money in trust, I mean, put your money where people can't get to it, and that includes you.

Where's your money going and will it be there when you need it most? Local, state, and federal governments keep raising taxes and fees, leaving each of us with less money to spend at our own discretion. The future of the Social Security program keeps coming up for legislative debate. Can you and I depend on that money being there when we need to tap into it? Unsecured, commercial investments are fickle and nerve-wracking. Many pensions and profit-sharing programs that millions of people once relied on for their retirement are now either broke or worth only a fraction of original expectations. In many cases, court-ordered child support—on which many single parents depend—stopped coming in, or became sporadic, at best. And, you're continuously bombarded by retail advertising schemes, their only goal is to get your money without any consideration for what happens to your over-extended family budget.

So how do you fight back against these seemingly insurmountable odds? My family and I have had to learn how to successfully fight them. My annual income of $25,000, with little or no child support, forced us to be thrifty, but at the same time allowed us to be peaceful and content with life.

I started my single parenting career with $15,000 from my half of the house sale proceeds, and about $200 a month for two years from the sale of a jointly owned business property. By the time I had recovered from the divorce and survived a couple of job losses, I was down to under $500. Today I'm totally debt free, own and operate a successful business, have two automobiles, eat well, dress well, take regular vacations, pay taxes, give time and money to my community, and have over $50,000 equity in my home. I'm far from being rich, but that's never been my goal.

Making money demands time, energy, and patience and those are precious commodities that I'd have to steal from the dedicated single parenting that is my top priority. My family and I live a happy, productive life. We do the things we want to do, and in the meantime, I'm reaching my long-term retirement goals.

My financial philosophy is to keep as many people away from my money as possible. Plus, I pay myself a salary that even I can't get my hands on. Since most of my monthly income goes to pay other people, I should at least get a small slice of the pie. Every month I pay taxes, the grocer, the dry cleaner, the gas station, the bank for the mortgage, the hardware store, the department store, the auto mechanic, insurance, the kids, and the list goes on and on. When do I get paid?

A neighbor of mine posed that question to me many years ago and it made sense. "When do you get paid? If you don't pay yourself something each month, sooner or later it'll wind up in someone else's pocket and you wind up with nothing." My neighbor concluded, "It can be horribly discouraging if, after working hard for several years, you haven't accumulated any property equity, investments, or savings." I'm not speaking about paying yourself a salary so you can blow it in Cancun or Las Vegas. Rather, I'm talking about putting your money in trust, a place where you don't see it, and where it can't tempt you when you're low on funds. The monthly amount doesn't have to be much to start a small treasure for yourself. Paul knows that's true from his stockpile of $5,600. I know a lot of single parents who would love to have $5,600 in their savings accounts, drawing interest.

I started by paying myself a salary of $50 a month and soon bumped that up to $100, and then to $200. I explored money-saving options by visiting with a couple of investment firms, but didn't feel comfortable with their "experts." In fact, one man who worked for a large, well-known investment firm had a downright ridiculous approach to money. He "shared" the "wisdom" of leveraging. That is, to buy something you can't really afford, but hope that the return on your investment will pay the initial purchase price. I told him, "I think that's a dangerous and risky type of investment." "Not actually," he said.

TACKLING SINGLE PARENTING

"Conrad Hilton, the successful founder of Hilton hotels, coined the term, 'leveraged to the hilt.' Leveraging has become a way of life in the business world." After that preposterous assertion I thought to myself that this man is not going to get my money. The "hilt" to which he was mistakenly referring is the handle on a sword, not Conrad Hilton. Furthermore, I'm much too cautious with my meager funds to spend sleepless nights thinking about leveraging and risky investments, much less handing my money over to someone who had showed very little interest in my personal financial goals, needs, or concerns.

I believe that the way to make big bucks through the stock market is with proper timing. You need to have the time and resources to pick through the daily criteria that affect your investment, and then buy or sell based on that information. An article from an investment journal reported, "Financial experts say that for most investors, trying to time investments in the stock market is too difficult. They often end up selling when prices are low and buying when they are high." The implication is that you need to keep your money in these investments over the long term, riding the highs and the lows. Thanks, but I don't need to add more anxiety to my life. As a dedicated single parent, I already have all that I can bear.

I realize there are professional money managers who can help investment funds grow. I also realize that leveraging can and does make many people very wealthy. I simply had come to the conclusion that these money-making strategies were not right for me, not at this time in my life, anyway.

I made the decision to pay myself by putting extra money into my house payment. Every month, regardless of the difficulty, I reward myself with a salary used toward the principal of my mortgage. It's a money saving strategy from which I receive many benefits.

My initial house loan was for $80,000 in 1986, a conventional 30-year loan at 9 1/2 percent interest. My monthly payments, not including insurance or taxes, but just principal and interest, is $672.68 per month. If I paid that amount for 12 months a year for 30 years, I would eventually pay the bank $242,164.80. That's a whopping $162,164.80 more than my initial loan of $80,000. The difference is interest comprised of my hard earned money, paid directly into the bank's coffers.

If I pay myself an average monthly salary of $163 and apply that money towards my mortgage principal, I can accelerate my loan payoff by 15 years. My monthly "salary" will earn a healthy 9 1/2 percent interest, and it'll cut my total mortgage expenditure by almost $92,000. More money for me, less for the bank.

When the 15-year loan period is over and my mortgage is paid, I'll be able to pay myself a monthly salary of $835.68—the total of the original mortgage amount of $672.68 plus my initial salary of $163. It'll be up to me whether I invest my "salary" in the best interest-yielding investment plan I can find, or take a couple extra vacations a year. It'll be my choice. Either way, I'll have a home that's rent free, mortgage free, and worth well over $100,000, allowing for inflation. I'm excited about this prospect and it'll happen as long as I pay myself that salary. It's an investment program that's safe, stable, easy, and productive.

Another way to keep people away from your hard-earned money, I teach my children, is to get involved with the public issues that involve your money. Whenever the government tries to control more of my money through taxation, I object loudly. I believe that given the option of allowing the government to raise my taxes by 10-15 percent so they can "improve my life," or allowing me to keep 10-15 percent of my income so I can improve my own life, my family and I will do much better with the latter.

A perfect example of government trying to assume more control of my money comes from the Metropolitan Council for the Minneapolis/St. Paul and surrounding region. Many metro areas have similar, central, policy-making organizations. The Council is the chief policy maker for several giant public programs in a seven-county system. It operates on annual revenues of over half a billion dollars. The Council sets standards and goals for community programs which include highways, air and water quality management, woodlands, land pollution, parks, airports, public transportation, and the economic growth of the area. The state legislature has given the Council authority to levy taxes on local communities to carry out the Council's plans. It's the plans for "economic growth" that has many area citizens, including me, concerned and upset. Out of almost a dozen primary work projects at the Council, the area of economic growth, which includes Housing and Redevelopment, consumes the lion's share of

TACKLING SINGLE PARENTING

staff resources. Over 30 percent of Council planners and administrators are used in this department with fighting poverty their #1 mission. I've learned from experience that when government "do-gooders" try to fight poverty, it's time to hold on tight to my wallet.

The Metropolitan Council has proposed in their Regional Blueprint, released in September of 1994, that they will aggressively make changes to areas where poverty is concentrated. The Blueprint reports that among the nation's 25 largest metro areas, poverty rates for the white population and for people of color living in Twin Cities suburbs rank in the middle. However, poverty among Twin Cities urban residents of color is highest among the 25 areas. A significant number of these households are headed by single parents, many of whom are not in the labor force. Quoting from the Blueprint: "A household with only one adult is more vulnerable to economic setbacks, with the children more vulnerable to the physical and emotional stress of poverty." The Blueprint continues: "Hopelessness, anger, and crime may develop in a community that does not offer future opportunities for its residents. One approach to alleviating the effects of poverty is to improve conditions within areas of high poverty concentration. That would include creating jobs, upgrading housing conditions, and adding stores, services, and community centers in the neighborhood. A second approach would provide additional housing choices in suburban locations; where education, job and other opportunities can improve conditions in people's lives."

I believe that helping the poor, elderly, and afflicted meet their most basic needs of food, shelter, health care, clothing, and education is a noble cause. After all, there isn't one person among us who isn't susceptible to falling on hard times caused by age or unforeseen circumstances that can profoundly affect our physical, mental, or financial ability to survive.

The question that I ask my boys is how many more public assistance programs need to be enacted before it's made clear that money isn't the cure-all answer in the battle against social ills in America?

In free-spending states, like Minnesota, a whopping 30 percent of the state's total biennial budget of $18 billion is already being spent on social services. Those numbers, from the State Legislative Library, reflect a 100 percent increase since 1967. On the national scene, a preposterous 58 percent of the total annual budget of $1.5 trillion goes to social appropriations.

Private businesses are forced to spend huge amounts of money to keep unemployment funds afloat. In states like Minnesota, the unemployment tax for business owners is as high as 9.1 percent for each employee taxed on wages, up to $15,100 per year. Therefore, a small business that employs ten people must pay out almost $14,000 a year in benefits to unemployed people.

Social Security and Medicare/Medicaid programs take almost 8 percent of the gross income of working Americans, up to an individual annual maximum income of $61,200. Those mandatory contributions support the Social Security Retirement Fund, health care programs for the elderly and poor, plus disability and survivor's benefit programs.

On top of the Social Security tax burden, every American worker must also pay state and federal taxes. In many cases, that adds up to an additional 35-40 percent of their gross income. For the sake of comparison, when I was born in 1947, a median income family of four paid virtually no income taxes, and only about $60 per year in Social Security. And, be sure to include the ever-increasing fees and sales tax that are tagged onto purchases of licenses, gasoline, and other consumer goods and services.

Why this enormous increase in tax demand? Take a look at the hundreds of billions of dollars that the nation spends on welfare-style appropriations every year. The dictionary defines "welfare" as "charity."

There are Aid to Families with Dependent Children (AFDC) style programs. There are the federal food stamp and the Earned Income Tax Credit programs. There are school breakfast and lunch programs. Billions of dollars are spent on student grants and loans—often defaulted on. There are medical assistance, child care vouchers, and public housing programs. According to the 1995 Taxpayers Guide to Federal Spending, these programs alone account for close to 40 percent of the nation's total annual budget.

"Bullshit to more spending," I tell advocates of welfare. The current system is set up in such a despicable manner that a person who earns only $12,000 a year, and who takes advantage of all the available government handout programs, has more discretionary spending cash than the hard-working, dedicated single parent who earns a respectable

TACKLING SINGLE PARENTING

$35,000 a year, and who must support herself and two children out of her own pocket. Where's the incentive to get off welfare? The system is absurd, and unfair.

At the very top of this heap is the massive tax fraud that occurs every year. In 1994, the I.R.S. reported fraud of over $5 billion from the previous year on a single tax item—the Earned Income Tax Credit. Many economists say that's only the tip of the iceberg. How much more hard-earned tax money is simply forfeited to fraud each year? $10 billion? $50 billion? $100 billion? More?

Even though there are major government spending cuts continually proposed in congress, I'm reporting the enormous amount of social spending for 1995. I challenge anybody to show me another country in the world that's had more public assistance programs phased in, and more charitable money dished out to its citizens in the last 30 years, than the United States. Yet, in spite of colossal social spending programs, the public demand for more keeps rising. Every day, while the federal budgets are being analyzed, the media reports about conservatives who "want to reward the rich by taking food from the mouths of children." I can assure the media that my moderate income family will fare much better if the spending budgets are slashed.

The problem that my family has with the rising tide of public spending is that my business, general, and property taxes keep rising. My property taxes have doubled in the last five years because our local school district keeps asking for more money, and almost 60 percent of my property taxes go directly for education demands. Plus, the state, county, and city keep taking more money because they're also finding more ways to spend it. At this point, there are no "circuit breakers" to keep my taxes from doubling again in five years, and again in another five years. By then my house will be long since paid off, but my property taxes will constitute more than 70 percent of my current mortgage. That's especially frightening to me since that's the money I plan to put away for retirement. I'll literally be taxed out of my modest three bedroom, rambler-style home unless the rampant spending slows down. I don't see any end in sight.

During the 1994-1995 Minnesota State House session, a Minneapolis legislator, Representative Myron Orfield, re-introduced legislation for the third consecutive year that's referred to as the

Metropolitan Area Fair Tax Base Act. The bill would force area communities to contribute tax proceeds to all other area communities that fall below the metropolitan average in net tax capacity. In Minnesota, it's an ongoing 20-year concept that's been limited to business and industry tax. Orfield's legislation proposes to include residential property tax that would directly impact hundreds of thousands of metro area homeowners by raising property taxes.

The proposed tax-sharing legislation most certainly fits the poverty fighting strategy of the Metropolitan Council, tactics that I characterize as "Let's throw more money at it." That philosophy is warmly embraced by the Twin Cities news media. Their attitude is summed up by Doug Grow, a well-known newspaper columnist in Minneapolis:

"Sure I'm for it, Steve. We all need to work together. You people in white suburbia don't have any idea what's going on in the inner cities."

I get much the same feedback from the Metropolitan Council. When I've appeared before the Council to share my views and strategy for combating inner city poverty, I get disbelieving smirks and rolling eyes in return.

Here's a clear example of the lunacy and shortsightedness of Orfield-style legislation. It would be logical to assume that since the metro area of St. Paul and Minneapolis has 73 percent of the State's AFDC recipients, that all or most of the newly generated funds would go to help these two communities. That's not the case. With the flawed manner in which the program is designed, even my bountiful, little suburban community of Apple Valley—lightheartedly referred to as "Happy Valley"—will be on the receiving end of this liberal gift to the tune of $1 million per year. We don't need the money, and the communities who are being asked to ante up should be outraged. Besides, if history repeats itself, it's just a matter of time before Orfield's gang gets into my family's pockets by expanding the program.

When publicly voicing my opinions on this issue in the newspaper and on the radio, I've been called racist, greedy and cold-hearted by "freedom fighters" like Doug Grow who salve their consciences by throwing money at poverty, but don't want to take the time and effort to get involved in any other manner—they take the easy way out. I don't want to live in a vacuum. I've often told my boys that we should be shepherds and not sheep, leaders and not followers. I'm assertive and stand up for my rights, and I lobby against legislation that I think is destructive to society. I make phone calls and write letters to the governor, legislators, and organizations like the Metropolitan Council to voice my opinions. I want to keep more of my hard-earned money in my family's pocket, not the government's, because they just keep pumping it into endless rat holes with their enabling subsidy programs.

For the third year in a row, Orfield's grandiose scheme narrowly passed the House and Senate. Fortunately, for the third year in a row, Governor Carlson vetoed the bill saying that "it punishes communities that are successful and rewards others for being inefficient." I'd like to feel that my input helped to make a difference defeating the bill and keeping the lid on my property taxes.

The Damn Thing Is Broken

Here's a prime example that I've shared with my boys of the exorbitant expense and relative ineffectiveness of many subsidy programs. In the "continuing battle against poverty," the Metropolitan Council in the Twin Cities, and public policy organizations like it across the country, are the primary conduits for Section Eight Housing. Section Eight is an extremely popular and expensive, federally-funded, rent subsidy program run under the umbrella of Housing and Urban Development (HUD). It's implemented through a state's Housing and Redevelopment Authority (HRA).

To qualify for funds, the applicant's annual income must be at or below the median income. For a family of four, the current qualifying income is a generous $25,500 or less. In 1994, the Metro Council assisted 4,600 households with an average monthly assistance of $471 to help pay rent. That's a total annual outlay of $26 million from just a single HRA office. There are eleven other offices in the Twin Cities region. The combined offices in this region serve over 13,500 families. Imagine the enormous amount spent throughout the 3,200 public HRA regions across the country!

In addition to Section Eight rent subsidy funds, the Council can create an escrow fund for the families they support through the National Family Self-Sufficiency Program. The Council, through this federally funded program, matches the assisted family's additional income, dollar for dollar, for five years. For example, if the family earns an additional $100 per month while on Section Eight, the Council will match that $100 by putting an equal amount into the family's escrow fund every month, up to five years, after which the escrow funds are dispersed to the family. The purpose of the escrow program is to provide an incentive for the family to earn more money from work, build a nest egg, and eventually get off public assistance. A primary indicator of the program's success or failure would have to be the number of active escrow accounts on deposit. As of early 1996, the HRA at the Metropolitan Council reported that out of all their Section Eight customers, only ten families had active accounts. The dollars on deposit in these accounts ranged from a few dollars to a couple hundred. Those feeble savings spell FAILURE!!!

The two HUD programs—the Section Eight Rent Subsidy Program and the National Family Self-Sufficiency Program—create lots of public controversy. Each tax funded program is enormously expensive, and some critics feel that enabling, government programs like Section Eight create a mentality that they'd like to avoid. That philosophy was emphasized by a Twin Cities newspaper article that was written by a single mother who was angry about a subsidized housing unit going up next to her townhouse. In earlier, related stories, the newspaper had expressed its support of the subsidized housing project, and the single mom was loud and clear about her disapproval.

The following excerpts begin by making reference to an already existing controversy among HUD, the City Council, and local residents.

> "What kind of country are we living in that allows the HRA to threaten residents and our City Council members in any community with lawsuits if we don't agree with their proposals? Or better yet, threaten us with higher density housing, accusing us of being ignorant. Who are you (newspaper) to accuse us of lacking morals and of being ignorant?
>
> "Everyone has a right to protect and be emotional about their home and family.
>
> "Our outcry (as you put it) was not against the poor. Some of us have had personal experience living in subsidized hous-

ing or in areas with low-income housing. Why shouldn't we be concerned about our safety when comments that come directly from law enforcement officials lead us to believe that they respond to four to six times the amount of police calls to low-income housing than they do to any other residential areas? Are you suggesting that this information is erroneous?

"I once was a single mother with four children to raise on an $800 per month income. I remember my experience with housing. Have you lived a similar experience? I do not live in one of the expensive homes. My townhouse has a market value of around $69,000. Some of the homeowners in our association don't have an income of as much as $30,000 and some earn much less. Are you saying that because we live where we do the system has distributed wealth to us disproportionately? I will not apologize for working hard to make a better life for myself and neither should any of the residents in question. You are doing what you accused us of, stereotyping and putting the concerned citizens into one class of biased individuals. We have a right to our opinion and to protect our families and homes when we feel a possibility of threat."

I spoke to this single mother on the phone, and I told her how much I supported her concerns. I suggested that she send a copy of her article to the governor and to the Metropolitan Council. I knew immediately that this person wasn't your typical social activist when she said she hadn't heard of the Metropolitan Council, and was nervous about sending a letter to the governor because, as she stated, "I don't want to make trouble." This single mom spoke from her heart and from her experience. She didn't like what subsidized housing was going to bring to her neighborhood. Imagine her distress when I told her that drug addicts and alcoholics are now being classified as "disabled," and are qualifying for subsidized housing assistance through HUD.

So, Let's Fix It

Government handouts only serve as crippling enablers and thwart a person's initiative to make personal improvements. Private organizations like Minneapolis-based, Up and Out of Poverty Now, who often rally on the steps of the State Capitol to protest welfare cuts, only aggravate the problem. In a phone interview with Mark Thisius, the group's leader, I asked him how he helps his members get "up and out of poverty." He said, "Our main function is to publicly protest budget cuts to welfare programs and to train our members (welfare recipients) to canvass door to door, educating the public on the benefits of welfare programs." I told him that sounds like begging. He said, "call it what you want," and he hung up on me.

There need to be more constructive ways of breaking the cycle of poverty than throwing money at it. Organizations like the Metropolitan Council could be more tenacious in promoting technical and vocational schools. With new and useful skills, many people on public assistance could skip the $6 an hour burger-flipping jobs and move into better paying jobs that are certainly available.

During the spring of 1995, the owner of an automobile repair center—where I have my car serviced—told me that he recently spent over $200 in metro-area want ads trying to hire a mechanic. "I ran the ad for over four weeks and didn't get a single response," he said loudly, "and I want you to know my guys make good money, about $35,000 a year."

During the same period, I had a field repairman at my home to service my water heater. He told me that his company, Minnegasco, was looking for 30 to 40 field technicians, starting at $14 an hour, but couldn't find them.

So, when I hear the same old sloppy excuses about quality jobs not being available I suggest that learning a skill provides a solution. Learning specialized skills was how generation upon generation of Americans found work and supported their families. The good news is that many vo-techs already offer financial aid and on-site child care facilities to help struggling, untrained single parents learn new trades so that they, too, can become productive and self-sufficient.

Another solution might be to reinstitute a military draft for 18-year-olds. This time around, the draft could include male and female single parents and their children. Think of it—the parents could learn a specific skill in the military, while their children were safe and sound with on-post child care. At the end of the duty day, mom or dad would pick up the kids after a productive day of learning new skills and earning money. They would carry home a positive attitude, pride, and a hope for the future that they could share with their children.

How about resurrecting a version of President Roosevelt's Civilian Conservation Corps (CCC)? Recruits could learn skills working on bridges, highways, fence lines, waterways, in forestry, and health care programs, while their children were in secure child care programs. Every day the entire family would receive lodging, three square meals, and health care coverage, while the adults earned money and built their futures and self-esteem. The December, 1994 Smithsonian magazine interviewed dozens of former CCC workers and, to a person, they claimed that a program like the CCC should be instituted again. A man from Tennessee recalled, "Just timid, I didn't think I could talk to people. I'd only gone to third grade. The C's gave me confidence that I was as good as anybody. It made me know I could do things, gave me some push. I'm proud that I worked on that Crossville dam. I wasn't afraid to tackle anything after that."

Americorps, the federal program that pays citizens, mostly 18–25 years old to work on community projects, survived its inaugural year in 1995 in spite of much congressional scrutiny. Advocates claim that it's affordable, helps students get through school, teaches skills and does a great deal of good for communities. Individual group leaders boast that the program creates that "can-do" spirit within its workers. Criticism of the program comes from those who say the program is much too expensive for what it delivers. Debate continues.

More legislators in office now recognize the benefits of hard work over cold cash. Minnesota Representative Todd VanDellen came up with a work program that featured creative and affordable financing.

VanDellen's Minnesota bill sought a federal waiver to create a jobs program to have the state contract with employers to hire eligible welfare recipients, specifically AFDC recipients. The monthly AFDC grant would be diverted to the employer as a subsidy, and the welfare recipient would be paid a monthly wage equal to the grant amount plus $2 an hour. Recipients would receive work experience and employers would pay only $2 an hour per worker.

I tell my sons that it's work experience that makes the big difference. It fills people with pride and confidence. It sure did for me. One of the most grueling days I spent as a teenager turned into one of the most rewarding and memorable. I was working weekends and summers at a horse ranch for only $1 a day plus room and board. You might think we were chumps to work for that measly pay, but most of us would've worked for free, the way we loved horses. I was 14 the first summer I worked there. One day, five of us picked up 1,300 bales of hay from the field and hauled rack after rack of hay back to the barn, unloaded it and stacked it. I was so tired at the end of the day I could hardly walk, but I'll never forget the gratifying feeling of accomplishment I had that night before I fell asleep. The fond memory of that personal reward has stayed with me all these years.

I Don't Fall For The Guilt Trip Anymore

I was fortunate to have been raised with solid values and principles by parents who cared about me. That experience gave me strength as an adult. I know that there are plenty of people who had lousy upbringings, with little or no love or concern shown to them. Many of those people were poverty struck, orphaned, or victimized by war and oppression. Yet today's research shows a multitude of those people are now successful and well-adjusted. They made the best out of a bad situation.

I try being generous with the gifts I've been given. Besides the community work with which I stay involved, I volunteered my time and talents at three United Way agencies during the winter of 1994-1995. Not one of them returned my repeated phone calls. I regularly volunteered to speak to African American organizations about my success as a single parent, as well as before single mother groups about starting a business. The black groups told me, "We only invite black speakers" and the women's groups told me, "We only invite women speakers."

I hear members of my society cry out for help. I extend my hand to them, but few grab hold. They just want my money. I tell my kids that the decision to better one's own life has to come from within. Continuing to throw money at people is not the answer. In fact, it only worsens the matter.

My boys and I have seen the babies who are held up as hostages supported with resounding battle cries of, "Give us money! The children are suffering!" Yes, some children will suffer, but it won't be the direct result of a reduction of public assistance funds—millions are already suffering, today. They're being suspended from schools for behavior problems in record numbers. They're engaging in dangerously promiscuous sexual practices, and killing each other on the streets over drugs. They're being arrested for theft, violent crimes, and rape, and they can't read or write. Could their parents have instilled in them more self-esteem, responsibility, discipline, and communication skills? Those are personal qualities that require little or no money to foster, just a lot of dedication. Many of those kids have been armed with phony excuses explaining why they can't succeed by groups like Up and Out of Poverty Now, and corps of crutch-bearing, government enablers who kill the initiative of these kids with their hand-out programs. The values that these kids have learned places their top priority in life on the convenience that money buys, rather than the power of personal accomplishment that comes from hard work. Those children are the result of a cold, deceitful, uncaring, and selfish society—not a loving one.

I approach public assistance programs understanding that they're needed for some people who simply cannot help themselves or their families. However, for the most part, I lobby against public assistance and encourage legislators to scale it back, and instead create alternate, more constructive programs that build skills and self-esteem. Besides, as a dedicated single parent, my family and I can't afford to pay for any more public assistance programs with our taxes. It's time once more for hard work and determination to take the place of the hand-outs from sea to shining sea.

Advertising Is Another Vacuum That Sucks Away Your Money

The government is a greedy monster out to get your last hard-earned dollar. I believe that my lobbying efforts are serving me well, helping to keep my money for my family and out of the hands of others. The government, however, isn't the only money monster to watch our for, and maybe not even the most ferocious. I make it very clear to my sons that the most insatiable money monster is a product of our free-wheeling, consumer-driven society: the diabolical forces of advertising and public relations.

From the time we wake up until we go to bed at night, most of us are bombarded with hundreds, maybe thousands, of commercial messages. We hear them on the radio, see them on TV, and read them in newspapers and magazines, on billboards, buses, and taxicabs, at sports stadiums, on people's clothes, in restaurants, in department stores—they're everywhere. They're clever and well thought out messages designed to get as much of our money as possible by persuading us to buy products and services.

A large part of paid advertising and public relations campaigns focuses on our emotions of pride, fear, pain, hunger, thirst, comfort, joy, sex, and love. If we perceive that the advertised product or service fills an emotional need of ours, then we're more likely to shell out money to make the purchase, whether we can afford to or not.

Today's ad and PR campaigns are extremely effective, and many people needlessly succumb to them. Beer companies portray the image of fun, youth, and a feeling of restrained recklessness for those who drink a special brand of beer. Automobile ads give the impression that independence, prominence, and popularity will result from buying a certain style of car. Credit card companies play on our sympathies with slick PR campaigns that "pledge to help the homeless" if we patronize their cards.

When advertising tempts me to buy a product or service, I pause to analyze the message. Which emotion of mine are they targeting? Will I really benefit from the features and "advantages" of the product or service? Will the product or service fill a genuine need of mine? Maybe I'm buying out of "revenge indulgence." That is, to indulge myself for "all the hard work I do and sacrifices I endure." Will revenge indulgence satisfy my emotional needs? Those are a few of the screening questions I ask myself to determine the value that an advertised product or service claims to offer me. My questions help me to be a more prudent buyer.

The art of persuading people to spend money by means of advertising and public relations is here to stay. The better we learn about the thought processes behind advertising and PR, the more discriminating we can become as shoppers. I applaud the district where my boys attend school for offering courses about advertising. The kids learn advertising concepts and how to attract customers to a store or product. As my boys become more consumer-oriented, they will have acquired skills to help them evaluate whether the product or service promoted really serves their needs, or if clever ads have merely convinced them they will do so.

The Resulting Problem Is Debt

We fall prey to glittering ad campaigns and pretend to satisfy our emotional needs by buying more goods and services than we can afford, and end up in debt. Debt is overhead. Just like the struggling store owner who can't make a profit because of too much overhead, the single parent can't put money into savings if there's too much debt—it's failing to live within one's means.

We hear lots of stories about the difficulty of two parent families staying financially afloat, and the need for both parents to work outside the home. Here's a story from a financial magazine which I read to my sons. I told them that this pretty much pinpoints the problem.

> "My husband is 34 and I am 28. We have no children. We have a combined income of $60,000; a home with a $58,000 mortgage at 7.5 percent interest; $1,200 in savings and $200 of "free" money once the bills are paid."

The story goes on to ask the purported financial expert how they should invest their "free" money. The key words are, "once the bills are paid." These people make more than twice the money I do, don't have kids, yet I have more money in savings and more disposable income than they. Why is that? I wonder what kind of workout these people's credit cards get each month—for new clothes, entertainment, and even groceries. What kind of monthly finance charges are they paying on their new car, boat, and expensive furniture? Maybe there are other luxuries they couldn't afford but paid for with credit, like last winter's vacation or this summer's his and hers 20-speed, titanium bicycles.

The reason I have more disposable income than this couple is that I've scaled my life down to a manageable level, with little or no unnecessary overhead. I don't have bills other than my monthly mortgage, utilities, normal business expenses, and insurance, and I do my best to keep it that way. To me, having bills is like the old adage of paying for a dead horse: the thrill and enjoyment are gone but the burden of debt remains. I keep my monthly debt under control by not spending my money until I've earned it. I pay by cash or check, and leave the credit card tucked away in my wallet. That way I cut out buying things I can't afford, and keep from paying a lot of interest charges on purchases.

Long time baseball mainstay, Calvin Griffith, recognized the wisdom of avoiding unnecessary interest charges, and because of it he was the envy of many other team owners when he retired. Griffith, the former owner of the Minnesota Twins, is a man with a long and successful history in professional baseball. He's fondly known as the "Last of the Dinosaurs" because he preferred to do business "the old fashioned way," by keeping a low overhead, paying cash when he could and not buying things he couldn't afford.

As the player's salaries rocketed during the '80s, Griffith was often called a cheapskate by the media and fans for refusing to borrow money to satisfy the player's salary demands. Griffith's philosophy was, "Why borrow money when you just have to pay it back with interest?" So, he sold the franchise rather than overextending himself and falling into the merciless pit of high debt. He received $33 million for the club and settled for a carefree retirement in Florida. That's what I call playing it smart.

Another way to expand my disposable income is to restrict my everyday purchases. It's a matter of limiting myself to planned purchases only, and not buying on impulse. It's also a matter of not buying things I can do without—extra TV's, VCR'S, computers, cellular phones, or a new set of golf clubs while my old set still works just fine. I'm not tempted to spend money on "sales" or "bargains." A popular sales pitch is: "Hurry and save 30-50 percent. Buy Today!" My philosophy is "Don't buy anything and save a full 100 percent." Most people are surprised to discover how well they can get along without something they thought was necessary. When I make a planned purchase for something considerable, like clothing or an appliance, I shop and compare at three or more different stores. That way, I get a good feel for what the market is offering in price and value.

It doesn't take a genius to spend money. That's child's play. However, as a hard-working single parent on a tight budget, it takes thought and creativity to enjoy life without spending money needlessly, and I get great satisfaction from that.

I'll never forget our 1992 family vacation to Walt Disney World. I had to go there on business, so I made arrangements for the boys to join me. Each of three days we enjoyed a different theme park. We took in the rides, ate at the food stands, bought a few souvenirs, and did a lot of sightseeing. On the third day, I was tired of spending money, so I packed a lunch and some snacks to keep expenses under control.

It was a gorgeous spring day and the crowds were down. We enjoyed many of the free attractions and leisurely roamed the park. We ate our sandwiches under palm trees in a grassy area. Then, we took off our shoes and tossed a Frisbee around. When we were thirsty we filled up on ice cold tap water from faucets that were scattered throughout the park. Later in the afternoon, we sprawled out in a lovely garden area to eat the oranges I had brought along. By this time, we all agreed we had had enough of Mickey, Donald, and Goofy, so we headed for the car.

On the way out I spotted an old, wooden, flipper-action, baseball game in an arcade. I tossed a couple of quarters to Paul and J.J. so they could each play a game, and then we left. Just outside the park something interesting occurred to Paul, "Gee, Dad, we got through the Magic Kingdom on only fifty cents. I bet that's a record." I laughed and told him that I'd bet he was right. There we were, the three of us, in the land of Disney, where every five or ten steps there was a new and exciting way to spend money. Still, we didn't feel that we had been denied anything we really wanted. All day we had jumped right into the action, had a ball, and beyond the general admission charge, spent only half a dollar.

I had beat the system and that made me feel pretty damn good.

I've taught my kids to realize the benefits of my philosophy about money: "Why work hard just to buy more crap?" The more "crap" you buy that you can't afford, the more you go into debt, and the harder you have to work to pay it off. Consequently, you spend more time concerned about money problems than you do with your children. Forsaking the children can further complicate life because they don't get the TLC they need, feel neglected, and then act resentful, causing trouble. It's a vicious cycle caused in part by falling victim to the alluring images created by advertising and public relations: buying things you don't need and can't afford, and falling into the bottomless pit of debt.

My frugality has occasionally earned me the nickname "Caveman," bestowed by my kids. When they first referred to me that way I laughed: "Is it because of my girlfriends?" "No!" They shot back. It's because we're the only ones we know with no dishwasher, no VCR, no video games, no home computers or microwave oven." I told them, "And I bet you're the only kids in town who know how to wash dishes by hand."

I'm sure that my kids have not suffered an agonizing and deprived life without all the electronic goodies that are on the market. In fact, I think it's been good for them.

I remember many summer evenings when my boys have had friends over playing outside night games like ditch, hide'n go seek, and tag. From the sounds of laughter and monkey play, there's no doubt in my mind that interactive outdoor games are much more fun and productive for children than being glued to a TV or video game.

I'm glad that my boys have learned to have fun without lots of money and expensive toys by enjoying night games, sports, reading, hobbies, and the like. It's a lifestyle that has kept the pressure of debt off of me, and will also keep it off my boys and their own families in the future.

A couple of years ago, a person with whom I do business referred to his cross-country skiing, jogging, and bicycle riding when he said to me, "The things I enjoy most in life don't cost a lot of money." That rang a bell with me. I said, "Come to think of it, I feel much the same way." Sure, it's great to buy new clothes now and then, buy a new piece of furniture, or take a vacation. However, many single parents don't have the extra money for luxuries, so they have to make the most out of what they do have while trying to maintain a positive outlook on life.

Being debt-free helps me keep a positive outlook on life. It helps me feel secure and in control of my future, while being independent of others. Keeping as much of my money out of the hands of the free-spending government and money hungry advertisers as I can is an important ingredient that helps me save money and stay free of debt.

TACKLING SINGLE PARENTING

My In-House Management System

I've discovered other methods to conserve funds that help me be successful at tackling single parenting. They're derived from practical business principles. I refer to these methods as part of my "In-House Management System." That term occurred to me while I was visiting with Mike K., one of my business customers.

Mike and his wife, Anita, have owned a large, regional furniture store for several years. I asked him what has been his largest struggle in establishing his business. You might think his answer would have been something like attracting customers, or handling deliveries. It was neither. Their biggest hassle had been to get the business systems in place, such as accounts receivable and payable, new orders, deliveries, returns, employees, taxes, and similar business concerns.

Mike said, "When we finally developed systems for each department, the wheels of our business ran much smoother, required less of our time handling problems, and more time was available for growth. Once our systems were in place, it's just been a matter of preventive maintenance to keep our business running smoothly and going forward."

Setting up and maintaining management systems has also worked beautifully for me as a single parent on a tight budget.

With my In-House Management System, each component of the system relies on the strength and success of all the other components below it on the priority ladder. When a foundational component breaks down, all components above it suffer. Therefore, the most important aspect of the In-House Management System is maintenance and timely repair. Oftentimes that means doing the chores I enjoy least, first.

When I went into business for myself, a successful and wealthy business friend of mine gave me some valuable advice which I didn't see much worth in at the time. He cautioned me, "Make sure you get your bills out each month." Billing my customers seemed automatic to me, but as time went on, I understood the complexities behind his message.

I enjoy the challenges of selling and the face-to-face interaction with my customers that selling provides. Clerical work in my office, such as sending bills out, is the least favorite aspect of the job. However, as I've realized, if I don't bill, I don't get paid. If I don't get paid, I don't have cash to operate. Therefore, with the business system I have established at work, taking care of the "uninteresting and boring" office work, such as billing, is a foundational, business priority. It's more important than establishing new customers. For without effective maintenance of my current customers, my whole business would soon collapse.

The same principles hold true in my In-House Management System. As soon as my clothes washer or dryer breaks down, or when I start having problems with the plumbing in my home, I put almost everything else on hold and make the needed repairs to my "foundational" operating items. Without proper plumbing or clean clothes, everything else shuts down. My life gets more complicated and troublesome by washing things by hand, air drying, and running to laundromats.

There arises a lot of needless down-time, that is, time away from tackling projects that are more productive.

Preventive maintenance on priority equipment like washers, dryers, and plumbing is important. I keep filters cleaned and water hoses turned off when not in use. My basement floor drain has a tendency to back up if I don't maintain it properly. So, to prevent trouble, once a year I rent a 50-foot power snake for $20 and run it through my floor drain, keeping the line free of sludge so it doesn't back up, causing down-time, damage to my basement, and complications to my life.

That same preventive maintenance philosophy goes for my car, which is also one of my foundational operating items. When my car is down, my family and business life are down. I've read my owner's manual several times over the years, and maintain the car according to manufacturer specifications. Timely oil changes, rotating my tires, and fixing the small problems, like burned out dashboard lights, as well as the bigger problems, like air conditioning and cruise control, have proven to be wise investments. I have over 190,000 miles on my 1985 mid-size automobile, yet the entire vehicle performs practically like new. I keep the body looking good with regular washings, wax and semi-annual spot-sanding and paint jobs that I do at home. Most auto parts stores are happy to give free how-to advice. All you have to do is ask. They also have do-it-yourself videos available.

TACKLING SINGLE PARENTING

Maintaining an older car that runs well and is dependable provides many benefits. First and foremost, the car is paid for, so I have no monthly loan payments. The cost of maintenance, repairs, and tires have averaged only $90 per month for the last five years. My automobile insurance is considerably lower because of the older age of the car, and so are my annual license tabs. Another factor that helps keep my insurance costs under control is my careful driving habits. My insurance agent told me that two speeding tickets in a year would double the cost of my insurance, and one DWI would quadruple it. Those numbers help make me a cautious and responsible driver. All in all, I drive a clean, good looking automobile, with all the modern conveniences, for under $1,700 per year, including maintenance and insurance. I know many people who spend $6,000 a year, or more, to drive their cars. When I'm finally ready to buy a new car, I should get much more money than typical market value for my car because of the high quality care it has received.

Here's another way that my family's In-House Management system helps keep our lives running smoothly. The latest technology at the checkout counter at your local store scans the item you're purchasing and automatically deducts the item from the store's inventory. This system helps to prevent untimely and costly inventory shortages. We use the same system at home. When one of us uses the last of the peanut butter, or nears the end of the toilet paper or shampoo, he writes the item down on our shopping list. That way, when any of us reaches for a regularly used staple item, we know it'll be there. This system not only saves down-time and money by eliminating unnecessary runs to a convenience store where prices are higher, but also on frustration, which is a huge benefit to me.

Every person has his or her own priorities in life so your In-House Management System might be different. Just a little effort and thought will prioritize your life and keep the maintenance and repair levels where they need to be, to allow you and your family to keep moving forward in life at a smooth, steady pace. I save on headaches, downtime, and expenses by keeping my foundational operating items in order. Whenever I ignore them and hope that they'll magically disappear, I end up losing money and patience, and spend unnecessary time picking up the pieces. Some people have a more difficult time than others focusing on their priorities.

I dated a woman who lived in an elegant, well-kept home of her own. When the mortgage interest rates moved downward, I suggested that she consider refinancing her mortgage to save well over a hundred dollars a month. Her focus, however, was to repair a broken window screen in her basement that cost a mere $15. For some reason, she wouldn't prioritize the real money-saving matter in her life.

When I personally took the refinancing plunge and bought my mortgage down from 9 1/2 percent to 7 1/2 percent interest, I shared the prioritizing story of the woman I dated with my loan officer. She told me that it was very common for people not to want to leave the comfort of their daily schedules for the grueling task of crunching numbers, even if it was quite apparent it would save them real money.

It's much the same as my dreading doing the end-of-the-month books at my business. There are chores I'd much rather do, but I've learned that procrastination can be the weak link in my management system. So, I force myself to do the work I like least, first. Then, the rest of the chores seem much more enjoyable and my system runs smoothly. This allows my boys and me to move forward. Once again, knowing what the problem is—in this case, procrastination—is half the battle. The system follows the philosophy of my good friend, Willy. I've never known a person to get more done in one day than Willy.

"Don't put off for tomorrow what you can get done today." I can't count the number of times Willy's work philosophy has come to my rescue during unforeseen circumstances such as bad weather, illness, or automobile breakdowns. Instead of worrying how I'd get groceries during a huge snowstorm, I had shopped the day before, when I was able to find time.

Another way I keep my In-House Management System working well is by streamlining. I don't like having a lot of extra machines around, because they translate into maintenance, added cost, and more work. Many times I've had business people ridicule me for not owning a fax, computer, or a word processor. I've responded by telling them that I see more negatives than positives owning that equipment, and I'm quite successful without them. Some people might consider my old-fashioned practices keep me in the "ice-age." I prefer to think that my resistance to "progress" helps keep me happy by simplifying my life. I've had many stressed out and overspent business people tell me that they envy my prudence. Some have told me that faxes and computers increase their work-loads by shortening deadlines. The common complaint is: "Everyone expects more work to be done faster."

I'm fully aware that if I decide to expand my business in the years to come that new and efficient office equipment will benefit me. I definitely advocate using the right tools for the job. My point is that I've resisted the pressure of public scrutiny to buy expensive equipment without which I've been successful, anyway. That's the same philosophy I live by with my In-House Management System. While I'm on a tight budget, we live nicely without the latest high-tech gadgetry. My boys get practical hands-on experience with computers at school, and most of their friends have the newest video games to keep them in touch with the latest graphics. I'm happy to keep this clutter out of my life. It helps keep my life simple and manageable by eliminating added expenses and time-costly maintenance and repair. And besides, think how frantic life gets when we're without electricity for a few hours. I don't want my family to evolve into short-circuit hostages by building that same kind of dependency on computers and high-tech gadgetry in order to enjoy life and be productive.

If you think that I'm a cheapskate, you won't be the first who thought that. Just know that not spending money needlessly is a large and successful element of my In-House Management System. It's the same frugal philosophy of most of my business customers. You've heard the old saying, "birds of a feather flock together." I've noticed that many of my customers, like me, do their daily business from very humble work spaces with a minimum of luxury. Yet, every one of my customers has an extremely successful business with high, net operating revenues. They, like me, have worked hard to scale their businesses to manageable levels so they can enjoy their families and whatever else they value in life. That's my on-going objective during these years of full-time dedicated single parenting—to make a living and plan for the future while spending as much time as possible with my kids and doing the other things I enjoy. My In-House Management System helps me achieve that goal.

STEVE HORNER

More In-House Management Tips

I buy items that are repairable and reusable, instead of disposable and non-repairable. It saves money, and makes me feel good about treating the environment more kindly, from both manufacturing and disposal points of view. One of my most prized possessions is a Westclox alarm clock that Santa Claus gave me in 1953. All it calls for is a shot of oil every five to ten years, and it keeps on running like a clock ought to. I also believe in the practicality of buying rebuilt equipment instead of new whenever possible. I purchased my rebuilt clothes washer and dryer when we moved into our house in 1986. They've been dependable, and cost less than half the price of new machines. I found them in the Yellow Pages under appliances, new and used.

Unfortunately, much of the equipment on the market today, including clocks and most appliances, are designed to make most repairs and rebuilding cost-prohibitive. When I had to buy a new television, two of my main concerns were: which fancy features would I really use, and how easy is it to repair? My old television console was 19 years old before lightning destroyed it. During its years of faithful service, repair was easy and affordable. That's why I was able to keep it so long.

My philosophy on repair stresses preventive maintenance. When I buy a new piece of equipment, I read and save the operating manual. I've taught my kids to do the same. I keep all my equipment manuals in a box on a shelf in my clothes closet.

I bought my power lawn mower in 1986. It runs beautifully, and has never needed professional repair because of the timely maintenance I give it. I refer to the owner's manual at least twice a year, for a mid-season lube job, and to winterize it before I store it in late fall. I save my receipts and warrantees in the same box in my clothes closet. If a product breaks down due to a manufacturing error, my receipt helps me get a refund or exchange. Many product manufacturers offer lifetime warrantees. Many people, however, discover they've lost their warrantees when it comes time to replace the product. My car has a lifetime muffler. I've replaced it four times with my warranty, saving $75 with each replacement. It pays to hang on to product receipts and warrantees.

TACKLING SINGLE PARENTING

When it comes to technical repair and handiwork around the house, I rate myself about 4.5 on a scale of 10. I'm comfortable doing most fix-it carpentry, and I can usually get through the discovery stage of an electrical, mechanical, or auto breakdown. However, I've learned from experience that a novice like me working in technical areas can cause further damage. Like Clint Eastwood once told a villain: "A man has got to know his limitations." I hire a professional. This philosophy holds true for most specialty work.

While the professionals I hired were getting the specialty work done right the first time, saving me time, effort, and money in the long run, it allowed me to be productive with my business and jobs around the house. A good example is my practice of hiring an affordable professional to handle my taxes. I keep track of my annual income, expenses, credits, and deductions and my hired tax expert stays current with the ever-changing tax laws, assuring me a maximum return. Hiring a tax pro who files for all available tax benefits on my behalf has served me well. Otherwise, like many other single parents, I might've missed out on filing for all the benefits due me out of simple ignorance. Bill Knight, a public affairs official at the Internal Revenue Service told me, "There are millions of single parents who aren't receiving the proper credit that is owed them because they don't know about the existence of the various programs and haven't filed for a refund."

An investment of $150 to my accountant netted me over $1,500 in "single parent" refunds for 1994, alone. Given my hectic lifestyle as a single parent, it's likely that I would've forfeited thousands of dollars in refunds over the years had I not hired an accountant. And, now that congress is once again overhauling government spending, there's sure to be a whole new list of laws, deductions, and credits that will need to be sifted through. I'll leave those headaches up to my accountant.

My philosophy for achieving positive results in my business, or at home, is that people, such as the tax expert or auto repairman, are hired to do what they excel in, making sure the job gets done right the first time. That philosophy saves me money and time, and is a big part of effective management.

Accounts Payable is an important department in business and is just as important with my In-House Management System. When bills arrive, I ascertain the due date. Then, I go to my daily schedule book—or "planner"—and jot in a reminder to pay the bill a week prior to the due date. Then, I put the bill in my "to be paid" rack in my office. When a bill shows up in my planner, I pay it. There are three advantages to this system: I keep from losing the bill by putting it in my "to be paid" rack; I eliminate interest charges by paying the bill on time; and by logging the things I need to do in my planner, I eliminate the need to worry about details. My daily agenda simply shows up in my planner because I log, in advance, the functions I need to track. It's an effective way to keep my mind free of clutter while staying current with my responsibilities of school activities, family affairs, business deadlines and paying bills on time.

My planner came to the rescue the year I was audited. The tax examiner asked me, "Do you have records to verify your daily business activity?" I handed him my planner. He opened it towards the middle, saw that each page was packed with my chicken scratch writing, circles, arrows and red stars that highlighted the "must-do's." He studied it for a few seconds before he closed the book, handed it back to me and said matter-of-factly, "I can see that you keep busy."

Eating out is a nice luxury to enjoy from time to time. There's no meal preparation required, nor cleanup needed. However, you pay dearly for the convenience. My boys and I eat the vast majority of our meals at home. I do weekly grocery shopping as a foundational priority of my In-house Management System. We spend around $300 a month on groceries. A little extra planning for meals and time in the kitchen pays off with big dividends for single parents like me. Especially when you compare a $300 monthly food budget to a restaurant bill of $30 for the three of us. That's roughly three times what it costs us each day to eat breakfast, lunch, and supper at home.

I'm not one to take time to clip coupons, and when my boys were about seven and ten they became concerned about that. They believed I was wasting money. I told them that I'm fairly brand loyal to the tried and true products that have served us well, and most manufacturers use coupons to urge shoppers to give their product a sampling and ultimately switch brands. So my kids devised a clever money-making scheme, to which I agreed. Each week, they combed the Sunday paper looking for coupons for items that we normally use. They clipped them out and stacked them in a "J.J." pile and a "Paul" pile next to the cookie jar on the kitchen counter. Whenever we went grocery shopping, the boys would cross-check the grocery list with their coupons and hand them over to me at the grocery store checkout. I'd realize a cash discount on my grocery purchases and would give that same amount to the boy who had the coupon. The way I looked at it, the boys got extra spending cash from the food manufacturer and I just served as the middle man who rewarded them for their enterprising spirit.

Being prudent and hanging onto the money we already have, plus looking for ways to make additional money, are popular concerns of many dedicated single parents. Making money and being a full-time, dedicated single parent, however, do not always go hand-in-hand. Making money takes time, energy, and patience, and that's time, energy, and patience away from the family.

Many single parents rely on shortcuts to a secure future by placing their dreams in winning the lottery, marrying into money, getting favorable government funding, or receiving an increase in child support payments. Most of them become angry, frustrated, and poor because their fantasies served as crutch-bearing enablers. I chose to take the independent route and depend on my own actions to forge a secure future. I've described it to my boys as, "You can't sit on your butt and wait for opportunity to come knocking. You have to go out and make it happen." Buying a house was a good start in that direction for me.

I shopped long and hard for the "just right" house, and the result has been my best investment. It provides me with tax benefits now, and security for the future. I wanted a home close to where I was employed so that I wouldn't have to spend a lot of down-time traveling to and from work. Plus, I wanted a home within walking distance to parks and schools so that I didn't have to run a taxi service for my kids and their friends. To me, time is invaluable.

I was able to move into my $82,000 home in 1986 with only $2,000 as a down payment. My loan was guaranteed by the Veterans Administration. If you have a steady income and are determined to be a homeowner, there are lenders and plenty of housing experts ready to reach out to you. A person with zero down payment, an annual salary of as little as $18,000, combined with enough determination, can become a homeowner. For a list of resources ask your local Housing and Redevelopment Authority, the Federal National Mortgage Association (Fannie Mae), or a bank loan officer. You might also call a real estate office and ask to speak to the finance manager. The programs are out there. You just have to show your good credit, good will, and be ready to jump through some hoops. It was definitely worth it for me.

Another way I make my future more secure is to become more valuable to the people for whom I work. Let's face it, companies are in business to make money. If the people they employ make money for the company, they become more valuable to the company and therefore should earn more money. Here's an example. I used to work for a small town radio station as an announcer. I was paid a paltry salary because I wasn't seen as a valuable asset by the owner. Another announcer could've filled my position practically overnight.

Finally, one day it occurred to me that the people who sold radio time to advertisers were the ones making the bucks. I asked the owner of the station if I could try my luck at selling, and he told me to go ahead. Soon, my list of advertising clients was longer than any of the other salespeople, and I began to make a pretty decent living. My job was secure because I became a rare and valuable commodity—someone who performed well and made money for the owner.

Even today, as the owner of my small marketing company, I'm able to succeed in my business because I help my clients make more money. That's the key to earning a good living in our consumer-oriented society. Ask yourself, "How can I become more valuable to the people for whom I work?" The way to find out is by asking these two questions to the people around you at work: "What do you want to see happen as a result of my efforts?" and "What do you want to prevent from happening most?" Those questions will help you assess the goals, needs, and concerns of the company and how you can make yourself more valuable by helping the company be more successful. As a follow-up, and to keep the fact-finding dialogue flowing, try to make frequent use of our three most valuable critical thinking questions: "What do you mean?"; "Can you give me an example?"; and, "What do you think of this (or, that?)."

TACKLING SINGLE PARENTING

The ongoing process of building and establishing your personal worth with the people for whom you work requires that you be inquisitive, assertive, persistent, patient, responsible and productive. This process clears the way for you to effectively make more money.

Magic Formulas

Single parenting doesn't have to be a pauper's existence. Nor does being a successful single parent necessarily translate into having a lot of money. For me, being a dedicated single parent means living a happy and productive life while my children learn to be well-adjusted and productive members of their family and community.

Properly managing my family finances as a dedicated single parent requires that I provide for my children now, while at the same time I anticipate and provide for my personal financial security for after the kids are grown and left home. To reach those goals, single parents, like me, need to hang onto as much of their money as they can, be prudent spenders, wise investors, and focus on earning new money. There are no magic formulas, as internationally-known businessman, Curt Carlson, proudly professes.

Carlson owns one of America's largest private corporations who started out as a delivery boy during the Depression. His hard-working mother was a great influence on him as a youngster. She taught him about hard work, keeping commitments, money management, never asking for handouts, and not giving up. Today, Carlson the billionaire tells his audiences that there is no luck involved in achieving financial success.

"Hard work and persistence are the keys to success. The harder I work, the luckier I get."

From my personal experiences, the same rule applies for us dedicated single parents.

The harder we work, the luckier we get.

Child Care

I Learned The Hard Way

I'll never forget the phone call as long as I live. It was about four o'clock on a snowy afternoon in early December. I was down the hall from my office visiting with a friend who shared business space with me in a strip mall. I heard the phone ring, and I hustled back to my office. It was six-year-old J.J. He was crying, and as he tried to get the words out between his heavy sobbing, I was getting increasingly frantic. "Try to slow down J.J., and tell me what's going on." "It's Dawn," he said, referring to our new sitter. "She's acting really weird." I had hired Dawn two days earlier to come to my home each day to meet my kids after school and take care of them until I got home, usually about six o'clock. That night I had business scheduled into the evening, and had planned to be home at ten.

I told J.J., "Please get Dawn on the phone." I had known her for only a few days, but I saw her as an up-beat, bubbly, responsible, and I must add, quite attractive young lady. She appeared to be about 20. I didn't recognize her voice when she got on the phone. "Hellllloooo," she said, in a deep, ominous monotone. When I asked her what was going on she responded, "nothing," in the same deadpan voice, then the line went dead. I called right back. The line was busy. I tried again, and J.J. answered. He was still crying. I asked him if Paul was okay. He said he was and I told J.J to get Paul and go outside, or to another part of the house away from Dawn, and that I would be home in 10 minutes.

I thought about calling the police, but I figured that by the time I was able to explain the circumstances, I could be halfway home. The people with whom I worked overheard my conversation and sensed the urgency of the call. I ran out of the office; I remember the deep concern on their faces. They, too, had kids at home, and could relate to my fear.

I jumped in my car, flipped on my flashers, and headed for the freeway. As I drove, I prayed for the safety of my boys. Gruesome thoughts raced through my mind. I couldn't bear to think of my children being harmed, or much worse, killed. I just hoped to get home before it was too late. I tried to drive as fast as I could without jeopardizing the lives of other people on the road. I hoped for a cop to come up alongside so I could signal him to follow.

Dawn was the second in a string of "bad luck nannies" for my boys and me. I had hired her through an ad I placed in the local paper. I should've taken more time to interview her and check her references, but I was desperate. I had to fire Marlene, the young lady for whom Dawn filled in, for repeatedly missing work, and I was in a rush to find a replacement. Marlene had lived with us since September but had lately stopped showing up on Monday mornings after being gone every weekend. I had met Marlene's dad when I hired her and I felt confident that she would do a good job for me. The boys liked her, and even though I knew she was a bit flighty, I believed she was safe to have around. As I discovered later, she was pregnant when I hired her in September and she had been shacking up with her boyfriend on the weekends while in my employment.

I pulled off the freeway and raced through the residential area of Apple Valley towards my home; My heart was pounding. I just hoped that I'd be home in time to put a stop to whatever made J.J. place such a frightening phone call.

I blasted into my driveway, jumped out of the car, and dashed into the house. "Paul! J.J! Where are you?" I yelled. They came running from Paul's bedroom into my arms and said they were okay. What a relief. I asked what had been going on and they started crying again.

Apparently, Dawn had showed up at three, in time to meet the kids at the door after school. Soon after, however, trouble started. "She started drinking the liquor you have under the counter," Paul told me, "then she got on the phone and started telling her mother what a couple of little creeps we are. We really got scared." J.J. said she started making all sorts of scary sounds. "She started saying real bad things to us," Paul told me. "She came into my bedroom when I was lying on my bed looking at my baseball cards and she laid down on the bed next to me. Then she put her leg on me and talked real sexy." I assured my boys that everything was okay, and that I was very proud of J.J. for calling me at work when he knew there was trouble. I told both of them that we would talk a lot more about the episode later, but right then I wanted to talk to Dawn.

They told me she was downstairs.

I walked down the steps and noticed wavy, red lines etched into the paint on both sides of the stairwell. I discovered later that it was Dawn's fingernail polish that she left behind as she meandered down the stairs in a drugged and drunken stupor, scratching the walls.

I found Dawn fumbling around in Marlene's bedroom. There was a pipe on the bed that the police would later tell me had been used for smoking crack cocaine. I saw that $80 in twenties was missing from Marlene's dresser. I had seen the money there earlier as I gathered up Marlene's belongings to return to her if she ever showed up again.

I told Dawn I wanted the money she stole, then to gather her things and get out of the house. She denied having the money. That's when the meaning of the term "tackling single parenting" took on a whole new dimension. She yelled at me in frenzied, incoherent gibberish and tried to leave the room. I grabbed her and attempted to dig into her jean pockets to retrieve the money. All the while she was hitting and scratching me. I was tempted to slap her, in return for the scare she put my children through, but I knew that would only complicate matters. I was finally able to grab the money. I kept the pipe for evidence, booted her out into the snow, and tossed her jacket out after her. Then, I called the police.

When the police arrived, we were still pretty upset over what had happened. I gave the officer Dawn's pipe and a few other things she left behind. He told me that he was familiar with Dawn and her family, and that they had a long history of making trouble in Apple Valley. He said she probably wouldn't bother me since she was the one in the wrong. So, I told him I didn't want to pursue the matter any further. I just wanted her out of our life. That was many years ago, and we haven't seen a trace of her. I hope it stays that way.

After the police officer left I apologized profusely to Paul and J.J. for hiring Dawn before I checked out her references. I told them that I really learned my lesson about the dangers of child care. I kept questioning them about what happened and how they felt about the experience until I was convinced they were talked out about it. Needless to say, I called my business contact and told him that the business I had planned for that evening would have to be postponed.

I brought up the Dawn incident several times over the next few years just to make sure my boys weren't harboring any anxiety about the event. They shared their contempt for Dawn with me and how scared they had been, but after enough time passed, the topic became old news.

The Dawn incident is something we'll never forget. It could've been a lot worse had it not been for J.J.'s phone call to me. I don't care to think what might've happened had J.J. not called to report the news before I left the office for my evening business appointment. Thank God.

I remind parents that we live in an extremely unsafe time for hiring child care for either day or night sitting. The dangers abound. In the spring of 1995, the Minneapolis police reported about a 14-year-old boy who was hired by a single parent to watch her two youngsters for a few evening hours. The children were a four-year-old girl and her six-month-old half sister. During the course of the evening the boy stabbed the four-year-old to death. He later told authorities, "I just grabbed her and did it. I wanted to see what it felt like."

What can we expect? Society has indoctrinated children with horribly violent movies and television from the time they were born. In many cases, kids come from homes where there's rarely a parent or adult around to teach them right from wrong, and to help them realize that violence in movies is scripted, and shouldn't be acted out.

The Dawn incident taught me a couple of important lessons in child care: always check references, because a pretty or innocent looking face can hide a troubled mind, and, if your kids are old enough, be sure they know how to reach you when you're away. The issue of safety quickly became the primary rule with my children's child care and after the Dawn incident I vowed to never violate that rule again.

Hiring A Nanny

When my next nanny, Mary, responded to my newspaper ad, I asked her for references, and then made the extra effort to check them out. Mary was a middle-aged woman without professional child care experience. However, she did have several grown kids of her own, and from what I could gather, they seemed well-adjusted. Mary was a nice lady but couldn't put up with the daily routine of the job. After four months of almost steady whining about trivialities, such as the temperature in the house and not enough snacks in the cupboards, she quit.

That fall, winter, and spring of 1987-88 were particularly difficult to find quality child care. Marlene, Dawn, and Mary—what a trio. They sure were nothing like our first nanny, Rochelle. We really had a gem in Rochelle, and we appreciated having her work for us.

I hired Rochelle the day the boys and I moved into our house. During my house hunting it was important that I buy a house with a finished basement and a full bath, one that could accommodate a live-in nanny. Rochelle had kitchen privileges, and we often invited her to join us for supper, television, and other family activities, like playing board games and cards.

Rochelle came to us through an ad I placed in the Help Wanted section of the paper. We spoke on the phone and I invited her to come to the townhouse we had been renting so we could meet face-to-face. She was in her mid-twenties and was from a large family in a small town in Iowa. She was friendly, outspoken, and had lots of experience with child care, having taken care of her younger siblings. She grew tired of small town living and moved to the city. She lived with us for 15 months. Then, as was inevitable, she met her sweetheart, got married, and moved into a place of their own. We were honored to have been invited to the wedding, a big family affair in Iowa.

We really lucked out with Rochelle. I failed to investigate work and character references before I hired her, which, as we learned later with Dawn, is an absolute prerequisite when looking for child care. I told her the pay was $75 per week, plus room and board. Evenings and weekends were her own time, except when I needed to be away, and then I paid her overtime. I tipped her an extra $100 three or four times during the time she worked for us. I could do that when business was especially good, and I had extra cash. Other than that, it was a flat $75 per week. That was in 1986-87.

Many parents pay a lot more than $75 a week for their live-in nannies, but that's their choice. I'm confident that even today, if I advertised for a nanny, and screened carefully, I could find someone like Rochelle for $75 per week.

In the spring of 1995, I discussed child care concerns with a woman with whom I had business contacts. She told me that she recently hired a live-in nanny. The nanny had been looking for a place to live while she went to night school to become a registered nurse. Her word of mouth nanny search took only three days. My business friend has three children and doesn't pay the nanny anything except room and board. All the people involved agree that it's a great deal for them. This example proves that live-in child care doesn't have to be overly expensive. You just have to look for the person whose goals, needs, and concerns match the opportunities that you can provide. You can do so by asking questions like "What are the features of this job that you need to have present to be happy working for me?"; and "What don't you want to have happen while working for me?" If you get sincere and complete answers to these important questions, then the two of you will have a better understanding of what to expect from one another. There will be a higher likelihood that the working relationship will be a success for you, the nanny, and most importantly, your kids.

If you're hiring a live-in nanny, remember that there are taxes to consider. As an employer, you must withhold state and federal taxes and issue a W-2 form, and, pay half of your nanny's Social Security and Medicare taxes. However, there have been some recent changes in the laws. Social Security taxes need to be reported just once a year instead of quarterly, and a household employee who earns less than $1,000 per year is not subject to these taxes at all. Naturally, these laws may change quickly, so you need to review the current IRS publications.

Not paying the proper taxes as a household employer can come back to haunt you, as happened to several presidential federal appointees in recent years. They were not confirmed because they failed to pay full and complete taxes for their domestic help. Even if you're confident that you'll never have to come under the same scrutiny as a presidential appointee, I assure you that interest and penalties can be devastating if you're cited.

Fortunately, there are tax benefits as well as expenses to hiring a nanny. I was able to take advantage of the Child Care Tax Credit. I claimed wages, employment taxes, food, lodging, and all other work-related expenses as tax deductions. The current maximum for a person in my situation with two children is a generous $4,800. Even if you don't have a nanny, parents who pay for any type of child care can receive credit for child care expenses on their tax returns. You may want to hire a tax accountant to help you through this maze and retrieve the tax benefits due you. It served me well.

How Not To Lose The Help Of A Family Member

After Mary, the third of my "bad luck nannies" left, I put an ad in the paper again; plus, I tried other sources. I checked with a couple of social service agencies who generally keep a list of child care providers, and I spread the word throughout the neighborhood.

The day that I went to the grocery store to tack a help wanted ad to the community billboard I ran into my dad. He said, "Why don't you call your mother and ask her to help? She wants to help." I'd been reluctant to ask my mom because she had been so gracious to help me with child care during the first year after the divorce. I didn't want to become a burden to my aging parents, and I wanted to prove my independence.

I swallowed my pride and drove to my parent's home to visit with my mom. She was a sweetheart. She told me immediately that she would be happy to take the job of driving over to my home at three o'clock each school day to meet Paul and J.J. when they got home. What a relief.

Peace of mind and welfare of the children are two of the biggest reasons why relatives offer many single parents the best child care available. Relatives usually feel they have a vested interest in the kids and treat them as their own. Their value system is usually the same as the parent's, and in most cases the cost is considerably lower. When my mother signed on as a child care provider for my kids, she came up with a grand idea. Instead of providing the service for free, which would've made me feel awkward with indebtedness, she asked for a small monthly fee that I was happy to pay.

By bringing money into the arrangement, I didn't have to feel obligated to visit with my mother every day after work when I came home tired. There were no strings attached. My mom could also feel comfortable leaving right away to get home to her own chores.

There were a few heated disagreements between us over child-rearing techniques but that's a common problem among single parents. Both the grandparents and the parents want the children to do well, and there are as many different ways of parenting as there are parents in this world.

When I felt that my mom stepped over the boundaries of grandparent and parent, instead of getting angry and defending the hard work that I was proud of accomplishing, I simply asked my family's three important, critical thinking questions. They helped separate biased opinions from objectivity.

Once again, those questions are: "What do you mean?"; "Can you give me an example?"; and, "What do you think of this (or, that?")" For example: Your parent says, "I don't think Eric is doing well in school. He used to do a lot better." Instead of starting an argument by saying, "You're wrong! He's doing great!" It might be more constructive by asking, "Can you give me an example?" Then listen carefully to see if there's a legitimate concern that needs to be investigated. Otherwise, you could show her a recent school project on which Eric did well and ask: "What do you think of this?" The goal is constructive dialogue, not confrontation.

I've discovered that effective communication with relatives who help with child care is a lot more productive than arguing over biased opinions. Opinions can run the full gamut when it comes to the children you care for and love. Effective communication helps to establish the facts, keeps the bitterness out, and most importantly, helps to keep your valuable child care person from angrily walking out the door and out of the job, leaving you with larger problems.

My kids and I were really fortunate to have my mom help us with child care. Most of our time together provided all of us with terrific memories. My mom tells me she has saved all the notes I left for her before I went to work each day. They mostly filled her in on the day's agenda, along with a few words of appreciation for her efforts. I always signed them, "Love, Steve."

During this same period, when the kids were young and my funds were extremely limited, my dad also helped me with child care. He'd come over two or three times a month so I could have a few evenings to myself, away from the kids. Single parents need a break from their kids for their own personal entertainment. It rejuvenates the spirit and helps us stay inspired to tackle the rigors of this job. Responsible and loving child care, like my father provided, gave me a few hours to relax on my own, a real benefit for my kids and for me.

There Are Many Other Child Care Options Available

As I began to get more settled into my single parenting career, I wanted to gain independence and lessen the child care burden on my parents. I looked throughout the neighborhood for sitters on whom I could rely for occasional evenings. I found that there were plenty of good kids, from loving families, who were just waiting for me to ask them to help out with child care.

Emily was one of our favorites. I discovered her one morning after my kids had left for school and I had hustled down to the park for my morning workout. There was a group of middle schoolers standing on the corner waiting for the bus, so I approached them.

"Would any of you kids be interested in doing some evening child care for me?"

Without hesitation, Emily said, "I would." We didn't have any more time to visit because their bus pulled up so I gave Emily my phone number and asked her to call me. That evening her parents called and we had a nice visit. Emily was just two years older than Paul, but she was quite mature for her age. I felt comfortable with Emily watching my kids because I knew her parents were taking an active and positive role in Emily's life, and were just two blocks away in case of an emergency.

When I needed a sitter on the spur of the moment and Emily wasn't available, I often relied on the hourly, child care centers. Even though I paid more, the convenience was worth the extra cost. I loved the security of being in touch with my boys by means of the pager I was provided, and the kids always enjoyed their stay there. In fact, there were a couple of nights when they were having such a good time they didn't want to leave.

Working single parents who don't have the benefits of a child care provider come to their home, or the luxury of relatives to watch their children while they work, must rely on commercial child care.

From the information I gathered in interviews with several child care directors, the greatest concern parents have about their child care is location. Parents need to find child care conveniently located near home or work to reduce down-time. Coming in right behind "location" as a popular, parental concern is cost. I thought safety would be in at least third place. I was wrong. The directors said that it's extremely important to most parents that their children are happy, and have fun. "Probably has something to do with the guilt factor," I told one director. She laughed and said, "I think you're right." Most parents are interested in the activities the child care center provides, and how structured their child's day will be. There are concerns about illness policies, discipline and punishment procedures, safety measures, the competency of the staff, hours, food and snacks, diapering, and transportation to and from school for the older kids. The owners of the "in-home" centers told me that the parental concerns are about the same for them as for the larger centers with the addition of two: many parents want to know if anybody in the house smokes, and if there are pets in the house.

I asked the child care directors about their screening process for hiring new employees. I generally heard three criteria: dedication to kids, the understanding that child care is a hard and demanding job, and child care experience. A common problem throughout the industry is high employee turnover.

One major factor often overlooked by parents who are searching for reliable child care is proper hygiene practices of the provider. The Journal of the American Medical Association reported in 1994 that children younger than two who attended child care centers are 36 times more likely than stay-at-home children to have problems with earaches, pneumonia, and meningitis. Illnesses related to fecal contamination, such as the spread of giardia, which can cause chronic diarrhea and even death, most often find favorable breeding grounds in child care centers. Most health professionals agree that proper hygiene is essential to prevent illness-causing germs from being transmitted from child to child in these centers.

During the early 1990s, I represented the National Association of Diaper Services as a legislative counsel. One morning, while I was meeting with nine metro area health care professionals, most of whom were registered nurses, I heard some startling tales about flagrant hygiene abuse at child care centers. One of the nurses reported to the group that a provider at a large child care center had been washing the dirty diaper pail with the lunch dishes. Another provider had told the nurse, "I prefer to work with disposable diapers because then I don't have to wash my hands after each diaper change."

Research results from a 1994 study at Vanderbilt University show that diaper types, plastic or cotton, make no difference in the presence of diarrhea-causing bacteria in child care centers. The major variable was proper hygiene and frequent hand washing by the staff.

Nationally known pediatrician and author, Dr. William Sears, warns caregivers and parents alike from what he terms the "real issue" to helping prevent child care illnesses. "I believe that caring caregivers and their adherence to sound, hygienic practices, including regular hand washing, required over-clothing and frequent diaper changes, are the best insurance against disease for our children."

Proper hygiene practices at the child care facility is an invisible, but often one of the most troublesome problems for parents and their kids in child care. Keeping a close and careful watch for safe hygiene can make a big difference in helping to keep your child healthy while in child care.

If I've painted a guarded picture of child care, it's because I believe that parents need to be aware of the dangers. Most parents have good experience with child care most of the time. For several years, while Joyce and I were married, we both worked outside the home and took our boys to in-home child care. Most of our experiences were positive. The caregivers were loving, conscientious people whose first concern was the children. I have fond memories of picking my boys up from child care. From the time Paul and J.J. could express their thoughts, they were eager to show me their friends and what they'd been doing that day. To me, their eagerness was a sign that child care was a positive experience for them.

The cost of child care varies. Metro areas are usually more expensive than rural areas, and the age of your child can make a big difference. Infants require the most attention, and therefore cost more. The large commercial child care centers in the Twin Cities area average about $140 a week for infants, $120 a week for toddlers, $110 for preschool and $60 a week for school-age children plus transportation costs to and from school. In-home child care usually runs about 30 percent less. It pays to shop around to get the most value for your money, but most importantly, to find a person or staff with whom you and your child feel comfortable.

Many single parents qualify for county, state, or federal funds to help them with child care costs. There are many kinds of programs available for people from all walks of life. There are programs for people on AFDC, those not on AFDC, those working, and those looking for work, educated and not educated, going to school, not going to school, and combinations of the above. A person who has been working with government child care funding for over four years told me, "The funding programs can be very confusing. Sometimes there are meetings that I feel as though I'm struggling to get all the information and still I come away feeling confused with all the issues. Part of the reason is that each case is different, plus the fact that public child care funding is constantly being adjusted." She told me, "The best advice to give anyone is to begin by calling their County Human Services Department and setting up an appointment to see how and if they qualify for support funds."

More Options

What happens to the single parents who don't qualify for AFDC, don't have relatives on whom they can rely for child care, are on the waiting list at their County Human Services Department, yet who need affordable child care so they can continue to earn a living? That's the question I asked Sandy Pietig, the Financial Assistance Supervisor of the Self-Sufficiency Support Unit at Dakota County Economic

Assistance in Minnesota, during a phone interview. "It takes a lot of work and dedication but it can be done," said Pietig. "There are viable options, such as forming a child care cooperative in the building or neighborhood in which you live or creating a bartering system."

A successful child care co-op has at least one thing in common among its members: It's made up of parents who need dependable child care for their children. A co-op utilizes parents who have time off from work to care for children of other parents at work. A co-op needs careful management and planning so that each parent receives as much child care in return for as much as they have provided others. Otherwise, a feeling of resentment can grow and the co-op can fall apart if parents believe they're contributing more than their fair share.

The other alternative, the bartering system, works well if the single parent knows someone, like a senior citizen, who will provide child care in exchange for domestic favors, such as lawn work, cooking, handiwork, or grocery shopping. The single parent exchanges personal skills and abilities for child care. Pietig concluded: "Not only does the barter system usually work out well for the children, but both adult parties benefit from the exchange, as well."

Here's a partial list of other ideas with which many single parents have had luck securing reliable and affordable child care.

- Look in the yellow pages under CHILD CARE.
- Look for ads in your local newspaper.
- Place ads of your own.
- Look for notices on bulletin boards in grocery stores, churches, community centers, and in other public places.
- Tack up your own notice.
- Network. Tell friends, neighbors, co-workers or classmates that you're looking for child care.
- If you're employed, or interviewing for work, ask whether the company offers on-site child care or credit for outside child care.

- If you're attending school, ask about child care arrangements or funding through the financial aid office. Many innovative child care programs are being initiated in schools and offices, and it might serve you well to seek them out.

Change Is The Very Nature Of Child Care

My mother helped me with daily child care in my home for about a year. Finally, as my kids grew older and less demanding of my time, I moved my business out of the strip mall and into the basement of my home. Then, it was up to me to meet my boys every day after school, take time to visit with them, and then get them into their next activity. The added responsibilities cut into my business day, but it's been worth the effort and the reduction in pay. Three words have become music to my ears over the years as the boys have come storming into the house after school, the screen door slamming behind them, "Dad, I'm home!" Sometimes the music has been more like Van Halen than Mozart, but nevertheless, I'm grateful to experience it.

I'm proud too, because it wasn't luck that got me here. It took lots of hard work, dedication, and sound management. There were plenty of times when I didn't think I would make it, but I kept plugging away.

The challenge of securing responsible child care is one of the most formidable tasks facing dedicated single parents. You can ask almost any single parent to name the biggest hassle in keeping the family afloat and moving forward. Nine out of ten times the answer will be "responsible and affordable child care."

Because we're the sole breadwinners for our families, we have no choice but to spend several hours each day making a living. We need child care that we can trust, and that provides peace of mind while we're away from our kids. I know that when I felt good about my child care, I was more productive at work. When my child care was on shaky ground, I couldn't perform as well because I was distracted with worry about the welfare of my children.

My child care arrangements were always changing. Just when I felt that my boys and I had stable child care, something would change. Change might be the very nature of child care—it never stays constant, and there's no convenient road map to follow that makes it easier. I've discovered, however, that there are information signs along the route to successful child care. The largest sign says: SAFETY FIRST, which alerts single parents to the potential dangers of child care. Another large sign says: CHANGE, which forecasts twists and turns in the road ahead. The third sign says: CREATIVITY, which is what you'll need to overcome the obstacles in the road, so you can reach your goal of securing affordable child care that also provides you with peace of mind. It's peace of mind that's essential in helping you win the ongoing battle of effective and productive single parenting.

Teaching Disipline: Obedience to Rules

Turn Out The Lights, The Party's Over

When my boys are grown and have left home, and my child-raising days are behind me, I want to have the satisfaction of knowing that they are law abiding citizens. I want the pride of knowing that their compliance to rules benefits their families, society, and themselves.

I want to be able to say that I not only "did my best," but that I succeeded in teaching my boys the principles of discipline, in spite of the outside forces that always worked against us. Not the least of these forces are the poorly managed policies of our own government. I got a firsthand look at how these policies violate the basic principles of discipline, and how they interfere with my teaching discipline at home. The incident began in September, 1992.

The early evening was unusually warm for the first week of fall. My day had been one of those hectic and frustrating ones to which most single parents can relate. My sons had been back in school for about three weeks. Paul was in eighth grade, and J.J. was in fifth. It seemed like every day they had been coming home from school with a new batch of school rules, sign-up sheets, and permission slips. Each batch needed my attention, sorting, and signing. My stressed-out state of mind had me irrationally wondering if the teachers had a diabolical plan to burden parents with such an overwhelming amount of notes and information that they wouldn't want to bother the teachers for the rest of the school year.

TACKLING SINGLE PARENTING

In addition to the notes and information, there was the regular confusion of the three of us adjusting back to the school year routine: getting homework done, getting to bed on time, getting up early, having fresh clothes, eating breakfast, and getting to school on time. While the kids and I were getting back into the swing of school, I had to keep my business customers satisfied. It's a family juggling performance that gets rusty during the summer, and that needs brushing up on in the fall.

On that particular evening, I decided that I needed a break away from the kids and my routine for a couple of hours. Besides, Paul was just coming of age where I could leave him in charge of the household for a short time—this would give him some experience. The new Mall of America had opened a month earlier, and was only a 15-minute drive from my home. I hadn't been there yet, so I decided to head there for a cold beer. I had $10, and a thirst.

The first place I went was Gators. It looked like a lively joint, so I stood in line to get in. I thought the people at the door were just checking I.D.'s but they were also collecting a cover charge. I figured if it was only three or four bucks, I would still have enough for a couple of beers. The issue turned out to be a lot more than a cover charge.

It was Ladies' Night.

During Ladies' Night, the women get in free and enjoy drink specials, and the men pay a cover charge and full price for drinks. I asked the guy at the door, "You mean to say that the women get in free because they're women, and the men have to pay because they're men?"

"That's right, buddy. Ain't you ever heard of Ladies' Night? Where you from, North Dakota?"

With that snide comment several people in line laughed at my "stupidity." So I asked to speak to the manager.

When the manager came out, I explained my grievance. "I'm sick and tired of some women taking every opportunity to sue for sexual discrimination. Yet tonight, I'm being discriminated against based purely on my sex, and it doesn't seem to be important." By that time my thirst had turned to anger. I told the manager, "I should sue Gators. That would certainly make a bold statement about discrimination." He said, "Go ahead, pal. Frankly, I don't blame you."

I left the Mall in a huff and I don't even remember if I stopped somewhere else for a beer. All I know is that I was pissed. The next day I filed a formal sexual discrimination complaint with the Minnesota Department of Human Rights against Gators.

Getting somebody at the Human Rights Department to take my complaint seriously was a challenge. On at least two occasions, female employees at the Department questioned my motivation. One of them, Pam Kelly, who later joined St. Paul mayor, Norm Coleman's administration, asked me, "Why are you filing this charge, Mr. Horner? Don't you think it's about time that women get a break in society? They only make seventy cents on the dollar compared to a man." That kind of rationale only inspired me to press on with the complaint. I told her, "Well, hell, if that's the case, then let's pass a law that says women only pay 70 percent for the cost of groceries, for a new car, and on their taxes." My answer seemed to quiet her down. At least I got a good idea of the Department's sentiments about discrimination.

A couple of weeks passed with no response to my complaint, so I asked the Human Rights Department to send me a copy of the state statutes on discrimination. In a few days, I received a little white pamphlet, Department of Human Rights, Human Rights Act, Chapter 363. I found what I was looking for on page 18 under subdivision 3. It read, "It is an unfair discriminatory practice to deny any person the full and equal enjoyment of the goods, services, facilities, privileges, advantages, and accommodations of a place of public accommodation because of race, color, creed, religion, disability, national origin or sex."

There it was in black and white. I had definitely been discriminated against. Now, to get the Human Rights Department to act on my behalf was another matter.

After months of haggling with the department, I brought the state attorney general's office into the case. That expedited the matter. In March of 1994, 18 months after I filed, the Human Rights Department came to the formal conclusion of "probable cause" that my rights had been violated. Somewhere along the line the attorney general's office attached a dollar figure to the settlement that I received from Gators. It was a little more than $100. However, as far as I was concerned, the matter was founded in principle, not money.

TACKLING SINGLE PARENTING

Before I signed on the dotted line I asked the Human Rights Department to issue a press release to the media so that my case would have an impact on society. The Department balked, saying that they only issue press releases on cases that are "unique and have far-reaching effects." I countered by stating my case was the first in Minnesota—one of a few in the nation—and Ladies' Night affected several thousand bar patrons throughout the state every week. Still, they wouldn't release a press release on my behalf. So, instead of the press release as a stipulation of the settlement, I asked that the attorney for Gators inform the Minnesota Bar and Restaurant Association about the ruling. I also asked the Human Rights Department to send me a copy of all the sexual discrimination press releases they issued during the previous year, 1993.

A few days later I received a batch of 40 press releases from the Human Rights Department. Every single one of them was a case that involved women filing discrimination charges against men. None of them was about men having been discriminated against, even though there had been a few cases during 1993 that were found in favor of men. That confirmed my hunch about the Department's discrimination biases.

Several months after the case was closed I called the director of the State Bar and Restaurant Association to find out if the attorney for Gators had informed him about the outcome of the case, as the ruling stipulated she must. No word had been received. I informed the attorney general's office and asked them to enforce the ruling, and they assured me that they would. Several months passed again.

It was now April of 1995. I made a last ditch call to the director of the Bar and Restaurant Association. He said: "Horner! Your timing is excellent. We received notice of the ruling a few weeks ago and I have inserted the piece into May's newsletter. All the members should have it in their mail by next week."

I picked up the phone and called the first Twin Cities television station that came to mind to report about the newsletter mailing. That's all it took to ignite the wildest media frenzy I could've imagined. The scene was like a wild prairie fire on a hot and windy afternoon—fast and furious. The front page headline of the next day's newspaper read: "TURN OUT THE LIGHTS, THE PARTY'S OVER." For the next week I had cameramen and news people at my home every day. The story ran on the front page of four metro newspapers. Every TV station in town covered it, and every Twin Cites radio station wanted an on-air interview. National radio and TV picked up the story, and the CBS radio network featured me on one of their coast-to-coast talk shows.

The public feedback sparked by all this media attention absolutely amazed me. It was a terrific study of contemporary issues and human nature. There wasn't a bar, restaurant, or business office in the Twin Cites that didn't have people expressing their viewpoint about Ladies' Night. Sociology professors at the University of Minnesota were discussing the issue with their classes. I heard from past acquaintances whom I hadn't heard from in over 20 years, some of them living in other parts of the country. They all called to express their opinions about Ladies' Night. Overall, I'm sure I fielded well over 200 phone calls at home.

The first wave of feedback was emotionally charged with anger, split about 50-50 between men and women. Some said that I was gay; "you must not care if you ever get laid again;" I was weird; or that I had too much time on my hands to deal with such a trivial issue.

I received four death threats, my house got egged, and people publicly blamed me for squelching their social and sex lives.

A television reporter asked disparagingly, "Why didn't you just go to another bar?" I countered, "Why didn't Rosa Parks just get on another bus?" Bar owners across the state were up in arms, complaining that I ruined their livelihood, and as one St. Paul newspaper columnist wrote, "Steve Horner is the most hated man in Minnesota."

After the first avalanche of bitterness subsided, I began hearing constructive and supportive feedback.

The phone calls at home turned positive. Several women said, "If women want equal rights then we should have equal rights across the board. That means taking the bad with the good."

Dozens of men called to lend their support. The most memorable was a call one evening while I was watching the story on TV. In a very earnest tone of voice the caller said, "Thank you, Steve," then he hung

TACKLING SINGLE PARENTING

up. A leader of a state-wide men's rights group was quoted in a newspaper article as predicting, "The Ladies' Night issue will be remembered as a turning point for men's rights and Steve Horner is a folk hero." My son, Paul, praised my efforts when he said, "Gee dad, one guy *can* make a difference."

A man stepped up to me at church, eagerly shook my hand and said, "My family hasn't had such a hot debate among ourselves for years. It was great!" Meanwhile, his wife standing next to him, was snarling at me. After the service an elderly woman in a wheelchair made a special effort to shake my hand and said, "Way to go! I support you 100 percent."

A woman called into a radio talk show that I was on and said, "Susan B. Anthony would've been proud to walk hand-in-hand with you on this issue." Another woman called to applaud my efforts and said, "Ladies' Night is just another example of men thinking they have to help out women. Women don't need help, thank you!" And, while being interviewed on the CBS radio network, I spoke to a woman caller from Connecticut who said, "Ladies' Night promotes the sexist concept of rounding up the herd, getting 'em drunk, and taking 'em home to screw 'em."

Why did the Ladies' Night issue stir up such widespread controversy? Many of the people to whom I've posed that question are amazed by the amount of dialogue the issue stimulated. I've heard answers that pertained to gender rivalry and gender equity. Those are some of the obvious issues that lie on the surface of Ladies' Night, but there's something else that runs much deeper. I've had several business customers and friends comment about the "mystery issue." They've said, "There's something else there, but I just can't put my finger on it."

The Four Elements Of Discipline

While the smoke was clearing from the Ladies' Night controversy, I arranged a meeting with our local school district's director of secondary education, Dan Kaler, to discuss an unrelated issue. Kaler grew up in mining country in Northern Minnesota. When he was a kid, his father worked in the mines and Dan worked on mining support jobs, such as keeping the rails straight so the ore cars could move smoothly.

I was impressed by the hard work on which Dan was raised, and I asked him what he thought were the components of discipline. I defined DISCIPLINE as the adherence to rules. The director stated quite matter of factly, "Most educators believe there are three elements involved with effective discipline: consistency, firmness, and fairness."

As I drove home, it occurred to me that DISCIPLINE was the mystery issue in the Ladies' Night debate. Ladies' Night was a blatant violation of the elements of discipline: consistency, firmness, fairness, and through my own personal observations and experience with discipline, I'm including the element of convenience.

The dispute over Ladies' Night followed the same course in which discipline runs amuck in government, in schools, at home, and in society in general, and has been running amuck throughout the country for the last 25 years. The stampede of controversy that Ladies' Night stirred up reflected the popular discord and confusion that weak discipline policies generate.

From the very beginning of the Ladies' Night controversy, dating to September 1992, I was never angry with Gators. As a matter of fact, the whole concept of Ladies' Night never really bothered me that much. Ladies' Night became a vehicle through which I was able to shed some light on the irregularities surrounding gender laws. I was angry with the state lawmakers and the Department of Human Rights for creating laws that were designed to prohibit gender discrimination, and yet violated the fundamental principles of administering the rules they created. The element of consistency was clearly missing.

Even though the anti-discrimination statute, created as part of the Civil Rights Act, had been on the books since 1964, it was inconsistently enforced. The law worked for women and minorities, but as I found out from dealing with the Department of Human Rights, it wasn't intended for men like me. It was inconsistent of the Department of Human Rights to preach and promote the righteousness of gender sensitivity and gender equity in schools and work places, but then to allow blatant violations like Ladies' Night to occur. It was the confusing, mixed message of a double standard. Consistency means that if you're going to "talk the talk" then you need to "walk the walk." Ladies' Night was not "walking the walk," and that made me angry.

TACKLING SINGLE PARENTING

I felt as though I'd been swindled by hypocrites.

If rules are going to be effective they also need to be firmly enforced. The discriminatory practice of Ladies' Night had been around for many years, but the law that says it was illegal was never enforced. A law that doesn't have any teeth is a law that's ignored. If a law isn't important enough to be enforced then why does the law continue to exist?

Rules need to be fair. If rules are unjust, discipline will be ineffective. Ladies' Night was unfair. It's unfair to deny a person goods or services based on something they have no control over, such as gender. Ladies' Night allowed women preferential treatment over men based on gender, and that was unfair. When people are treated unfairly they get justifiably angry, resentful, and lose respect for other people. I lost respect for the Human Rights Department because of the unfair treatment I received.

It's often inconvenient to practice the fundamental principles of effective discipline. The Department of Human Rights found that to be true with the Ladies' Night issue. It wasn't convenient for the Department to stand up and speak out for the sexual discrimination laws which had been failing to serve me and thousands of other Minnesota men. The Human Rights Department didn't want to make waves. That's why they balked at releasing a press release on the issue. It was much more convenient for the Department to keep the issue quiet, rather than to stir up the flames of dissent that they knew were inevitable. Typical backlash against the Department's ruling came from the Opinions Editor at the Minneapolis Star Tribune: "That the Department says it has time to pursue any and all individual complaints of gender discrimination (referring to Ladies' Night) should raise questions about its priorities. In a world where serious discrimination still exists, how can officials find resources to tackle ubiquitous business promotions? It can't, and it shouldn't. Minnesotans would be better served by a Department that cracks down on discrimination that causes harm."

That tells me that the newspaper doesn't see any harm in my rights having been violated. They sure seize every opportunity to speak out whenever they think women's rights are being breached.

More importantly, are some civil rights more important than others? Who decides? Another confusing double standard.

That suggests another reason why it was inconvenient for the Human Rights Department to stand up for what was right. The delicate issue of Ladies' Night—allowing preferential treatment of women, based on gender—was too closely connected to the politically sensitive issue of affirmative action. That's exactly the definition of affirmative action: preferential treatment based on a person's race or gender. Many politically powerful minority and women's groups promote affirmative action. It's not convenient to go against their agenda. It's more comfortable to agree with them. When people compromise their principles for the sake of convenience, it's termed "selling out." The Human Rights Department sold me out for the sake of their own convenience.

It was also inconvenient for the Human Rights Department to support my discrimination complaint because of the imminent wrath from the bar and restaurant owners. The bar owners claimed, "Some types of discrimination and bias should be allowed in situations where commerce (money) is involved." That's why the St. Paul City Council scrambled to draw up a resolution a week after the Ladies' Night issue was made public. That resolution was in response to angry bar owners. It requested that the Minnesota Legislature enact an amendment to the Minnesota Human Rights Act that would exempt business promotions, such as Ladies' Night. It passed six to one. I called the City Councilman who initiated that action and told him that in light of his resolution that we might as well go back to the Stone Age again and allow all sorts of discriminatory acts. I told him, "Let's not stop at Ladies' Night. Let's include Blacks' Night and Jews' Night." No response.

Teaching Effective Discipline Begins At Home

The Ladies' Night issue was a matter of discipline. The state legislature created laws that were designed to fight discrimination. Those laws were supposed to be enforced by the Department of Human Rights. The Department violated fundamental principles of its charge regarding those laws. Eventually, that violation led to public dissent that resulted in resentment, anger, and confusion.

TACKLING SINGLE PARENTING

Resentment, anger, and confusion are the same volatile emotions that can rise to the surface of a child if fundamental principles of discipline aren't practiced at home. And home is the make-it or break-it element in the success or failure of a child learning the features, advantages, and benefits of following rules.

Research from the National Institute of Mental Health reported in a 1995 study of violent communities: "It seems clear that whatever factors are ultimately identified as important influences on adaptational successes and failures in children, they will almost certainly be related to characteristics of their families."

There's plenty of evidence indicating that discipline in the home isn't as effective as it should be for a healthy society to exist. School superintendents, principals, teachers and school board members have told me that the dramatic rise in school discipline problems is due to a lackadaisical and ineffective approach to discipline at home. Those same educators make one thing clear: discipline problems aren't limited to single parents and their children. Many two-parent families struggle with worrisome discipline problems, as well. Either way, the number of troubled kids just keeps rising.

My boys and I live in Dakota County, part of the Twin Cities metro area. Its population can be generally regarded as medium to up-scale in terms of education and income. Yet, county Community Corrections reported that juvenile arrests jumped 72 percent from 1992 with 2,695 arrests, to 4,638 arrests in 1995, while the county population rose only 8 percent. More than half of those arrests were for felonies. In the 1994-1995 school year, there was a 300 percent increase in the number of school suspensions in Minnesota public schools over the year before. Juvenile arrests and school suspensions result from a lack of adherence to rules, and many people are fed up with it.

These eye-opening comments from a couple of Twin Cities school teachers paint a vivid picture about the need for better discipline. Leah Stanek, a special education teacher for years, told a 1994 group of parents and teachers at a "site" council meeting that 1995 was going to be her last. "I can't go home and keep losing sleep over these kids who have no respect for property or authority. I went into teaching to teach, not to be a bouncer. I'm spending more and more of my time dealing with behaviors than I am teaching in the classroom." Julie

Wernimont, an 11-year teaching veteran, spoke to the same group and echoed the same sentiments. "I feel heartbroken that I spend more than 40 percent of my time in school disciplining kids."

The lack of discipline not only negatively impacts school teachers and the kids who come to school ready to learn—only to be distracted by troublemakers—but also every taxpayer. Dakota county placed over 1,500 minors in foster homes and other out-of-home facilities in 1995. Some of the placements were made to protect children from parents, but the vast majority of the placements were a direct result of juvenile crime. Each youth costs the taxpayer from $13,000 to $63,000 per year to care for, depending on individual need. Out-of-home placement numbers had been rising at the same terrifying pace as juvenile crime until county authorities had to relax their enforcement criteria due to budgetary concerns. Law enforcement officials and educators say that parents need to take more responsibility disciplining their children. Many single parents claim that's easier said than done.

All dedicated parents must battle the onslaught of outside negative forces, such as drugs and gangs, that can derail even the most valiant efforts to maintain discipline in the family. However, single parents have their own, unique set of problems and challenges to building and maintaining effective and productive discipline in the home.

The absence of a spouse of the opposite sex can tilt the family scales of discipline and justice too far in either direction. Many men are perceived as overly tough on their children, while many women are said to be not tough enough. A delicate balance and mix of gender styles is missing from the single parent family.

Another disciplinary handicap of the single parent is that effective and productive discipline demands time, energy, and patience. Many single parents find those three elements in short supply.

Building And Maintaining Discipline

You have now seen the public uproar that ineffective discipline policies can cause, evidenced by the Ladies' Night debacle. Emotions of resentment, anger, and confusion were running rampant. You've seen the negative fallout of ineffective discipline policies through sky-rocketing problems in schools, and throughout society. How then, can moms and dads who are tackling single parenting put practical discipline policies into effect at home, where teaching discipline begins? For my family, the solution began with consistency.

Consistency

When my children were much younger, maybe six and nine, I used to smoke cigarettes. I was a light smoker—about a pack a week. I used to tell the boys, "Smoking is bad for you and I hope you're never tempted to take up the habit."

For a long time they listened to my preaching about cigarettes without saying much in response. I rationalized my hypocrisy with the standard cop-out, "Do as I say, not as I do." There came a time, however, when things changed. My boys began coming home from school with fresh insights to smoking. They were learning how harmful it is to your health, and how many people died from smoking-related illnesses each year.

Eventually, through their love and concern for my health, my sons persuaded me to quit smoking. How could I have possibly expected my children to accept the hazards of smoking had I continued to smoke?

How can we adults teach rules to our children when we break them ourselves? It's not consistent. Children don't have the wisdom or experience to sort out the "do as I say, not as I do" mentality. We are their role models. Have you noticed how young children emulate the activities and musical tastes of their parents? If the parent plays sports, the child wants to play sports. If the parent spends a lot of time on the computer, the child wants to work on the computer. If the parent listens to rock music, the child wants to listen to rock music. If the parent listens to country music, the child wants to listen to country music. Sure, children soon acquire their own personal tastes and interests, but their first look at life is through the eyes and examples of their parents.

Impressionable children are watching and listening when their moms and dads drink and drive, take things that don't belong to them, walk across the street against a red light, or use foul language. The kids soak up negative behavior like a sponge. However, when kids see their parents drive within the law, refrain from the temptations of stealing, stand patiently at busy intersections waiting for the walk light, and communicate with words that are creative and constructive, they also soak up those positive qualities. It's part of setting a good example.

What are we supposed to do when our children know that we have broken rules yet we warn them against breaking the same rules? When Paul was 16, he told me that he knew lots of kids who smoked pot and did other drugs. "Dad! You're a hypocrite for telling me not to smoke pot. You told me you smoked pot in Vietnam." I replied, "Let's look up the word hypocrite in the dictionary." The definition says, "One who feigns virtue or piety, a pretender."

"Paul, I'm trying to teach you a valuable lesson. If we're wise, then we learn from our mistakes and we pass those lessons on to our children. I learned from experience that smoking pot builds a false sense of happiness and pleasure which I've seen collapse on a lot of people. I'm trying to pass that lesson on to you. It's the same as if I jumped off a bridge and broke both of my legs when I landed. You don't need to jump off the same bridge to find out if you'll break your legs. You can learn from my experience that jumping off the bridge isn't a wise thing to do."

With that logic, my discipline teachings have consistency and credibility. However, they wouldn't hold up if I was still a pot smoker. Then I would be a hypocrite, which could arouse confusion and build anger, resentment, and mistrust in Paul toward me. My repeated warnings about the negative impact of smoking pot wouldn't be very persuasive, and would probably not discourage Paul from smoking it. Our family fares much better in discipline when I not only "talk the talk" but actually "walk the walk."

Firmness

If rules are going to be effective, they need to be firmly enforced. If a rule doesn't have teeth, it will eventually be ignored. Children learn to recognize toothless laws in school and throughout society, in general. They realize that certain rules can be violated without penalty. Ineffective discipline policies are in direct conflict with the techniques that work for my family and me. They create confusing double standards for my children. I was involved with a toothless law while working as a clean-up volunteer for the local park department.

My boys and I had volunteered our cleaning services for three years. We were assigned to a city park close to home, and each year we did thorough spring and fall cleanings. During the rest of the year, we picked up litter at the park once or twice a week. It was an excellent family project that we enjoyed working on together. It helped build our camaraderie, and rewarded the three of us with a feeling of accomplishment, knowing that we had chipped in to help our community.

One spring day, while I was at the park shooting hoops, I noticed several garbage barrels floating in the pond. It was nothing new. There was always something being destroyed at the park. I felt disgusted and remember promising myself that I'd retrieve the barrels the following day, but not then.

The next day I drove past the park on an errand, and I saw a group of kids by the pond near the barrels. I parked and walked over to see what was going on. There were eight kids, ranging in age from about 10 to 13. There was an adult woman with the group, but I didn't notice her. She was the same height as the kids and didn't make herself known when I approached the group. I asked them if they were the guys who tossed the barrels into the water.

At that, the woman spoke up and said she was the foster mother to several of the kids, and that one of them, David, was being asked to fetch the barrels. I asked David if he tossed the barrels in the pond and he told me to "fuck off." The foster mother said that David had admitted earlier to throwing the barrels in the pond.

After ten minutes of hearing David insult both the foster mother and me and seeing that no progress was being made in hauling out the barrels, I stepped behind David, gently put my hands on his shoulders and began to walk him down to the water. The whole time David was laying his insulting and vile language on me. Then he stopped and spat in my face. I instinctively slapped him across his shoulder. That's when the kid went ballistic. He started swinging wildly at me. I did my best to dodge his attempts to hit me. The foster mother abruptly stepped in, took David by the arm, and the whole group marched away, cursing me and threatening a lawsuit. I thought that their words sure echoed what a lot of crybabies were saying these days—Lawsuit! Then I finished my errand. On my way home, I saw the same group back at the pond. This time there was a policeman with them. I knew I'd get in trouble if I went down there but I also knew that I had to stand up for my principles. I decided to confront the situation. A week later I received a summons to appear in court for fifth degree assault.

As soon as I received the summons, I got on the phone to Tom Adamini, the superintendent of park maintenance. He told me, "Steve, we'll support you in every way that we can." Tom told me how frustrated he was, "The destruction of park property is at an all-time high," he said. "We used to have the public outhouses knocked over from time to time. Now they get torched. Last summer we had five outhouses totally destroyed by fire." He told me the problem is that the city attorney's office "won't touch these kids." He was right.

Annette Margarit, a lawyer representing the City, wrote to me saying that civil action, which I tried to file against David for vandalizing the barrels, was inappropriate. "The City has experienced no damage as a result of the boy's actions." I vehemently disagreed. I told Ms. Margarit that it was likely that the group was responsible for much of the damage at the park, and someone needed to step into this kid's life and make a statement about discipline.

"He apparently is not getting the message at home, or in school." Still, she refused to file a charge.

When I appeared in court, I was adamant about not pleading guilty to an assault charge. I felt that such a harsh charge did not fit the situation. In fact, I felt that had it been 20 years earlier, David would've been instilled with more respect for adults. He wouldn't have cursed at me, spat at me, and would've taken my orders to remove the barrels from the water. There shouldn't have been any charge leveled against me. I know that I didn't harm or frighten David at the pond because a week later, while I was shooting hoops, he rode his bicycle right up to me. "Hey! Aren't you the guy that tried to make me get the barrels out of the water? Can I play basketball with you?" This kid needed some discipline in his life, not people encouraging his destructiveness.

As I was sitting in court waiting for my name to be called, I was able to get a good look at today's level of law enforcement. I saw eight people with speeding violations plead their case before Judge Mary Pawlenty. In each case, she reduced the severity of the offense so that the violation wouldn't go on the speeder's insurance record. I was sitting there wondering, "Where are the teeth in the speeding laws?" One young woman, who looked about 20, who just had her violation reduced, walked by me on the way out of the courtroom. She was smiling broadly and, referring to the judge, said quietly under her breath, "Sucker-r-r-r." I doubt she'd be singing the same tune if her insurance premiums were raised 30 percent. A hefty insurance hike might also encourage her to be a safer driver. The only encouragement she received from the judge, however, was to maintain her same driving habits.

When my name was called, I pled not guilty to the charge of assault and stated my case. I was found guilty of a reduced charge of disorderly conduct. Instead of hassling with an appeal, I agreed to serve 15 hours of community service.

The pond incident was a unique learning experience. I learned that society is anxious for us taxpayers to show our love of children by throwing more money at them, but when it comes time to show our love and concern by means of firm discipline, which is often referred to as "tough love," we end up in court, and the kids learn that they can get away with breaking the law.

After my hearing, I called Ms. Margarit, the attorney for the City, and expressed my anger at her refusal to take measures against David. I predicted, "David will end up with a gun one of these days." Sure enough, about a year later, I was shooting hoops and along came one of the kids who had been involved in the pond incident. He didn't recognize me. I tossed him the ball and started a conversation. He told me there are "Blood" gang members who hang out at the park, "but I'm not scared of them," he bragged. "My brother has a gun. It's a real one. Just a little baby one," as he stuck his thumb up and his finger out to resemble an under-sized gun and demonstrated how neatly it fit into a pocket. He told me his brother's name was David. When I got home, I called Ms. Margarit and told her my prediction had come to pass. She assured me that necessary steps would be taken and thanked me for the information. I wonder what kind of "necessary steps" were actually pursued.

In the case of the pond incident, David had violated the law and should've been punished. But with today's ineffective policies on discipline, David was labeled as the victim, and I was the bad guy because I slapped him across the shoulder. A year later, David was toting a gun. I thought, "Where's David going to be in another year, in a grave?"

Supreme Court Justice Clarence Thomas referred to this type of ineffective discipline in a 1994 speech to the Federal Institute and the Manhattan Institute. In that speech, Thomas blamed a well-intentioned "judicial rights revolution" for accelerating urban crime by treating underprivileged perpetrators as victims rather than criminals. "No longer was an individual identified as the cause of a harmful act. Rather, societal conditions or the actions of institutions and others in society became the responsible causes of harm," he said. "In the long run, a society that abandons personal responsibility will lose its moral sense," he warned. "And it's the urban poor whose lives are being destroyed the most by this loss of moral sense."

My definition of "moral sense" is a sense of right and wrong behavior based on standards of honor. I define honor as being "upright," formulated from accepted, traditional guidelines: not to use foul language; to obey rules at home and in society; to respect your parents; not to harm others with words or actions; to keep a pure body and mind; not to steal; and not to lie. I've worked hard to teach my children these moral guidelines. The merits of firm discipline have helped me succeed.

Firm discipline has been an on-going process for my family. It hasn't been a single, shoot from the hip lesson. Firm discipline is a way of adhering to a system of guiding principles. There are three important elements to my definition: ANTICIPATION—to expect, to foresee, to recognize beforehand. PERSUASION—to prevail upon by argument, to convince. And, PUNISHMENT—to inflict a penalty for violating a rule.

ANTICIPATION

The first element of guidance, ANTICIPATION, serves as preventive maintenance to discipline problems. You become pro-active by taking steps to prevent problems, rather than always having to react after the fact. The benefits of ANTICIPATION include helping your child to better understand rules, plus accumulating positive experiences from which self-esteem blossoms. ANTICIPATION is often used successfully in sports.

During the summer of 1995, I coached J.J.'s soccer team. I told the goalkeeper that he needed to keep his eye on the ball and anticipate from where the ball might be kicked. I told him that one moment the ball might be up front to your left, then quickly passed to an opponent positioned right in front of your net for a quick shot on goal. "The goalkeeper needs to anticipate the pass and take care to avoid being scored on. He has to continuously consider all the factors involved." It's the same philosophy for being effective when using ANTICIPATION for firm discipline in the family: It's wise to take precautions against trouble. One important way that we've done that is to ask for God's help.

Our family accepts God as a wonderful force in our lives; there are measures we take to benefit from His presence: We pray together daily, my kids are involved in religion classes, and we attend Sunday services. I've also tried to set a good example for my kids as a religion teacher. I believe that God should be at least as prevalent as sports in our lives and if I'm going to coach sports, I should make the extra effort to "coach" religion. It's a tough world riddled with complications, challenges, and temptations. By keeping God active in our lives, we're anticipating the ever-present need for His strength and support to help us over the hurdles. His presence safeguards us from the poison of boredom, gives us a fresh sense of direction, and helps to take dissatisfaction out of our lives; all of which are precautions against trouble.

There are other, secular techniques that have also helped me be successful with firm discipline through the use of ANTICIPATION.

When J.J. was a baby and Paul was just out of his toddler stage, we lived on a hobby farm in a rural area near Willmar, Minnesota, about 100 miles west of the Twin Cities. Both boys were born there. We had a lovely home surrounded by rolling hills and a panoramic view of rustic Lake Solomon. The house was set back about 100 yards from a busy county road. From the time Paul could walk, I anticipated that our county road was a potential hazard. I often took Paul by the hand and walked him out to our fence line, and stopped. I pointed to the cars and recited the word "danger." That was our code word to beware. We would stand at the end of our driveway and watch the cars speed by. Day after day, I walked Paul to the end of the driveway, and repeatedly discussed with him the dangers of walking beyond our fence line. Through my ANTICIPATION, I was trying to prevent an unspeakable tragedy.

We used our code word, danger, to anticipate other trouble areas, like being too near our horses, a hot stove, or playing behind the truck. Then, after I noticed Paul made a conscious effort to abide by the rules, I praised him for his effort, further reinforcing his actions, and building a stockpile of positive experiences to nourish his self-esteem.

The repetition and ongoing process of ANTICIPATION provides growth for young children by teaching them about the importance of rules. It remains, though, no substitute for adult supervision, especially with dangerous situations like, "Don't go near the busy road." Supervision needs to be ever-present whenever the youngsters are active.

ANTICIPATION doesn't accommodate failure, it discourages it. Like when I took my boys to a friend's home for an outdoor wedding. I had them dressed in their best clothes. I told J.J., who was about seven or eight, that we weren't going to be there very long, so I didn't want him playing and getting dirty. I had to remind him a couple of times, but he generally abided by the rules. I had anticipated a potential trouble area and laid the rules down beforehand. J.J. abided by them, so I praised him later for his success.

I'm certain that the story would've ended differently had I told J.J., "Don't get dirty, but if you do, there's a clean-up area in the basement." In that case, I would've accommodated a young boy's normal inclination to test the rule, and set him up for failure.

ANTICIPATION means that I try to spot potential trouble areas and set rules beforehand for the welfare and success of the child.

Another time, one of the boys' cousins, 11-year-old "Nicole," spent the night. Nicole's mother told me that Nicole had a bed-wetting problem. She had brought a bed pad along for her to sleep on. I recognize that urinary problems can be symptomatic of more serious medical or psychological concerns, but from what her mom said, I thought the only malady Nicole suffered from was laziness.

That night, while I was tucking the kids into their beds, I told Nicole that she wasn't to use the pad, but that I would leave the bathroom light on. I said, "If you feel the need to pee, then I want you to make the effort to get out of bed and use the bathroom." Nicole succeeded, and the next morning she felt great when I praised her for her success. The bed pad had been accommodating Nicole's inclination to linger in bed and pee. It was setting her up for failure. 'ANTICIPATION means that you identify potential trouble areas and set rules beforehand for the welfare and success of the child. Even if Nicole had failed in her efforts the very next night, at least she would've experienced success the previous evening giving her a positive foundation on which to build.

It helps reinforce the rule if you have the child repeat it back to you. This practice helps eliminate any misunderstanding about expectations. I asked Nicole, "So, when you wake up and feel like you have to pee, what are you supposed to do?" "I'm supposed to make the effort to get out of my bed and go to the bathroom to pee instead of peeing in my bed," was her answer. "Very good," I told her. "That's exactly right." Now the rule was crystal clear.

I've found success disciplining my boys through ANTICIPATION by becoming educated on the matters involved, and then setting appropriate rules. For instance, I ask my boys a lot of questions to get their feedback about topics such as school work and their other activities: "Where are you going?"; "With whom?"; "When are you coming back?" When I feel as though I've learned enough, I set the SUBSEQUENT RULE: "It's a school night and I want you home by nine o'clock." I can ask their school teachers for suggestions on how to improve certain grades. The fact: "Your teacher said you're screwing around in math class and that's why your grades are suffering." SUBSEQUENT RULE: "It's time to shape up and quit screwing around in school." I can visit with law enforcers to learn about crime trends and about the early warning signals of drug use. When I learn about the issues, then I can make the rules that are applicable. SUBSEQUENT RULE: "The police report that drug use is up at the high school. The temptation to use drugs will be stronger than ever, so be on guard." After I set a rule I try to remind myself to praise the kids when they abide by it. Praise for a job that's well done is praise that's long-lasting.

I remember telling J.J. to be home by six o'clock because I'd have supper ready. Right at 5:59:30 he came bursting through the kitchen door, out of breath from running, opened his arms wide like a circus performer looking for applause after a daring act, and exclaimed, "ta-da." It was great. I could have left my praise go unsaid and told him to get washed up for supper. Instead, I dropped what I was doing, urged Paul to join me in giving J.J. a well-deserved applause and a big hug. All the while J.J. was blushing and saying, "I know, I know, I'm great." Our acknowledgment rewarded J.J. for following a rule, and therefore encouraged him to continue following rules. It also helped refine J.J.'s character by building standards of discipline from which to grow into an up-right, successful, law-abiding adult.

The element of ANTICIPATION is an excellent parenting tool to use from childhood through adolescence, and into adulthood. It helps me through many of the on-going concerns of child-rearing: keeping rooms tidy, doing household chores, teaching courtesy and safety, getting home on time, getting to school on time, doing school-work, morals, drugs, crime, and any other issue that involves rules.

PERSUASION

The next element of guidance that helps me be successful with firm discipline is PERSUASION. PERSUASION helps me enforce the rules that I have already set in place for my children.

Business experts have extolled the importance of persuasion for years: "Selling is when just one side wins, PERSUASION is when both sides win."

In the case of discipline, both sides win when the child understands the benefit of following a rule. Most of us have heard comments like: "Why do I have to make my bed every morning? Nobody will see it."; "Why do I have to keep my room clean? It's just going to get messed up again."; "Why do I have to do this stupid homework? It's stuff that I'm never going to need." Answers like "Because I said so," or, "Because I'm the boss," are not very convincing. Communication skills that emphasize PERSUASION are much more effective in getting children to follow rules.

Rules are more effective when children understand the reasons behind them. Reasons translate into benefits. Creating dialogue, with pertinent questions and patient listening, helps to discover the benefits. J.J. used to ask, "Dad, why do I have to keep my room clean? It's just going to get messed up again and besides, nobody's going to see it." I asked J.J:

"What do you want to be when you grow up?" He repeated what he had been telling me for years, "A magazine publisher." I asked him about the duties that a magazine publisher must perform to be successful. "Certainly, an important ingredient of the job is management. You need to learn to keep things in their proper place so they'll be there when you need them. Keeping your room tidy is good practice for your business skills." Learning business skills, which will help J.J. achieve his goal of being a magazine publisher, was a benefit for him. He quickly saw the connection, and that has helped to inspire him to keep his room clean and tidy ever since.

Here's another dimension of PERSUASION to which many parents can relate. My mother was effective with this form of PERSUASION when I was a teenager: "If you don't get that lawn mowed, you won't be using the car for your big date Saturday night." My mom knew that using the car was a benefit that resulted from mowing the lawn. She used that logic to persuade me to follow the rule of mowing the lawn. It worked. I was able to use the car and my mom got the lawn mowed. We both won.

There must be at least a million rules, both in homes and throughout society. Each rule has benefits: "Keep your bedroom neat and tidy because it will help you learn to be an organized business person when you get older." "Mow that lawn or you won't use the car." Asking questions, listening to concerns, and ultimately discovering what those benefits are, will help me continue to persuade my boys to follow rules. Following rules will help my boys live a happy and orderly life, meaning fewer hassles for them, and for me, as well. Fewer hassles for all of us is a goal that inspires me to keep practicing effective discipline through PERSUASION. Each side becomes a winner.

PUNISHMENT

The third element of guidance that helps me be successful with firm discipline is PUNISHMENT. Promoting PUNISHMENT is not seen as politically correct these days. Many educators and family counselors say, "It is an archaic paradigm that should be done away with." I don't agree with them. PUNISHMENT has worked beautifully for me in helping to raise my children.

It would be a much better world if those in authority were able to effectively implement the first two elements of discipline, ANTICIPATION and PERSUASION, and nothing more was needed for people to abide by the rules. Unfortunately, rule violators often don't get the full message of discipline through ANTICIPATION and PERSUASION; that's why we need PUNISHMENT. PUNISHMENT means to inflict a penalty for breaking rules. It's much the same principle as in playing sports. In soccer, for example, if a player commits a foul, the player's team is punished by awarding the opposition a penalty kick. PUNISHMENT works to deter future rule violations.

Since the late '60s, there's been a terrific amount of debate about what methods of PUNISHMENT are acceptable and effective at home and in school. Many people claim that everybody would benefit by eliminating all forms of punishment, that punishment itself is the cause of much of the world's evil. Others claim that society has "gone soft" on punishment, that the lack of punishment is the cause of much of the world's evil.

Here are some contemporary philosophies about punishment that I've gathered from several Minnesota state-funded organizations. They include the Early Childhood Family Education Center (ECFE), which works with my local school district and has been regarded as a model program for the nation. ECFE's focus is on parenting skills for young families. I also include data from the Minnesota Extension Service at the University of Minnesota, and from the Minnesota Department of Children, Families, and Learning. Formerly, the Minnesota Department of Education.

I find it interesting that all the directors and discipline policy makers at these agencies, including a 32-member task force at the ECFE, are women. No men. Why don't these agencies embrace a wider view of the goals, needs, and concerns of their discipline policies by including a male perspective? Maybe the lack of gender balance happens when men decide not to get involved in child guidance and discipline policy-making.

Whatever the reason, I think the single gender discipline policies, and those that discredit the use of PUNISHMENT, have a negative influence on my discipline efforts at home. They conflict with the techniques that work for my family. They set confusing double standards for my children, at school, and throughout society in general.

How These Agencies Define Punishment

Punishment may be physical—spanking, hitting, causing pain—also called CORPORAL.
Punishment may be psychological, which includes disapproval, isolation, loss of privileges, and shaming—making a child feel remorseful.

Their Policies and Guidelines on Punishment

Punishment focuses on past behavior.
Punishment may do little or nothing to help a child behave better in the future.
Punishment can leave bad effects on children such as shame, guilt, anxiety, and increased aggression.
Children who are punished learn that those they depend on the most for love and care can also inflict physical and psychological pain on them.
Children should be allowed to misbehave, rather than disrupting them by causing skirmishes.
Violence is never an acceptable form of punishment. When children learn that violence is acceptable, they may imitate it.
Spanking should be against the law. Spanking teaches that hitting others is morally correct.
Those who are spanked as children grow up to be spankers.
Spanking chips away at the bond of affection.
Spanking can escalate into physical abuse.

Spanking leads to spousal abuse.
Spanking instills fear.
Spanking hurts the child's self-esteem.

The groups theorize: "Effective discipline can be achieved almost entirely through ANTICIPATION and PERSUASION." Penalties for rule offenses should be limited to "time-outs," sending the child to a "safe but boring place for a certain amount of time," and "loss of privileges for a certain amount of time can be effective."

I told the psychologist in charge of policy making at the Early Childhood Family Center that I disagreed with many of the contemporary policies on discipline. "As a matter of fact," I told her, "I think much of the challenge of tackling single parenting would be a lot easier without outside forces like you working against my efforts at home." After she got past the initial shock of my candor, she showed me the results of studies that supported her theories about discipline.

The topic of discipline oozes with subjectivity. I told her, "Research on the topic can reach any conclusion that you're striving for. Obviously, you've reached some conclusions on discipline with which you feel comfortable." Her conclusions couldn't stand close scrutiny. I asked the psychologist: "What would you say if I told you that 10 out of 12 student council members at Apple Valley High School, which prides itself on high scholastic merits, admit to having been spanked as youngsters?" It really didn't matter whether I actually surveyed the students—she was tongue-tied. A slight contradiction to her permissive, highbrow theories about discipline completely baffled her. She muttered something about my rudeness and abruptly left the room.

The conclusions reached by those "experts," that spanking encourages future spousal abuse and other anti-social behavior, are easily contradicted. The National Institute of Mental Health stated in its 1993 report about improving children's chances for success in society that not all children raised in violent environments suffer unfavorable consequences. The report states, "Many children exposed to even the most desperate of circumstances manage to not only survive but also thrive." The report further says, "The presence of violence (which the dictionary defines as: "Acting with physical force") does not destine children to poor developmental outcomes."

TACKLING SINGLE PARENTING

The Public Policies For Teaching Discipline Are Broken And Need To Be Fixed

Something is drastically wrong with current discipline policies. We've seen the results of those ineffective policies splattered across the headlines at a steadily increasing rate over the last 25 years. An FBI report released in November of 1995 showed that the number of teens under 18 arrested for murder rose more than 158 percent from 1985 through 1994. Rates for other teen crime and sex offenses are soaring, as are drug abuse and school suspensions. Metal detectors are placed at school entrances and armed guards are used in place of hall monitors. It has become routine to read about a kid who has brutalized a teacher or a parent. That kind of behavior was considered appalling—almost unheard of—when I was a child. Experts recount the biggest discipline problems in public schools in 1965 as talking in class and chewing gum. By 1995, the biggest discipline problems involved violence and drugs.

Much of the popular anti-punishment philosophy in schools and homes has its roots in a concept that was tested in the '60s. The concept known as "empowering" was originated by Dr. William Coulson, among others. Coulson, a psychologist, helped develop a "nondirective" theory of education in which students were encouraged to make their own choices rather than be directed to predetermined answers by their teacher. It wasn't long before the nondirective theory of teaching curriculum also took over as the fashionable way to teach discipline.

Over the span of 25 years, Dr. Coulson had evidently seen enough education go awry with his inane nondirective approach. He joined the education lecture circuit in the early 1990s to argue against its use. When referring to education about drug use and children, Coulson mocks the discipline philosophy of "choice." "And why would they do that?", Coulson implores his audiences with a rhetorical question that refers to parents, teachers, and choice. "It is because they have a wrong-headed idea that was tested way back in the '60s and found to be as wrong-headed as can be, that it's better when the children make up their own minds."

The word that's constantly invoked by proponents of empowering is "choice." They pride themselves when they tell kids, "Here are some consequences of making bad choices. It's up to you whether you want to make the wrong choice and suffer the consequences." As a loving guardian of my two minor children, I take a much more pro-active, directive stance, given the wisdom of my years, to prevent problems before they occur. I don't allow my children free reign choices to break rules. It's my responsibility as a nurturing, dedicated, and mature parent not to enable them with options of breaking rules—such options accommodate failure. I try to discourage my children's failures, and encourage their successes, instead. I follow the principles of ANTICIPATION and PERSUASION, and if my boys still "choose" not to follow a rule, the enforcement step of PUNISHMENT follows, a step that sometimes includes corporal punishment.

Corporal Punishment

I know that corporal punishment, when properly administered, is effective in encouraging children to follow rules. I asked Dan Kaler, the Director of Secondary Education in my local school district, one of the state's largest, if he was spanked when a youngster on Minnesota's Iron Range. Without hesitation and in a loud clear voice, he proudly proclaimed, "You bet!" Today, Dan is a successful, contented, contributing member of society.

When we were kids, my dad used to spank my brothers and me for repeated violations of family rules. My 5' 2" mother was never shy about paddling our butts when we deserved it, either. I remember one time specifically. I was 14, and my school grades were falling off because of my misbehaving. My mom warned me several times to get busy and improve my grades. I kept screwing around. Finally, one evening after a parent/teacher conference, my mother came home, grabbed a paddle, and started swinging. She had taken all of the disobedience from me that she could handle. I tried to talk my way out of the punishment, but she continued flailing away. I got walloped on the shoulders, back, legs, and butt. Wherever she could hit me, I got hit, as she chased me all around the house. She was furious, and made her point: "No more screwing around. It's time to get busy!" Soon afterwards, my grades made a noticeable improvement. Corporal punishment proved to be the right tonic for us

Horner boys. Today, we, too, are successful, contented, contributing members of society.

Corporal punishment effectively taught me about discipline because it was memorable. I was a smart-ass in my early teens, and more than one person wanted to take a punch at me. One summer day, while working at the horse ranch, a couple of fellow workers and I were giving another worker, Jimmy Theis, a hard time. Jimmy was a couple of years older, and a Golden Gloves boxer. He was a patient young man and warned us repeatedly to "quit bugging me, or you'll be sorry." He was unknowingly using the discipline elements of ANTICIPATION and PERSUASION. Still, we kept it up, calling him names and laughing at him.

Finally, Jimmy had taken all the abuse he could stand. He picked me out as the ringleader and the chase was on—around the yard, over the fence, in the barn, over the horses, under the horses, up the ladder into the hayloft, down the trap door, "isn't this guy ever going to give up?" I thought, "He wants to kill me." I ran out of the barn and around the back, where Jimmy caught up and tackled me. "I'm sorry, Jimmy, I won't bug you again." I kept apologizing as I scrambled to get back on my feet but it was too late. With two quick punches, one to the gut and then to the jaw as I was doubling over, I was knocked out. I came to, and Jimmy warned me as he walked away. "Don't ever bother me again."

I learned a memorable lesson that day about annoying people. Not only did I never bug Jimmy again, but I matured a lot with those two punches. I stopped being a smart-ass and got along much better with people. As a matter of fact, Jimmy and I became pretty good friends after that day. The corporal punishment that Jimmy laid on me was a rude awakening to the rules of courtesy, but I needed it. I'm glad it happened just the way it did. It made me a better person.

My Style Of Corporal Punishment

My main focus in disciplining my children is on ANTICIPATION and PERSUASION. I try to regard corporal punishment as a last resort. It's like the police officer who says, "I hope I never have to use my gun, but it's an effective deterrent to have around just in case." My goal when using corporal punishment is to act on behalf of my children's long term welfare.

When the boys were under 20 months old, they didn't yet have much of a handle on right and wrong. Yet, when they broke rules, like climbing on tables and throwing food from their plates, I'd discipline them with a stern and concise "DANGER" or "NO" in a matter-of-fact tone of voice that would get their attention. That would help them understand that what they were doing was unacceptable. I'd briefly explain the reason for the rule, such as "You might fall off and hurt yourself." I would then divert their attention to a book, or a toy, or back to their food.

As the boys got older, they came to recognize the difference between right and wrong. If, after repeated warnings, they were still throwing food on the floor, they received a sharp "NO" and a slap on their fingers. Not enough to inflict pain, but just enough to startle them. I would pick up the mess, settle the kid down, and explain what he did wrong, citing the reasons for not throwing food on the floor, such as wastefulness and bad manners. Then, I would finish eating with him, and make a final comment about the rule violation, to help him understand as much as he could for his early age. My words might've seemed insignificant, but discipline is a long-term process that requires patience and repetition. Each correction is a building block for the future. I could've stayed upset about the rule violation after administering the punishment and walked away in a huff of anger and frustration. Instead, I made the effort to explain the punishment in words that my young son could understand. That helped us create a positive learning experience. My punishment wasn't mean-spirited, and I didn't hurt the child. Yet, the message was a memorable one that helped him abide by the table rules in the future. Later, I lightened the conversation with a more pleasant topic, thereby reaffirming my love and commitment to my son.

As the boys grew older, to four, five and beyond, the corporal punishment for violations became more earnest. I believe that slaps or blows to the face are extreme and unwarranted, but a swift swat to the back of the shoulders will get their attention. In most cases, a couple of wallops on the leg or bare butt is all that's needed. I tried to make each disciplining episode a positive experience, explaining to my boys the purpose for the punishment and then discussing the rule violation with them afterwards. It's that delicate balance of firmness and love that I seek to achieve with corporal punishment. Any bully can beat up his kids, but the secret for success using corporal punishment is disciplining in a thoughtful, loving manner that turns an unpleasant action into a positive lesson. Words help make the difference between success and failure.

By the time Paul was four, I had repeatedly told him, "Don't go into the barn or corral without holding mom's or dad's hand." One Saturday afternoon, Paul and I were walking across the yard when we heard a commotion in the barn. I told Paul: "Stand here. Do not come through this gate." In the barn, the two horses were fighting over each other's grain.

I was settling them down when Paul walked up the ramp at the doorway, smiling. "Paul!" I yelled, "Get out of the barn." My yelling startled the horses, and they bolted for the door. Paul tripped and fell face down on the ramp. I quickly moved in front of the charging horses, like a football lineman, to shift their point of exit so they wouldn't run over Paul who had just risen to his knees. We were lucky that the horses got by Paul without trampling him. Thank God!

I was grateful that no accident had occurred, but I was furious at Paul for violating a rule that had been stressed—"Don't go into the barn without holding mom's or dad's hand." I was loud, and emphatic with him. "I've told you many times what the barn rule is, haven't I? Tell me what the barn rule is." Getting him to repeat the rule to me enforced his understanding of the violation, and the reason for his punishment. By then, the tears rolled down his cheeks, and he struggled to get the words out. I was on one knee with both hands on his shoulders looking right into his face. He said, "You don't want me to go in the barn by myself." I said, "That's right. And because you broke the rule, you could've been seriously hurt. Now I'm going to spank your butt to make sure you remember the rule from now on." I took him by the arm and forcefully marched him into the house.

The mere thought of getting a spanking inflicts suffering on a kid, so I figured he didn't need much more punishment to make it a memorable lesson. Back in the house, I walloped his butt a couple of times and said, "Now run to your room, close the door and think about this for awhile."

15 minutes later, after he settled down, I walked into his room, took him by the hand and said, "Let's sit on the bed and talk." With words, I told him how much I loved him, and that rules are made for the welfare of people and are meant to be obeyed. I again asked him to repeat the barn rule to help him understand the infraction and the penalty, and to help him remember the incident for the future. I asked him if he had any questions, giving him the chance to tell me what he felt about the rule or his punishment. We talked a while longer, and then I gave him a kiss and sent him on his way. He never broke the barn rule again.

Over the ages, parents have relied on rulers, belts, and switches, to make the punishment experience more memorable. A major drawback to using such a spanking tool is the difficulty in determining the extent of the punishment being inflicted. It's a wise and just parent who exercises a great deal of caution and discretion when using such an object. When I was a kid, my dad had a favorite spanking device that he used as the "last straw" measure with a rule violation. If we crossed the line too many times we ended up getting our butts beat with THE BLACK HAIR BRUSH. It was made of heavy plastic and was about ten inches long, including a five or six-inch handle. My dad would spank with the flat, smooth side, rather than the bristles. A couple of sharp blasts to the ass made the 'ol buns smart long enough to make the lesson memorable and help keep us from violating the rule again.

I preferred a spatula. The first time I used it on J.J., he was eight-years-old. Until then, I used the palm of my hand. By eight, I figured that J.J. was old enough to know that I shouldn't have to bitch about Saturday morning chores every week. The kids had their duties, and were told to get them done before their friends called to make plans for the day.

For weeks I had to light a fire under J.J. to get him to do his chores. I went through all the steps of ANTICIPATION and PERSUASION, but to no avail. J.J. sat on the couch watching television one Saturday morning, about 11:30. I grabbed his arm and told him to get the spatula, and I kicked him in the butt to hurry up his pace. When he came back I told him to whip down his pants and I gave him a couple of stinging whacks on the cheeks. He quickly realized that the gig was up. No more Mr. Nice Guy!

TACKLING SINGLE PARENTING

After I spanked J.J., I told him to get busy on his chores, "and when you're finished, I want you to go to your room and write a two-page essay about doing chores on Saturday." Having children write an essay as part of the punishment is an excellent way to make the discipline experience memorable, positive, and not mean.

I told J.J. that I wanted him to write down all the duties required of him as part of his Saturday morning chores. That way, both of us would have a firm understanding of what was expected and what wasn't getting done. Next, I had him write down all the negative effects that his failure to work had on the family as a whole, and on himself, which included his being unavailable to play when his friends started calling. I also had him describe how his failure to work angered me and contributed to my stress because I had to keep yelling at him to get his work done. I also made it clear that his failure to work was unfair to the rest of us, because we had to pick up the slack to keep our home a clean and pleasant place for all of us. Last, I wanted to know how he planned to take care of the problem in the future, such as getting up earlier, watching less TV in the morning, and maybe even doing some chores Friday night.

J.J. wrote his essay, forced to articulate on paper the reasons why he needed to obey the rule about doing Saturday morning chores. It made him consider aspects of the rule that he may not have thought about before. It helped him understand the importance of the rule. The essay lesson also improved J.J.'s grammar, syntax, punctuation and spelling skills, since I insisted that he arrange his sentence structure properly, and use the dictionary to spell words correctly.

The essay lesson requires extra parental patience, but it's effective in helping the child learn the importance of following rules. The formula I use for the essay lesson consists of three steps: Have the child define the problem; how it affects the people involved, including himself; and how the child intends to rectify the problem in the future.

After reading several proofs and helping him correct his errors, J.J. finally had an acceptable product that was the result of careful thinking and research. One that made him proud.

As we sat at the dining room table, reading his essay out loud, I pointed out many of the positives that he wrote down and applauded his efforts. "This really looks good, J.J." I told him. "I hope it'll help you understand the importance of rules and to get your chores done on your own from now on." He assured me that it would. I gave him a kiss, told him that I loved him, and to have a good day. A few minutes later he was humming a tune as he gathered some toys for outside play. I felt good about helping J.J. learn some new lessons about discipline, and he felt good about himself, having written an essay that passed my inspection. The next Saturday he did his chores without my having to say a word. To reinforce the essay lesson, I tape it up on a wall, or on an inside door where my son will see it, and I leave it there for a couple of days as a reminder.

That's pretty much the corporal punishment process that I've tried to stick to throughout my boys' formative years. Mostly, I relied on ANTICIPATION and PERSUASION for effective discipline, but occasionally I depended on corporal punishment to enforce rules when ANTICIPATION and PERSUASION weren't effective. Corporal punishment has helped me enforce many of the rules with which parents of youngsters must continually deal: "I want you to go to bed on time."; "Get the toys picked up."; "Don't go near the busy road."; "Don't play on the steps."; and "Don't throw things at people," among many more.

As my boys grew older, the occasional rule infractions changed in nature, but nevertheless, remained violations: "I've told you over and over to be home on time."; "Why did you lie to me?"; and "How many times do I have to tell you to get that homework done?" Corporal punishment helped me enforce the rules until they reached adolescence, at which time I began to rely on other discipline techniques that are discussed later in this chapter.

My philosophy is different from that of the proponents of "choice" and "empowering." They risk allowing their young children to experience the consequences of breaking rules, hoping that the negative results will deter future rule violations. I chose to be more directive in my approach, and occasionally resorted to corporal punishment to enforce rules. I believe that when kids are young, corporal punishment, that's used judiciously, more effectively enforces rules than "time-outs" and temporary "loss of privileges." Corporal punishment, when properly administered, has helped me be more proactive in teaching my children to follow rules. It has helped me eliminate small problems before they escalated into big problems. Getting trampled by a horse or run over by a car are what I call big problems. I didn't want my children suffering those negative, potentially fatal, consequences.

The long-term objective for my children that justifies my punishment techniques is to help prevent negative consequences from ever taking place, such as serious injuries, run-ins with the police, school suspensions, or unplanned pregnancies. I want to help my boys make right choices now, so they'll be more likely to make the right choices when they're older and on their own.

The Problem Is Abuse

No form of punishment is perfect; every style has its own positives and negatives. Corporal punishment is no exception; its main problem comes from its potential for abuse. The same failing holds true for guns, cars and fire. When properly handled, guns, cars, and fire are beneficial, but when they're abused by people, they can become destructive forces.

During my years of high school in Minneapolis, when corporal punishment was the rule rather than the exception, we had an attendance supervisor, Mr. Roach. He was a cockroach. He took every opportunity to exercise CORPORAL PUNISHMENT rather than emphasize ANTICIPATION and PERSUASION.

I remember a Friday afternoon in early spring when I caught the wrath of Mr. Roach. I planned to catch the early bus from school so I could transfer onto a suburban bus and get out to the horse ranch for the weekend. My plan was to go to my locker before my last class, so I could grab my jacket and leave school at the bell, without going back to my locker. Jackets weren't allowed in class, so I hid it by folding it into a tight wad under my armful of books.

On the way to my last class, I saw Mr. Roach walking down the hallway towards me. He spotted the jacket. He ripped it from my arms, sending my books flying. Then he slugged me in the stomach. He grabbed me by the front of my shirt, pinned me against a row of lockers, and slapped me across the face several times. He gave me a detention slip, told me to collect my books, take my jacket back to my locker, and report to class.

I never told my parents about the incident with Roach. I'd been in the wrong, and felt that I deserved the punishment. Since that beating, though, I had a deep-seated hatred for Mr. Roach that lasted all through high school. I wasn't the only student who was bitter and harbored resentment against Roach and his battering style. Soon after I graduated, I heard that a group of former students encountered Mr. Roach downtown, pushed him into a back alley, and beat the shit out of him. As far as I'm concerned, he had it coming.

Roach's haphazard beatings were destructive. Instead of utilizing patience to mold the spirit of his students, just as a carpenter would carefully bend and shape a piece of fine wood, Roach was enamored with his own authority. He chose to break the spirit of the students with strong-arm tactics as his way to enforce discipline.

Roach failed to appreciate the big picture, which is what I try to consider with my style of discipline. My reason for using rule enforcement measures, such as punishment, is to help my boys pay attention to rules. My goal as a dedicated parent, is to work for the long-term benefit of my children. I don't want to break their spirit, and instead create resentment, bitterness, anger, rebellion, or revenge. I want to build respect, trust, understanding, love, and an appreciation for rules.

Mr. Roach was a dictator. I remember the wisdom that a good friend, Dick Jones, who was a highly successful and widely praised college history teacher, shared with me about dictators. "Most dictators begin their rule as being well-loved because they've promised their followers revolutionary changes for which they have eagerly awaited and longed. However, when they're in office, they get hung up on a power trip and become assholes. They conveniently forget the goals, needs, and concerns of their followers. They abuse their power."

The Roach dictatorial beatings were abuses of corporal punishment. That type of meanness can breed violence in a child. That meanness might become an acceptable life style that spills over into the child's family and social life in later years. As a loving and concerned parent, I try to watch out for the welfare of my child, but not by being a dictator.

TACKLING SINGLE PARENTING

Out Of Control Anger And Corporal Punishment Don't Mix

I've tried to use Corporal punishment effectively to help my boys learn proper behavior. It has helped them live a productive and contented life. To be effective, corporal punishment must be continually monitored to hold it in check. The principle is similar to that of the social drinker who disclaims the possibility of becoming a problem drinker—he's either a liar or a fool. Early one June, my use of corporal punishment got out of hand. I'm ashamed of what happened.

The boys had just gotten out of school for summer vacation and were anxious to make the most out of it. J.J. was 13 and Paul was 16. It was my first summer raising two teenage boys alone. For awhile, during this transitional period, it seemed like an endless battle with both about rules and regulations. They wanted to go here, there, and everywhere, all of the time. They were away from home for most of the day, and they wanted to go out every night, staying out later and later. If I told J.J. to be home at 9:30, he would want 10:00. If I told Paul to be home at midnight, he would clamor for 1 a.m. Maintaining control is a strain.

One evening, J.J. wanted to go skate-boarding with some kids up at the school. I told him to be home at nine because it would be getting dark by then and besides, nothing else was going on.

J.J. had been pretty good about coming home on time, so when 9:25 rolled around, I started to worry. I rode my bike up to the school, looking for him. I discovered he wasn't there, so I rode home and found him casually skating home from the opposite direction. I was furious. I thought that he had intentionally disobeyed me by staying out later than he was supposed to, just to test the water. I was going to make a bold statement and set an early precedent for obeying the rules for the long, hot summer ahead.

"Where have you been?" I yelled at J.J. I grabbed his skateboard and flung it into the garage. Before he could say a word I slapped him across his back and shoulders, and quickly ushered him into the house. By this time, J.J.'s frustration and anger had brought tears to his eyes. After he went to his room and I had a chance to cool down, I went to talk with him. We replayed what was said earlier, when he left for the school after supper. As it turned out, I was wrong. I recalled that we had agreed on 9:30 as a "be home" time, and not 9:00.

I felt like a rat. I was ashamed for jumping at the opportunity to hit J.J. over a minor infraction of the rules, which turned out not to be an infraction at all. I humbly apologized to J.J., and asked for his forgiveness. Like the good kid that he is, he forgave me. Several days later I did the same damn thing, only worse.

It was a Saturday night and I had a hot date at 6:30. I'd been home every night during that week and had worked hard every day. I needed some adult time, away from the kids. I'd told them about my date, and that I wanted them home about 5:30 for dinner and to stay close to home while I was out.

Paul came home at 5:00 and did the dishes. I was feeling mellow and hopped into the shower, sure that J.J. would pop in at any minute. I was hoping he wouldn't disappoint me. By 5:30, J.J. wasn't home yet. He still hadn't returned by 6:00, so I called my date to explain that I'd be late. J.J. finally strolled in at 6:30. My mellowness had turned to rage.

"J.J.," I yelled, "I told you to be home at 5:30 so I could get you fed before I went out for the evening." "But dad," he countered, "I told you that I'd be home at 6:30 and you said okay."

"J.J., that is absolute B.S. and I'm tired of you guys working on me the way you've been. I'm in charge here and that's just the way it's going to be." Once again, I grabbed his skateboard, flung it into the garage: "That's going to stay there for a week." I grabbed J.J. by the arm and marched him into the kitchen, grabbed the spatula and told him to take down his pants. I saw his frustration and anger, and felt his humiliation as he fervently protested the punishment. Still, I was determined to make an attention-getting statement about following rules. I spanked his bare butt a couple of times and told him to get to his room.

I jumped into my car and left in a huff. After a few blocks I turned around and drove back home to talk to J.J. "Why did you come home late after I told you I wanted to go out tonight? Don't you have any concern for me?" "Dad! You never told me anything. I didn't know you were going out tonight," he pleaded, "otherwise I would've been home at 5:30."

This time I was intent on not wavering. I knew that I had told him to be home at 5:30, but whether he heard me could be another matter. Maybe that was the reason I was so angry—I was saying a lot lately, but not a lot was being heard.

I got back into my car, but by then the episode had ruined my evening. I had blown my cool. As I drove through town, I kept wanting to be right about the incident, but down deep I knew that I had overreacted again. It was maddening to come to that realization. Could it be possible, through all of the confusion in my life, that I had forgotten to tell J.J. to be home at 5:30?

There was a sharp, jagged sensation of parental failure gnawing its way through me as I cursed up and down the freeway. I wanted to chuck this whole parenting project, just lay down and give up. I was being bombarded with despair from all sides. "All I do is *try*, and I really *try* hard. I'm sick and tired of *trying*." By the time I picked up my date, I was an emotional mess. We went out to eat but wrapped up the evening by 10. I just couldn't find it in me to have any fun.

I didn't know how to approach J.J. I had abused my power again. I had allowed my anger to get out of control, and because corporal punishment was so easily accessible, I used it. I'm just thankful that I didn't hurt J.J., easy enough to do when anger mixes with corporal punishment. I told J.J. that I was sorry. But this time, I was going to make some changes so that we wouldn't repeat that ugly incident.

I struggled with self-doubt for a couple of days, and then was able to reassess the situation. I had to get to the bottom of the problem. The woman with whom I had supper earlier was convinced that corporal punishment, itself, was the problem. I didn't agree.

While shooting hoops, trying to restore my parental confidence, I thought, "I must be doing something right. I'm convinced that corporal punishment has been good for my family. Look at the results: The boys do well in school. They're industrious. They have lots of friends. They get along together. I've never known them to bully anyone. They're involved with extracurricular activities. They've never been in trouble with the police. They don't do drugs. I get lots of positive comments about them from teachers and parents. And, for the most part, they're good at following rules. I couldn't ask for anything more. I must be doing some things right."

I decided that the problem was not corporal punishment. It was the anger that occasionally gets involved. I had to take care of the anger.

Anger Control

I called the Hennepin County Children's and Family Mental Health Department in Minneapolis and spoke to one of the resident psychologists, Mike Sancilio. I introduced myself, and told him about the situation. I asked, "What causes anger?"

He paused, then I heard a slight, nervous laugh. "That's a great question. I wish I had all the answers, because it sure causes a lot of trouble. Stress is one of the big problems, along with being overwhelmed," which he described as feeling weighted down, or oppressed. "Frustration is another cause of anger. It's caused by not having your needs met. Your anger can be fueled when something unreasonable or unacceptable stands in your way and frustrates you. These barriers can be real or perceived." He continued, "Sometimes rules are set for our personal benefit. For example, 'be home so I can go out' (which reminded me of my episode with J.J.), then we get mad when our needs aren't met."

Mike said that anger is situational. "Being in a traffic jam is more frustrating for a person who's late for a meeting than for a person who's on a leisurely drive. Booze and drugs can affect a person's perception of a situation and turn what would normally be a controllable situation into an out-of-control situation. Being tired or in poor health can also negatively affect a person's assessment of a situation and allow anger to take over."

I could relate to everything Mike was telling me about anger. The strain of dealing with the demands of children on a day-to-day basis without the support of a spouse can exhaust a person's capacity to cope. The job just gets damn wearisome sometimes, and that can open up the door to the kind of situations that allow anger to step in and take command.

"We have to take steps to control anger." Mike said parents need to try to stay in control of schedules and routines. "Don't let the kids take over. It gets too frustrating that way, and invites anger. Set rules and limitations, and make sure they're followed." I reflected on how my kids had been running over me.

"Be sure to take care of yourself," Mike continued. "It's not selfish to take care of yourself when others depend on you. Get plenty of rest and exercise."

Mike went on to tell me if an angry parent/child confrontation is about to erupt, that it's a good idea to go to separate rooms until emotions are cooled down.

"Don't react immediately. Give yourself time to think about it."

I thought a lot about my conversation with Mike. I'd been losing control with my boys, causing complications. I'd always set clear limits in previous years but as this summer was upon us, I was buckling under to the pressure of kid-demands. Mike had opened up my eyes. It was time to tighten the reins by clarifying boundaries, rules, and regulations before the situation got out of hand, severing those invisible lines of authority. The consequence would be total chaos—something I wanted to prevent at all costs. Mike suggested that I discuss my expectations with my boys—that's what I planned to do.

I got Paul and J.J. together over supper and layed out my new strategy. "Fellas," I told them, "I'm getting too stressed out lately and we need to make some changes so we can avoid another incident like we had recently with J.J." I reaffirmed my love and commitment to them, and reminded them about the many good things they were doing, such as tidying their rooms and doing household chores. "But, some things need to change. I need to remain in charge to keep our lives running smoothly. When you're old enough to move out and be on your own, you'll be in charge of your own home and your own life. But until that day, I'm in charge here. Here's what we need to have happen."

I told them I didn't want any surprises. "If you're planning a sleepover, whether you're sleeping over at a friend's home or he's sleeping over here, don't tell me about it at 6 p.m." I'm not opposed to all impromptu happenings. It's just that last-minute plans might disrupt my schedule and can sometimes raise suspicions of trouble brewing, especially if there's a history of mischief. "I want to know about it by early afternoon. And, I want to talk to the mom or dad to make sure it's okay with them and to know if they're going to be home all night if you're sleeping over."

We layed out some other rules. "You aren't going to be out all day, every day. Several hours each week you're going to stay home and read a book from the library. Plus, you're not going out every night. If you're going someplace special, like a supervised party, you can stay out later. Otherwise, you'll be home at a decent time, with no arguments.

If you leave the house in the morning after I've already left, leave a note that says where you'll be. Phone at least once during the afternoon to let me know where you are, and to find out whether I've made any new plans for the evening. I also want a phone call if you're out for the night and your plans change." I made it clear: "All I'm asking for is a little courtesy so I don't have to worry about you."

A renewed enforcement of regulations and sharing of information helped me to curb my anger by putting me back in charge of my family. It helped keep the family operation running smoothly, controlled the frustration, and consequently helped to eliminate my anger. It's that anger control that helps keep the use of corporal punishment more judicious. It's an effective strategy for parents who make use of corporal punishment.

"Psychological Punishment"

People have told me that corporal punishment isn't right for every family. I agree. I dated a woman who had two daughters, 12 and 14. During the summer, her daughters would often be home on their own while their mom was at work. The two of them frequently fought. "I get infuriated when these girls fight because then they call me at work, asking me to settle their differences. Sometimes they call me three or four times a day over petty problems. It's distracting and disturbing."

I told her that if those were my kids I would start with ANTICIPATION and PERSUASION, and if that didn't work, I'd enlist more drastic measures. Before long, her girls pestered their mom at work again over trivialities. She was determined to spank them when she got home. The moment she layed a hand on one of her daughters, she felt something was drastically out of order. The daughter was shocked and the mom felt as though she had done something bad to her daughter. Corporal punishment was against the mom's behavioral style.

She had never used it before because it didn't fit her nature. Using it for the first time on her rapidly maturing daughter, the mom felt she betrayed her daughter, just as the daughter felt betrayed by her mom.

That's not the first time that corporal punishment didn't fit the behavioral style of the parent. While growing up in the '50s and '60s, when single parenting was a rarity, I remember numerous occasions when moms of my misbehaving friends threatened them with the popular warning: "Just wait until your father gets home, young man. Then you're going to get it."

The tendency of those mothers to wait for their husbands to do the "dirty work" of corporal punishment is what human relations and linguistic experts describe as a woman's sense of connectedness to others. Most women are more sensitive than men to the needs and feelings of others. Those moms of my boyhood friends relied on their husbands' personal trait of independence to dish out the punishment, a trait that may have given the husbands a greater sense of sovereignty over their children and allowed them to distance themselves from the emotions involved in employing corporal punishment that confronted many of the mothers. Corporal punishment was more in line with their behavioral style.

Single parents who aren't comfortable with corporal punishment can use other punishment techniques to supplement corporal punishment or instead of it. These techniques are often referred to by the purported discipline experts as "psychological punishment," a term that conjures up images of enemy interrogation during times of war. That's not the purpose of such techniques.

Like any other form of punishment, they're meant to be a deterrent to future rule violations. Such techniques, when used judiciously, are effective because they're memorable. They are FEAR, SCORN and SHAME.

FEAR

I define FEAR, when used as an effective form of punishment, as a declaration of action. It's meant to instill apprehension, not terror. For FEAR to be effective, these declarations—or threats—need to be carried out. They have to have teeth.

Consider an example of how FEAR works as an effective deterrent to future rule violations at a person's place of employment: "If you report late to work one more time you'll be fired." The fear of losing a job will motivate the employee to be more prompt, especially if the person making the declaration has a reputation of following through.

Another example was the young lady who walked past me in the courtroom while I was waiting to plead my case in the pond incident. The lenient judge had reduced her speeding violation so that the charge wouldn't raise her insurance rates. On the way out of the courtroom, smiling broadly and referring to the judge, she said quietly under her breath, "Sucker-r-r-r-r!"

Just think how much more effective it would've been for Judge Pawlenty to stand up, walk around the judge's bench to where the young woman was standing, get right in her face and shout, "Young lady, I am not going to reduce your charge. I hope your insurance premiums go through the roof. If I see you back in this courtroom for another driving violation within the next year, you're going to be in big trouble. Do you understand me?" This young lady would've quickly realized that showing up in court again within the next year would result in a more severe penalty. In all likelihood she would instead make an effort to improve her driving habits. That's how FEAR serves as effective punishment.

The new Alabama chain gangs are proving to be an effective form of punishment and deterrent to future rule violations. Past and current workers on the chain gang have been quoted as saying, "I don't ever want to come back here again." So, when a judge threatens a person with time on the chain gang, FEAR will undoubtedly serve as effective punishment by preventing future rule violations by that person.

The parent who utilizes FEAR as punishment at home has an effective tool in helping to curb future rule violations. One Sunday I needed to keep yelling at my two sons to get out of bed so we could get to church on time. Finally I said, "In 10 minutes, I'm leaving." They started hustling, but they didn't make the 10-minute deadline. I left and they had to run the mile to church. The next time that I told them to get out of bed so they could start getting ready for church I said, "I'll leave without you if you're not ready." The FEAR urged them to hurry because I had built a reputation for following through with my declarations of action.

SCORN

The so-called discipline experts claim that SCORN and shame can cause bad effects on children because these punishment techniques can produce anxiety, which is defined as "uneasiness of mind."

TACKLING SINGLE PARENTING

I wonder how my Army drill sergeant would've reacted had I told him that his loud voice and sharp reprimands were causing me to have an "uneasiness of mind." I think I would've been the laughing stock of the company, and probably been forced to pump out a couple hundred push-ups for my crybaby attitude.

In the Army, SCORN was part of the regimen for when you screwed up. It's an effective form of punishment that consists of verbalizing disapproval at a rule violation. It's done in a memorable manner so that it serves as a deterrent to future rule violations. It's meant to cause "uneasiness of mind."

Since Paul became a teenager he has enjoyed talking with friends on the phone. I usually allow it, unless it's too late at night or if he has more pressing obligations. If the obligations are his chores around the house, or other duties that remain unfinished, I can be quite impatient with him.

Corporal punishment doesn't seem appropriate to get a kid off the phone, but SCORNING can work wonders. After repeated warnings the scorn rings out. "Get off the phone," I yelled at Paul in a commanding voice. A voice that he knew meant business. "Is everybody supposed to wait around until you decide to finish up your conversation? Especially when you're just chit-chatting? Well, that's not the way it works around here. And I don't care if I am embarrassing you in front of your friend. You've put yourself in a position to be embarrassed. You have exactly 20 seconds to get off the phone or I'm going to hang it up for you."

One of the keys to success with effective SCORNING is a firm, authoritative voice that commands attention. It gets quicker response than a voice that's timid and submissive. Can you hear it? "Now, Steve," the drill sergeant says in a calm, resigned tone of voice, "I'd like you to please put yourself in a prone position and try to complete 200 push-ups." How effective would that be?

Many parents might argue that a firm, authoritative voice can be effective with an 18-year-old Army recruit, but that it's not appropriate for "fragile" elementary age children. Maybe it's that overly protective philosophy that allows many children to ignore the commands of their parents. I remember the Memorial Day services that my fourth and seventh grade sons and I attended. The speaker was a seasoned, two-star

Army general. He greeted the crowd and invited the youngsters to gather up front, near him, so that they could hear his message. The kids grouped together and sat on the grass, many of them visiting among themselves, while others laid back in a lounging position. They showed the general little consideration as he spoke. After a few moments he shouted, "Be quiet and sit up!" All the parents, who had been standing in a semi-circle behind the kids, chuckled with astonishment as the youngsters sprang to attentiveness and stayed posed throughout the general's speech. A firm, authoritative voice definitely commands attention and gets quick response.

Here's another ingredient that I add to make SCORNING more effective as a deterrent to future rule violations. I had come home from a business appointment to discover that Paul had broken a crystal candy vase that I had cherished for years. I can understand accidents happen, and I can be quite forgiving. However, he had violated a steadfast rule. "Don't play ball in the house." It resulted in disaster.

In a scornful voice I asked, "What happened?" Paul told me he was playing ball in the house. "The ball hit the vase, knocked it over and broke it." Then I asked him, "Why were you playing ball in the house?" Instead of accepting the typical, "I dunno" response, I made him stop to think of a legitimate reason. When he couldn't come up with a valid answer while standing in front of me I told him to go to his room and think of one.

A short while later, Paul thought of a satisfactory answer. "You weren't home and I didn't think anything would happen if I bounced the ball around a few times."

I asked him: "And what did you learn from this lesson?"

"That I shouldn't bounce balls around in the house because things can get broken."

"That's right," I told him, "But don't forget the bigger message: Rules are there for a reason and are meant to be followed, do you understand?" He assured me that he did, and apologized for the mishap.

The added step of demanding a concise reason for the rule infraction made sure Paul didn't get off the hook easily. He was forced to produce a legitimate reason for deliberately breaking a rule. This exercise helped Paul realize that he needs to think before he acts so he can keep the brainless rule violations to a minimum in his life. It also gave me an opportunity to clarify the main theme behind rules: "Rules are there for good reasons and are meant to be followed."

SCORNING is an effective deterrent for future rule violations as long as you try to work for the long-term welfare of the child. Being a dictator is not effective. Cursing, ridicule, and name calling can hurt a child's spirit by being degrading. I know, because I've been guilty of it myself. When it happens, the only course I have left is to apologize and try to keep it from happening again by utilizing the same anger control techniques that are effective in managing corporal punishment mentioned earlier.

Effective SCORNING requires that a person be emphatic, rather than angry. Anger can lead to abuse, which leads to frustration, anger, and resentment on the part of the child. My goal is to get my children to understand the importance of rules so that we all learn to live in peace and harmony, now and in the future.

SHAME

I had just returned to active duty at the Fourth Infantry Division Headquarters near Pleiku, Vietnam after being off for about two months. I'd been recovering from shrapnel wounds and a bout with malaria. One of my first stops was Charlie company headquarters to report to First Sergeant Gunther. Gunther was a middle-aged lifer who resembled a younger Redd Foxx, and he had a foul mouth to match. "What the fuck, Horner. Do you think this is a fucking golf club? Take the fucking Hawaiian shirt off and get into fatigues."

I should've known better than to take up the issue of promotion, but I did anyway.

"First sergeant," I said, "I arrived in-country with Welsh, Ramsey and Flannery and those guys have been promoted to sergeant. Why haven't I?" I could see the smoke start to come out of Gunther's ears. "Are you fuckin' shittin' me, Horner? For the last two months you've been on a South Pacific cruise and partying in Okinawa and you want a promotion?" Gunther was in my face and talking very loud. "Let me tell you what Welsh, Ramsey and Flannery have been doing during that time." He then proceeded to describe every ambush patrol, every fire-fight, every lousy rain storm, and every canned meal for the last two months.

The more he yelled, the more I realized I didn't deserve to be promoted to sergeant. "Just putting in the fucking time doesn't cut it, Horner. You have to work to earn the fucking stripes. Now get the fuck out of here and start earning the fucking stripes. NOW!" I moved towards the door, and apologized for my smug attitude. He answered, "It's all forgotten, just get out." And that's what I did.

I'd been shamed for my insolent attitude. Gunther helped me see the situation from another perspective, which made me regret acting so cocky and self-centered. He filled me in on the circumstances that led to the promotions of my friends. I should've felt happy for them and honored them for their accomplishments. Instead, I was thinking only of myself.

Most parents realize that many children often have a problem with being self-centered. Most of the time it's just a part of growing up, but other times it can get out of hand. When it does, SHAME is effective punishment. SHAME can be damn memorable.

When Paul was 16, he would occasionally get on my nerves with his self-centered insolence. When I greeted him, he would grunt. If I asked him where he was going, he would grunt. He made me feel that I was a real burden on his life. I felt unappreciated, especially when he made catty remarks like: "Dad, do you think we can get some food in the house?" Or, "Dad, why do you have to be such a dork?"

Everybody has different hot buttons and kids seem to know exactly where to push to get a response. I don't know if they consciously do it to be mean, or subconsciously just to get a stir.

Sometimes, the kid goes over the line, and that's when I strike back with SHAME. "Paul! You've been giving me a hard time lately and I'm fed up with it. I don't think you appreciate me. What if I died right now. How would you feel? Let me tell you the facts. Someday I am going to die and it'll probably be before you. Then I'll be gone for good. Will you miss me?" "Well, yeah," was his sheepish response. "Then why can't you treat me with at least the same respect and regard that you show your friends? I'm only human you know. I think I deserve a smile now and then. You know, I do try extremely hard to keep things together around here. Somehow you have the impression that you're entitled to all the services I provide for you. You're wrong. I do them because I love you. My services are gifts and should be appreciated as gifts. I'd like to know what you've done for the welfare of the family during the last several days. What have you done for me during the last week? I've cooked for you, washed your clothes, done the grocery shopping and kept a roof over your head. What have you done for me?" Then I wait for a legitimate answer.

Some people criticize this discipline technique as a harmful "guilt trip" but there's a valuable lesson to be learned. "Besides," I tell my boys, "guilt is a useful gauge within our human make-up. It's like a red warning light in a car. When it comes on, it's wise to take time to discover what caused it to activate and then take necessary action." Anyhow, the lesson I wanted to make clear to Paul with this so-called guilt trip, was that while we all have our individual struggles, the world still doesn't revolve around any one of us. I told him, "We need to try to understand the challenges with which each one of us is faced, and try to appreciate the other person for who he is."

Paul began to get the message, as I noticed him shift to a more upbeat attitude. There are a couple of techniques I use to keep punishment by SHAME positive, and make it even more effective.

I was working in my office one morning, at the same time doing some laundry. I ran a load through, but I didn't have a full second load. The rest of the dirty clothes needed to wait for a day or two.

Paul came into my office. "Hey, dad, when are you going to wash my shirt?" I told him I did a load but there wasn't enough for a second load. "But dad," he insisted, "It's my favorite shirt and I need it for tonight." I calmly explained the situation again but it was no use. Paul acted like I was neglecting my duty and persisted. Finally, I told him, "Son, you can really get on my nerves sometimes. I tried to explain the situation, but that wasn't good enough for you. Now let me tell you what you've talked yourself into." I stood up, took Paul by the arm and led him into the laundry room. A few seconds later he was washing his shirt by hand and later hung it out on the line to dry. As a result, Paul was proud that he did his own washing, and was more inclined to do it himself from then on. A positive lesson in independence for Paul, and less work for dad.

The purpose of SHAMING isn't to belittle the child by making him feel less important, or less capable as a person. Telling the child that he's an idiot is belittling and demeaning. Instead, I try to focus my

SHAMING on the deed rather than the child. "That was a lame-brain thing you did. You're much smarter than that. Put a little more thought into your actions." That approach is much more positive, and will help them more in the future.

During and after a SHAMING or SCORNING episode with my kids, I reaffirm my love and devotion to them. "Paul, I'm getting on your case because I love you, and I want you to learn to follow rules for your own good. It's going to make your life a lot more fulfilling and productive." Affirmations of love help to keep the main purpose of punishment in focus—the long-term welfare of the child. Plus, words of love help keep tensions from rising during an already stressful time.

Further benefits can result from following up with the essay lesson to reinforce the central message of the SCORN or SHAME reprimand. It makes the message more memorable. Here again, the essay lesson consists of the same three steps that make corporal punishment more effective: listing the problem; describing how it affects the people involved, including himself; and identifying how to rectify the problem in the future. Taping the finished essay on a wall or door where the child will see it and leaving it there for a couple of days, reinforces the message.

Fairness

The third element of effective discipline is FAIRNESS. FAIRNESS instills the element of trust that needs to be present for discipline to be effective. When people, including children, feel that they have been treated unfairly, they can get justifiably angry, frustrated, resentful, and lose respect for the other person. The trust becomes marred.

As teen violence against parents soars, increasingly more parents and family abuse counselors are becoming alarmed. What's causing this turbulence? A therapist who works with domestic abuse cases in St. Paul claims: "You've got a child who's still a minor who's acting like an adult. What can you do with this person?" He's referring to 12 and 14-year-olds who swing wildly at their moms with their fists, and 15-16-year-olds who threaten their parents with guns and knives. "The end result is broken wrists, broken noses, gunshot and stab wounds, and slashed throats. And, we'll keep seeing increases until we start educating these kids and break the cycle of violence." Once again we have the so-called discipline experts working against the child-rearing efforts of single parents like me.

The problem isn't with children acting like adults, and the magic solution won't come from "educating these kids." The heart of the problem is with adults who treat kids unfairly. Children, like anyone, don't like being treated unfairly. They feel betrayed. They ultimately lash out in the mean-spirited, resentful ways they've learned through movies and TV, friends and peers, parents and siblings. What else can we expect from impressionable children?

One of the most unfair things parents do is betray the trust of their children by not keeping their promises. Promises can be verbalized: "I promise I'll be home by 5:30 so we can go to the park." Or, promises can be suggested through association, without directly expressing them: "I know I can trust my mom and dad because they love me."

How often have children of divorced parents had their hearts shattered over broken promises? How often has the child heard, "Honey, as soon as I get home from work, you and I will spend some time together" only to hear the same 5:30 phone call. "Hi, sweetheart. I'm sorry I won't be home right away, but I promise we'll get together later." How many weekend plans have gone awry due to vindictive ex-spouses who want to punish the other parent while innocent children stand in the line of fire? How many broken promises are children expected to carry inside before something snaps? And why are they saddled with the burden of fault when this thing does snap? Maybe it's that sense of betrayal that makes a child shout at a parent, "I hate you!" Being betrayed by another through broken promises can spark a flurry of human emotions. It's a lesson I have personally experienced.

The only time that I came close to striking my ex-wife was in the early days of our divorce proceedings. I just couldn't accept the fact that Joyce was intent on breaking our marriage vows. That feeling of betrayal frustrated and maddened me. Once, during a heated dispute over the divorce, we both pushed and shoved; I did my best to keep from hitting her. Betrayal can rouse the very human rage that's in each of us.

I've felt betrayed by members of my family as I struggled through single parenting. I felt that they disregarded our natural family bonds by denying me support. There were times when I felt so hurt that I lashed out in retaliation with angry phone calls and letters. Maybe I shouldn't have, but I did.

And others have felt that I betrayed them. When I was in Vietnam, a group of black guys called me "the blue-eyed soul brother," because they respected and trusted me. That sentiment changed.

While spending a couple of days in base camp, those fellas played their damn music loud, and late into the night, making it impossible to sleep. I asked several times, "Please turn down the music." It didn't work. Finally, I went to the first sergeant and asked him to enforce the rules about loud music. From then on I was an outcast. Those guys felt that I betrayed their trust.

One way to help keep children from feeling betrayed is to make your promises reasonable. If you can't afford Disneyland, don't promise Disneyland. And, do your best to keep the promises you do make: "I'll take you to the park tonight when I get home from work," or, "I'll help you with your homework," or "I'll help you fix your bike tomorrow."

Just as you're expected to keep promises to your child, your child is likewise expected to keep his promises to you: "I'll pick up those toys after this TV show"; "I'll do my homework after supper"; "I'll wash your car for you Saturday." Fulfilling promises builds trust between you and your child, and helps to create and maintain harmony in the family.

Another way to build trust is to show interest in your children. Kids want and need attention. They want to be noticed. Yet, I see many parents snub their children, even when they're making an obvious cry for attention.

I was at a dinner party at the home of my long-time friends, Fred and Mary. We were sitting at the table, when their 12-year-old boy, Andrew, walked by. "Hey, Andy. Come on over here for a minute." Andy had just gotten a new-age haircut, buzzed and chopped in different lengths. "Turn around and let me see your haircut." I saw that Mary was getting nervous. "I think your barber forgot to finish the job," I said. Mary was signaling me behind Andy's back to knock it off, but I wanted to ask Andy some questions about his hair: "Why did you get it cut like this? Do you have friends who have this kind of haircut?" Andy blushed as if he didn't have a good explanation for his haircut. He answered me the best he could, and then left the room after our short visit was over.

Later, Mary told me that Andy was going through "a stage" and Fred and she thought it best just to ignore it. That wouldn't be my choice with my own kids. I'd ask them why they wanted such a haircut? Who else has one? What it does for them? And other questions that show that I'm interested in what they're doing. I sure wouldn't ignore it. That's exactly what children don't want. Andy's unusual haircut was screaming out for attention. It could be the same with off-beat music, unusual clothes, and friends: They beg for attention so why not satisfy their need? Asking pertinent questions, and getting involved with children, is an effective way to build trust and to let them know that their opinions matter. Your interest and concern can defuse the child's frustration that comes from not getting the attention he desires and needs. I believe it's another positive step in helping children to become contented, law-abiding citizens. The next time I saw Andy, about two weeks later, he was sporting a more traditional haircut, one which Mary said he had requested.

My talking with Andrew was not intended to persuade him to get a traditional haircut and make him fit into some kind of conservative mold. My intention was to show an interest in him. I was giving him the attention he wanted, and that helped Andy build trust in me. It showed that I cared about him and the events in his life. Simply knowing that someone else cares enough to ask questions about your life can be a mighty satisfying feeling for millions of kids just like Andy.

Building trust in the family is a long-term process that begins early in life. Mike Sancilio, the child and family psychologist with whom I spoke concerning anger control, had some tips about building trust and being fair with discipline. Besides asking pertinent questions, Mike had other suggestions. "Try to become knowledgeable of what to expect from your child at different stages. Attend seminars and read books that can give you an idea about your child's individuality, abilities and limitations." Sometimes, parents can forget about their young child's abilities, and limitations. Here's an example.

I was walking briskly when I pushed on the door to the post office. I felt a thud and saw that I had accidentally banged the head of a three or four-year-old who had been standing behind the door, waiting for his dad. I apologized to the kid and his dad. The dad showed little concern for his crying son, and scorned him for being in the way of the door. "Ah, he's just a little boy who didn't realize where he was standing," I told the dad. "I shouldn't have come barging through the door like I did."

"It's the kid's fault," said the dad. "Maybe he'll know better next time."

The dad didn't show much tolerance for the child's tender age. Sure, the kid shouldn't have been standing where he was, and maybe the dad had been earlier telling his son to stand clear of the door, and the kid ignored the warning. Nevertheless, the child was hurting and needed understanding from his dad, an identification with his feelings that would help build trust. A scolding, while the child was hurting, didn't help build those bonds.

Tolerance is a balancing act that parents need to exercise if they want to discipline in a fair manner. Parents need to be firm, yet understanding. A wise and just parent learns not to blow up over every single rule infraction. Frankly, there are just too many of them: cuss words, heisting a dollar from a wallet or purse, school detention, sneaking a cigarette, saying that their chores are done when they're not, and other endless, minor acts of disobedience. There needs to be a balance of building respect for rules while keeping the kid's spirit intact. Sancilio claims you can find that balance: "Discuss your expectations with your children while at the same time learn what to expect from your children by talking to other parents." A good question to ask yourself before you punish your children is, "Will this punishment serve my child with a long-range benefit? Not just for the next hour, day or week, but for long term? If so, how?" If there's not a long-term benefit to the punishment, you might want to consider a different approach, perhaps another element of guidance, such as ANTICIPATION or PERSUASION.

I've discovered that occasionally going easy on a rule infraction can provide a lesson in positive rule enforcement. J.J. had invited a friend for a sleep-over. Early in the evening, I told them to be finished playing and in bed by midnight. At 1:10 a.m. they were still screwing around. I scolded both of them and told J.J. he was going to be grounded the next day. When I woke up the next morning, I happily discovered that before J.J. and his friend had gone to bed the night before, and prior to my scolding them, they had cleaned up the TV room and the kitchen. All the dishes and snacks had been put away, and both areas were neat and tidy.

When J.J. and his friend got up the next morning, I canceled the grounding, rewarding J.J. for his thoughtfulness. I told him that I was giving him a break: "I can understand how two young fellas can get carried away with talking and laughing, and I really like the way you tidied up the area." J.J. knows that I mean it when I say he's grounded, so when I gave him a break on the midnight rule, he really appreciated it. "Gee, thanks, Dad, that's great!" That helped reaffirm J.J.'s image of me as loving and fair, rather than as an ogre or dictator.

After all, everybody makes mistakes, "To err is human, to forgive, divine." I could've followed through on my threat to ground J.J. for his rule infraction. Instead, I took advantage of the opportunity to praise him for following the long-standing rule of keeping the house tidy.

I could've taken the issue to an extreme by holding a grudge against J.J. for breaking my rule, but grudges are mean. They show resentment towards another that can hurt much more than any of the psychological punishments that the so-called discipline experts have defined.

Grudges ignore one of the foremost components of fairness, that of forgiveness. Forgiveness is a time-tested principle of blessedness on which Jesus spoke in the Sermon on the Mount: "Happy are those who forgive, for they will receive forgiveness." Embracing that message helps me strive to be fair with discipline, out of love, and with my long term commitment to the welfare of my children.

Convenience

One Friday evening at about 11 o'clock, I was driving home on the freeway after visiting with friends. I was in the fast lane, going 10 miles over the speed limit, and passing the cars in the center lane. Still, the fella behind me was flashing his high beams on me. "What am I supposed to do, buddy? Drive faster and get a speeding ticket just to accommodate you? No way." Finally, I passed the line of cars, signaled, and moved to the right, out of the man's way. As soon as he passed me, I got behind him and flashed my high beams on and off once, to let him know I didn't appreciate his rudeness.

He slammed on his brakes.

I slammed on my brakes and was going to hit him until I swerved to the right, which forced a car in the middle lane to quickly move over. By this time the maniac had swerved back in front of me and slammed on his brakes again. I had almost come to a complete standstill in the middle of the freeway with traffic bearing down on us. I quickly accelerated to keep from being rear-ended. Just then, I saw that the fool had driven to the right hand lane and was signaling to exit up the ramp. He was a young man in his early twenties. He appeared calm and relaxed and his eyes were focused straight ahead as he rested his elbow on the open window frame. It was as if nothing had happened. He just casually drove up the exit ramp showing no apparent emotion over the chaos and the risk to human life he had just caused.

I relayed this story to an elementary school principal. She shrugged as if it was old news. "That's no surprise," she told me. "We see that type of indifference all the time. Over the last 20 years, many of these kids have been raised with little or no discipline at home, and our hands are legally tied. Many of these kids have absolutely no sense of the consequences for their actions."

To achieve effective discipline in the family, parents need to enforce rules, and that means laying out consequences for rule violations. The problem is that implementing consequences demands extra time, patience, and energy. For many people, there just doesn't seem to be an opportune time. Dishing out consequences can violate our convenience, or comfort zone. Conquering the obstacle of convenience is my fourth fundamental principle of effective discipline.

All parents are busy, whether part of a two-parent family, or single parents. They realize that time, patience, and energy are often in short supply. Many single parents, however, are confronted with additional situations that make dishing out consequences difficult.

Kathy, a single parent friend of mine, admits to being a victim of what she terms the "guilt syndrome."

"It's hard for me to strong-arm my kids because I know they're hurting from the divorce. I feel bad for them. It's like, they've already been punished enough."

My former sweetheart, Jean, would attempt to dish out consequences to her daughters when they broke the rules, but in many cases, she couldn't make the consequences stick. "If the girls broke a rule I'd tell them to stay in their room that night and not allow them to watch television. The problem is that later, as I watched TV alone, I'd get lonely and let the girls come out and join me. I'm a real pushover."

Other single parents have told me that they don't want to be too strict with their children because they're afraid of jeopardizing the child's love. In many cases it's the only love they have left in the world.

I've fallen prey to what I call the "jerk factor." The jerk factor might come into play when I try to enforce a rule with one of my kids. He refuses and then I yell; therefore, I become the jerk. "I told you to get to your room and read." He stalls, I yell—I'm the jerk. "I told you earlier to go to the store for milk." He stalls, I yell, I'm the jerk. "I told you to get your bathroom clean." He stalls, I yell, I'm the jerk, once again.

It's not that my children are calling me a jerk. Rather, it's because my ex-wife lives over 1,500 miles away and my children live with me full time. I'm the parent who comes down as the heavy because I'm the rule enforcer. It's not a comfortable feeling being the bad guy, therefore making it inconvenient sometimes to dish out the consequences.

The element of convenience can pressure a parent to compromise his or her principles. This pressure often comes from other parents as well. How many times have parents heard these popular pleas from their children? "But Mark's mom let's him stay out till midnight. Why can't I?"; "Jessica doesn't have to do work around her house. Why do I?"; or, "Ryan's mom lets him see R rated movies. Why can't I?"

Parental peer pressure is an outside force that causes me many more concerns than kid peer pressure. It's often uncomfortable to confront that type of pressure. There are times when my kids think I'm a jerk because they can't do what their friends do, and some of the younger parents support the jerk factor by saying that I'm old fashioned, and square. A few times it was just easier to give in than fight for what I knew was right.

Giving in to convenience always comes with a price. The price for not dishing out consequences is that the child quickly learns how to skip the penalty for a rule violation. If the kid puts up enough of a fight, he knows that he can wear his parent down. The parent threatens rule violations with consequences, but the kid has learned it's just a bunch of hot air. He simply works on the parent's comfort level and is able to skip the consequences.

The obvious result of a lack of enforcement is that the child doesn't learn to face consequences for violating rules. He doesn't gain respect for rules, and lack of respect will have a negative and disruptive effect on the child for the rest of his life. It will also present problems for the people around him, such as his parents, siblings, peers, future wife, and family. These problems combine as a huge price to pay simply for the ease of convenience. It's not worth it to me.

I've tried to keep my threats of punishment from becoming meaningless, regardless of the inconvenience to me. After repeated warnings, continued rule violations usually ended with a spanking. As Paul and J.J. grew older, and corporal punishment became less of a discipline option, I resorted to using loss of privileges as punishment. A weekend in the house is an effective deterrent to breaking rules for an active teenager. However, the punishment is meaningless if convenience cuts the punishment short, or worse, dismisses it altogether.

I'm perceived as a tough disciplinarian by peers, family, friends, and teachers. That's not always a pleasant title with which to live. The flip side is that I do get positive results with my style of discipline while maintaining the love and respect of my children. Enforcing the principles of discipline isn't always an easy course to take—It's usually the toughest. Research shows that kids need limitations set, and they need adults to enforce the rules. In fact, they thrive on it. Family counselors tell parents to "stick to your guns." They also say that it's never too late for an ill-disciplined person to learn to follow rules.

That was obvious in the Army.

For two years I saw 18-year-old draftees who had been ultra bad-asses back on the block. They were from the toughest neighborhoods of Los Angeles, New York, Chicago, Philadelphia, and other large cities. Those guys had bad attitudes and no respect for rules. In a relatively short time, however, they were marching in step with the rest of us.

The reason is that the military strives to adhere to the four principles of effective discipline.

> Military discipline has CONSISTENCY. Justice is impartial, and all rule offenders are treated equally regardless of rank, religion, gender, or race.
>
> Military discipline has FIRMNESS. Soldiers are expected and encouraged to follow rules through ANTICIPATION and PERSUASION. However, rule offenses are met with PUNISHMENTS that are strictly enforced.
>
> Military discipline has FAIRNESS. The military believes that a spirit of fairness is created by building trust, loyalty, respect, and camaraderie. Fairness encourages strong morale.
>
> Military discipline is not designed around CONVENIENCE. Military code teaches the concept of going the extra mile to get a job done properly, including the job of enforcing discipline.

We all make mistakes, and the military is no exception. That's why the four basic elements of discipline don't always work perfectly. Sometimes there are breakdowns, abuses, and violations. These four elements of discipline just seem to be the best we have in our imperfect world.

I do my best to hold my course in the midst of the outside forces that continually work against my disciplining efforts at home. It means being a jerk at times, and putting up with negative comments about my discipline techniques. It means to stand firm for the time-tested principles of discipline that I know will serve the long-term welfare of my boys. It means putting up with skirmishes from un-approving children. It means putting up with peer pressure from children and adults. Sometimes, it means feeling lonely, unloved, weary, and at the end of my rope.

But it also means that I've taken charge of my family's well-being.

Dan Kaler, the Director of Secondary Education in the school district where my kids attend school, shared an interesting analogy about effective discipline. "When elephants are young and untrained, a strong rope tied around their foot, attached to a four foot stake, pounded deep into the ground is needed to keep them in place. As they mature and learn the rules, all it takes to keep them in order is a couple of slight taps on a short stick."

Wise parents are the ones who have the foresight to realize that their five or ten-year-old son or daughter will someday be a full grown adult. Seasoned parents say: "That day comes sooner than you think." Wise and just parents exercise the four basic principles of discipline so that their children reap the rewards of being well disciplined in their lives:

- Consistency
- Firmness
- Fairness
- Convenience

They are the parents who will bear up to the challenges of effective discipline now, because they can't think of anything worse than having an angry, out of control "elephant" on their hands later.

Building Responsibility: Being Accountable

I Heard It Through The Grapevine

My business friend, Ernie, first introduced me to TRAM. TRAM stands for: The Ride Across Minnesota. It's a 350 mile bicycle journey from Big Stone Lake on the West to the St. Croix River on the East. It takes place during the last week in July, and participants are required to raise at least $150 in pledges for the Multiple Sclerosis Society. TRAM has been up and running since 1990 and attracts more than 1,500 men and women of all sizes and ages, and from throughout the nation. I rode in the second, third, and fifth TRAM.

"It's a people event," Ernie told me after the first year. "There's plenty of good food and great scenery, but if you don't take time to visit with all the different people you miss out on an important part of the ride."

Ernie was right. It was the "people" part of TRAM that I enjoyed most. Peddling between towns, you never knew whom you were going to ride next to. Beautiful women in colorful, skin tight lycra can take a man's mind off the lakes, cornfields, and forests in a hurry. Then there are the guys who want to talk sports, and the people who bend your ear about business.

I don't mind talking about business when I'm on vacation. I saw TRAM as an opportunity to learn new perspectives about life, so I asked a lot of questions. If I learned that the person riding next to me was a business owner, I asked, "What's the single, most troublesome hassle you have in business today?" Over the three years that I've rid-

TACKLING SINGLE PARENTING

den TRAM I'm sure I've directed that question to at least 30 different business owners. They consisted of men and women who owned large and small businesses from coast to coast. They always answered: "Employees!" I heard how difficult it is to find people with a good work ethic. "They lack responsibility," was by far the most common gripe.

The Problems Are Evident

I taught my sons that irresponsible people haven't developed the character to be accountable for their actions. In the work place, that deficiency shows up as persistent tardiness, unexcused absenteeism, or a lousy attitude. It means not being trustworthy, and in need of perseverance to finish a piece of work. It refers to weak integrity: lacking honesty and the courage to admit to wrong-doing. It means to be forthright with your intentions. It means not to blame someone else for your failings, and to accept your fair share of the work load.

My children don't have to be geniuses to see the results of irresponsibility throughout society.

It appears as crumbling morality, children born out of wedlock, absentee parents, discontentment, suicide, crime, trashy looking neighborhoods, high personal debt, and misuse of natural resources.

Where does irresponsibility begin? Research says it begins in the same place that responsibility needs to be taught—in the home, by the parents.

I interviewed John Richters, the Assistant Chief of The Child and Adolescent Disorders Research Branch at the National Institute of Mental Health in Washington, D.C. about a 1993 study he co-authored. It was a look at inner-city families and how their children do when the family is "stable and safe," versus "unstable and unsafe." He defined stable families as having parents living together, and unstable families as having parents who were divorced or separated. A home was defined as unsafe when guns and drugs were present.

The study found that only 6 percent of the children from *stable and safe* homes were suffering emotionally, socially, or scholastically. When the home environment was classified as *safe but unstable,* the percentage of children with anti-social problems rose to 16.7 percent. When the home was *unsafe but stable,* the percentage was 23.8 percent. When the home was found to be both *unsafe and unstable,* a whopping 100 percent of the children from those homes were considered to be suffering from anti-social symptoms.

Richter said that the negative symptoms he found included: clinical deviance, anti-social behavior, and displaying extreme forms of aggression. He said, "It all reverts to the subject of responsibility in one form or another."

Even though the Richters study was confined to the inner-city, evidence from suburban school principals and law enforcement agencies indicates that fallout from negative family factors don't stop at inner city borders. The Richter study concluded: "These findings are consistent with results from numerous other studies highlighting the central significance of family factors and/or their correlates in altering children's odds of adaptional success and failure." Irresponsibility knows no specific gender, race, age, or income level. It crosses all social boundaries.

A Higher Level Of Excellence

Teaching the principles of responsibility to my children has been a long, tedious, and often frustrating road. I often find myself up against one or more of the three common road blocks to successfully tackling single parenting: time, patience, and energy. If I realign my priorities I can usually find time for my children. If I take care of myself with proper exercise and rest, I can ordinarily come up with the extra patience and energy. It takes dedication, desire, love, and setting my sights on reaching my parenting goals that include: wanting my kids to be contented, productive members of their families and society, and not wanting them to come knocking on my door when they're 25, looking for a place to live. To help reach my goals, I demand a higher level of excellence from my children. I'm far from being the first single parent to use this method to successfully instill responsibility.

At age 43, Doctor Benjamin Carson was the youngest Chief of Pediatric Neurosurgery ever at Johns Hopkins Medical Institution in Maryland. Carson's parents had divorced when he was eight, and he remembers feeling sorry for himself because his father wasn't around, and because he and his brother didn't have the things that other people had.

Carson attributes his success to his mother, Sonya, who would work three jobs to support the family, doing domestic work and child care for wealthy families. She didn't allow the Carson boys to take the easy way out, and drift around the streets, getting in trouble. She would come home from work and teach her sons how successful people acted, telling them that they could do what other people were doing, and do it better. "She made my brother and me read two books a week and write reports on what we read," Dr. Carson recalls. "I didn't know until much later in life that my mother, with a third grade education, couldn't read those reports."

By forcing her sons to read, Dr. Carson's mother demanded a higher level of excellence. Reading changed Carson's life when he found that he loved to read books about science, nature, and animals. "I discovered that instead of not knowing the answers to many questions in school, I knew a lot of the answers."

With this revelation, he applied himself academically and excelled, graduating third in his high school class, and winning an academic scholarship to Yale University.

I tell my sons that people have a tendency to perform according to the expectations of others. If the expectation is high, as it was for Dr. Carson's mother, then the pupil's performance will most likely be higher as well. If the expectation is low, then the pupil's performance will likewise suffer.

A low level of student performance expectation was the #1 complaint about public education's tried and failed Outcome Based Education (OBE). With OBE, students didn't fail tests. If they didn't get a passing grade on a test, they were simply able to take it over until they did pass. At first glance, OBE appeared to be a fluffy, feel-good attempt by the public schools to build the much ballyhooed self-esteem of students. In reality, OBE was a survival technique to which the schools resorted to counteract irresponsible parents. "Many students live with little or no level of expectations at home and that's the mentality the kids take to school with them," several principals and school board members I've spoken to report. "However, if many of these same students take home failing grades, the parents come down hard on the teachers for inferior teaching."

A former school superintendent told me that many busy parents believe school work should be left up to the child and the child's teacher, and they resent being asked to get involved. I had a brief friendship with a suburban single mom who had three, young school age kids. One afternoon, we were at her home having coffee when her kids came bursting into the kitchen after getting off the school bus. One of the kids had a note from her teacher: "Please use the enclosed flash cards with Katie to help improve her spelling and math." The mom threw the cards on the floor and said bitterly, "If that teacher thinks I have time for that crap, then she'd better come over and do my laundry and vacuuming for me." Her kids and I were flabbergasted. That's a difficult and real attitude with which the schools must contend.

The schools are stuck in a no-win predicament. They've had to fashion education like Budweiser brews beer: produce a product that's the least offensive to the most numbers of people. And by so doing, the product has been watered down.

As a dedicated single parent, I don't rely on the school system—or any other system but my own—to raise the level of excellence in my boys. I encourage them with a higher level of expectation. Many other parents have a much different level of expectation for their children. Working as a little league coach gave me some insight into the level of expectation with which some kids have been raised, and how it conflicts with my child-rearing efforts at home.

During the Summer of 1994, I coached Paul's baseball team. The players were 13 to 15 years old. My style of coaching might be regarded as intense, but I never forget that it's only a game. I don't harangue players or belittle them. I tell them, "We're out here to have fun. Just remember, it's a lot more fun to win than to lose."

When we started practices at the beginning of the season, I heard a lot of excuses from players: "The sun was in my eyes"; "I slipped on the grass"; or "The pitcher is cheating and throwing curve-balls." I told them that I didn't want excuses, I wanted performance. "Get your hat down to block the sun; Get a good jump off the ball when it's hit, and wear shoes that give you better traction; and, it doesn't matter what the pitcher is throwing. Your job is to hit the ball." We won our first four games by healthy margins.

After the fourth game, I stopped at a local pub later in the evening for a couple of cold beers. I struck up a friendly conversation with Steffan Stenzel, a master instructor of Tae Kwon Do, who bears a striking resemblance to actor Chuck Norris. Stenzel was fascinated by my enthusiasm and philosophy of coaching, and I was interested in knowing more about his expertise. "Tae Kwon Do is the ancient way of the honorable warrior," he said. "It teaches a person to be a better human being every day that they live. Each day is better than the day before." I invited Steffan to put on a short demonstration and seminar for my players, and he accepted. I scheduled the seminar an hour before our next game. Every one of my players showed up. They were pumped to see Steffan break boards with his bare hands.

The kids were truly amazed by Steffan, exactly what we had hoped the board breaking would accomplish. It built Steffan's credibility with the kids and prepared them to pay close attention to what he had to say about The Seven Qualities of a Champion.

Steffan told the players about Grandmaster Jhoon Rhee, and the seven steps to building a higher level of excellence. "Jhoon Rhee refers to them as The Seven Qualities of a Champion." Steffan said, "These qualities can be used to excel in anything you attempt in life. Remember them. Most importantly, put them to work in your life."

- Power: for knowledge and wisdom
- Balance: to rationalize thought before action
- Flexibility: to be gentle with each other
- Posture: for integrity, fairness, and honesty
- Timing: for punctuality
- Endurance: for perseverance
- Quickness: to enhance alertness

Steffan translated each quality to the performance of a baseball player. "QUICKNESS means keep your focus on the game," he said.

"Be ready to move in either direction at all times when you're in the field and stay sharp when you're up to bat. Be sure to eat properly and get plenty of rest." Then he interpreted the other six qualities.

The message got through. We ended the regular season with a 13-0-1 record. However, when tournament time rolled around the team let their guard down and fell victims to a low level of expectation.

A few days before the first game of the post-season tournament, my two sons left for Arizona to spend six weeks with their mom, and I left for The Ride Across Minnesota bike ride. A couple parents had volunteered to coach while I was away. The team won their first two games. I returned in time to coach the third game. A win would've advanced us to the championship game.

I hardly recognized my team—there was no hustle, the excuses were back, and the parents encouraged it. When a kid struck out by watching three strikes go by, I heard the same old enabler chant from the crowd. "That's okay, Kevin. Good try."

Wrong.

That's the same low level of expectation with which my kids and I clashed at school. I told Kevin his at-bat was a poor effort. "I want you up there swinging. Your job is to make contact with the ball."

Towards the middle of the game several of the players told me, "All we have to do is wait to be walked. That's what happened the last two games." My response was clear, "I don't care what the substitute coaches told you. If it appears to me that you're not trying hard to make contact with the ball, I'll pull you out of the game. Same thing goes for fielding errors caused by lackadaisical play. They won't be tolerated." The kids listened but it was too late. We lost and fell into the losers bracket of the tournament.

We won the first game in the losers bracket, which earned us a berth in the championship game. The coach of the opposition was a veteran. He was well known throughout the community for consistently developing championship teams. This was my first year as a coach for any sport. It was an adventure to say the least.

During warm-ups, I recognized a meandering attitude among the players. As the infield practiced with ground balls, I yelled: "Fellas! You have to pick up your level of excellence at least five notches to compete tonight. I want total concentration, hard work, and positive results. That's how we're going to win."

The nay sayers were in the crowd with their accusatory glares and contemptible comments about my yelling: "Hey, coach! It's obvious you don't know how to inspire teenagers." I thought, *we'll see buddy. We'll see.*

The game was tied 3-3 going into the late innings. The pitchers were looking awesome, the fielding was sharp, and the bats were swung with passion. These kids didn't know the crowd existed. Their focus was on the ball with each and every play.

Finally, in the bottom of the eighth our bats caught fire and we started running away with the game. The boys were hitting, running, stealing, sliding, and scoring. Hell, we could've beaten the Minnesota Twins that night. As I was giving signals from third base, one of the parents yelled out to me, "They know what your signals are." I yelled back, "It doesn't matter. They can't stop us."

When it came to the top of the ninth inning, our defense glistened by making three quick outs and the game was over. The kids went bananas. They had won a well deserved championship, and I let each one know individually how well he had played. They had ear-to-ear grins as I presented the trophies. Even if we had lost, the kids had worked hard, and had played a great game. That's all we can ever expect from other people, that they do their best.

I gathered the team gear and headed for my car when a parent of one of my players approached to extend congratulations and compliment my coaching style. "You let the players do their thing. That's why they won." She had good intentions, so I thanked her for her comments but she couldn't have been further from the truth; I had pushed them away from doing their own thing, which had been mediocre play. I pushed them into doing something new, with which they were unfamiliar; a higher level of excellence. It paid off for all of us by winning the championship trophy.

The Lessons Begin Early

Promoting a higher level of excellence is the key to teaching responsibility, but where and when do children learn that new level of excellence? Some kids learn it at school, at work, or in organized sports. For others, it begins in the military, or during introspective activities, like Tae Kwon Do. After all, what defines the "champion" that Grandmaster Jhoon Rhee refers to with his Seven Qualities model? A champion is the winner of a contest which is defined as a struggle. Isn't life itself a struggle at times? Aren't we out to win at this struggle of life? "Most certainly!" said Steffan Stenzel. "The Seven Qualities of a Champion refer to the qualities of a responsible person."

For some people, a higher level of excellence doesn't begin until age 30. At least that's what a news article reported about a restaurant owner in New York City who was trying to get his irresponsible son into the business. He justified the kid's lack of responsibility with, "My son is only 29 years old. People don't start thinking until they're 30."

For others, the call for a higher level of excellence begins with rites of initiation, or the crossing of symbolic bridges into adulthood. I believe that striving for excellence is a learned behavior that begins early in a child's life, at home, with the parent or parents.

Knowledge, Wisdom, and Sexuality

There are numerous lessons in excellence that children need to learn to become responsible adults. One of the most important is to learn excellence in sexuality. Knowledge and wisdom have been powerful tools with helping me be an effective teacher of this lesson to my children.

The foremost social problem in this country is out-of-wedlock babies. 30 percent of the babies today are born out of wedlock, five times what it was 30 years ago. Two out of three black children are now born out of wedlock, up from one in four in 1965. Scholar Charles Murray asserts, "Children born out of wedlock is the single most important social problem of our time. These children are three times as likely to fail in school, twice as likely to commit crimes and, if they are girls, more than twice as likely to bear children out of wedlock themselves." I'm doing what I can to keep my two boys from fathering an unplanned child. It begins by showing good example.

President Franklin Delano Roosevelt said: "What good is the right of free speech for a man who does not say anything? What good is the right to go to church if you don't practice a religion?

What good is the right to vote if you don't register and vote?" Those words ring louder and louder, truer and truer, as the years pass; they speak to consistency. If you're going to "talk the talk," then you had better "walk the walk."

I've tried to "walk the walk" by not exposing my children to women sleeping overnight with me. As lonely as life can get without a bed partner, teaching sexual responsibility would be a difficult, if not an impossible lesson, if my kids thought that I was sleeping around. The message would be too confusing, and the stakes are too high.

That's why I think the distribution of condoms at schools is a bad practice. It's a confusing message. It says: "Having a child out of wedlock can be an enormous burden on you and the risk of catching a sexually spread disease is high, but if you're going to take a chance be sure to wear a rubber." Yeah, right. That's the same as telling your child, "Don't get into a car with a drunk driver. But, if you do, be sure to wear your seat belt."

The message accommodates irresponsible behavior. It doesn't cultivate excellence. It provides a convenient escape route from the chore of responsibility. Instead, I've taught my children about the merits and virtues of abstention. I've read articles to them about the innocent and frequent transmission of the AIDS virus and have discussed in a straightforward way the severity of the disease. I've told them that dating is for getting to know someone without letting lust get in the way. "The more time you spend getting to know her likes, dislikes, and general behavioral style, without being intimate, the better you can determine if yours is a lasting love, rather than infatuation. A lasting love is what you're striving for." I advise my boys, "Premarital sex can hinder a relationship by becoming its most important aspect. Sex should result from your love, not be the reason for it."

Those are sexual virtues I've taught my boys, and it's paid off. Both boys hang around with what appears to be a fun, well-adjusted group of young men and women. They play sports together, they good naturedly rib each other, and Paul confides that he gets a little kissing in when he's on a date. To me, that is good, healthy interaction with the opposite sex.

I've made it clear to my sons that if either one of them fathers a child out of wedlock they have a lifelong responsibility to be a good father. I caution them, "Once a dad, always a dad. That means total commitment." I showed them how big of a chunk child support payments would take out of their paychecks, and how an unplanned child would drastically change their teenage and young adult lives. I've tried to paint a vivid picture of extremely difficult circumstances. My kids also know, from past experiences, that in a situation such as an unplanned child, I would stand by the new child, and make sure my own son did, too.

I've warned my kids that promiscuous sex can be caused by booze, drugs, and late, unsuperivsed hours at friends' homes. "Booze and drugs can break down inhibitions that otherwise hold you in check. That can lead to sexual activity beyond what would normally take place. And if the mom or dad isn't home, the situation can easily get out of hand." I've tried to make my boys realize that five short minutes of pleasure can end up with 20 long years of extra duty.

Telling children to act responsibly can be productive as long as they have the knowledge and wisdom that goes hand-in-hand with responsibility. My baseball players wouldn't have been able to increase their level of play if someone hadn't taught them the basic skills of baseball. Simply yelling, "Catch the ball" would've been meaningless unless someone had extended the time, energy, and patience to show the player how to position himself underneath the ball, how to hold the mitt, and finally, spend lots of time practicing with him. That same work ethic is required to teach sexual responsibility.

In 1993, while running for the school board, several special interest groups interviewed us candidates individually to determine whom to endorse. When they asked me: "At what age should children be introduced to sex education?" I responded, "Just about the same time they're getting used to working with crayons."

That wasn't the answer they wanted to hear.

In subsequent years, I've been told that my answer was misconstrued by the members of the various panels. They interpreted my answer to mean that I would make an attempt to influence young children about ambiguous social mores of sexual behavior, including topics of homosexuality, condoms, promiscuity, and abortion. That wasn't my intent. I wanted to intervene early in student's lives to teach the biology of sex. For my family, teaching sexual responsibility began the same way as teaching a kid baseball—it works best when you start with the fundamental principles. "Knowledge and wisdom are a lot more effective than condoms." That's the philosophy I use to teach my boys about sexual responsibility.

It's easy to tell when a child first recognizes a biological difference between boys and girls. There are the awkward questions, like "Why doesn't she have a penis?" Or giggling over lewd jokes among a group of friends. As soon as I suspected that my boys had some sexually oriented questions, I discussed the topic openly. Usually around the supper table. Paul was in first or second grade when those discussions started. I filled J.J. in along the way, as he grew older.

I was quite graphic when I taught my kids about sex. At the same time, I tried to be sensitive to the impressionable ages of my sons. I wanted to share my knowledge of the mechanics of sex, and to put sex in a favorable light, something to be cherished and revered, rather than to cheapen and use frivolously. Parents who need to brush up on how the sexual machinery of the human body works can find dozens of books on the subject at their local library. They can also present their questions to their doctors, visit a medical clinic, or consult a public health department. Local family planning agencies and public human services agencies also might be sources for free literature.

A word of caution: I've discovered that there are plenty of self-styled "professionals" in positions of authority who dole out information about sexual reproduction. Much of it is untrue, and biased. Medical information nurses at major hospitals scrambled for manuals and research books to answer my simplest questions: "What time of the month do most women ovulate?" was answered with "Women can ovulate at any time during the month," and "It's always best to use protection." Those responses certainly emphasized the lack of sexual education in the public sector, and underscore the importance of again making sex education a priority.

After sorting through the opinions, literature, facts, and fiction about sexual reproduction, I shared some of my conclusions with my children. It's what I teach them to help them raise their level of excellence in being sexually responsible. The more correct information they have about sex, the more they will understand and appreciate its value. And then they will make wiser decisions.

The most important aspect of sexual reproduction that I've discussed with my boys is the woman's menstrual cycle. When they were much younger, they didn't have a clue to what I was talking about. Then, they began to understand that there were substantial differences between men and women. During the next round of discussions, they became more interested. Later, they were embarrassed to talk about sex. Finally, they began to ask for clarification about certain aspects of the subject, so I knew they had been thinking about it and that it was starting to make sense to them.

The sexual reproduction lesson I've repeated most often with my kids is how the woman's seed, the ovum, is released from the ovary during the course of her menstrual cycle, and how it makes its way down her fallopian tube. If the ovum meets a male seed, or sperm, during its journey, then the two of them unite. Together they travel to the uterus where they increase and multiply into a recognizable little baby. I've told my boys that there are only four or five days in a woman's cycle that she can get pregnant, but that there are many precautions and other variables to consider.

Most women's menstrual cycles last from 23-28 days. The cycle begins on the first day of her period, which lasts about five days. Many women keep track of their cycles by marking this first day on a calendar. A baby can't be conceived during the woman's period because a new ovum hasn't yet been released from the ovary. About midway through the menstrual cycle—on average from the 10th to the 14th day from the beginning of the cycle—a new ovum is released and travels down the fallopian tube in search of a male sperm. This process is called ovulation.

The vast majority of babies are conceived during this four day window but precautions need to be taken because the male sperm can live inside the woman for three days. Therefore, if intercourse occurs on day seven and the woman ovulates a day early, on day nine, there's a chance of conception occurring. Or, if intercourse occurs on day 15, and the woman is a day or two late ovulating, there's a chance of conception because the ovum can live 36 hours inside the woman's body.

Another precaution dispels a popular myth. Many people believe that it's safe to have unprotected intercourse during ovulation if the male simply pulls his penis out a moment or two before ejaculation.

TACKLING SINGLE PARENTING

"That's not a very good idea," according to a supervisor at Minnesota Family Planning, a division of the Minnesota Department of Health. "The pre-ejaculatory fluid on the end of the penis can contain live sperm and it only takes one to impregnate."

The practice of spacing intercourse before and after the woman's ovulation is called the natural family planning method. The family planning representative told me, "It's an effective method of family planning as long as the couple learns about the woman's menstrual cycle and knows when ovulation occurs, which can be determined scientifically by taking temperature readings." This procedure is called "basal body temperature graphing." The woman simply takes her temperature the first thing in the morning. Ovulation is indicated by a surge in temperature. More precise information on basal body temperature graphing is available from any of the family planning information sources mentioned earlier.

"The best part about the natural family planning method is that it works without chemicals," she concluded. "The down side is that it doesn't protect against the spread of sexually transmitted diseases, and for many people, it takes the spontaneity out of their sex lives."

As far as the natural family planning method taking the spontaneity out of having sex, I've told my boys that a person doesn't need to have sex every time he gets the urge. "Besides," I've added, "millions of people over thousands of years have built strong characters through self-restraint. It's a matter of taking control of your inclination to over-indulge yourself." I try to teach my boys to practice moderation in everything they do. "Too much work is not good, too much play is not good, too much food and alcohol are not good, too much exercise is not good. Each person needs to find his or her own balance, deciding on limits. Otherwise, negative consequences start to appear. Bulging waistlines and morning hang-overs are good indicators." I've told my boys that too much sex can make it seem routine. "Same as going to Disneyland every day for three straight months; the novelty and excitement eventually fades away. Abstinence makes the heart grow fonder."

The convenient, instant gratification that contraceptives provide, has cheapened the value many people place on sex and women. The image of women, for many young men, has deteriorated to where they casually refer to women as "holes." It's especially alarming knowing that many young women have that same cheap image of themselves. The effort I make to give my children correct information about reproduction results with their having a higher regard for sex and women in general.

The people who are concerned about sexually transmitted diseases might need to be a little more selective with whom they sleep. It gets back to the drunk driver and seat belt analogy. If a person is going to be irresponsible and ride with drunk drivers, a seat belt isn't going to be enough to save his life. Sooner or later he's going to wind up in serious trouble, or worse yet, dead.

It's like having sex without getting to first know your partner. It suggests a reckless lifestyle. Drugs, booze, and circumstances eventually undo the conscious regimen of using birth control devices. Pregnancy, disease, or both, can result.

Many people claim that condoms, like bicycle helmets, save lives. However, for some people, those safety devices encourage a devil-may-care attitude and a false sense of invulnerability. That's what I observed while I was bicycling on The Ride Across Minnesota. I saw dozens of people who were righteously wearing their helmets for "safety's sake." Yet, they were riding in an unsafe fashion. They rode three and four abreast in highway traffic, ran red lights at busy intersections, didn't signal their lane changes, and stopped to drink beer along the way. Many of these same people had the audacity to badger me for not wearing a helmet. When one would blurt out the same old interrogating question, "Hey, you! Where's your helmet?" I silenced most of them by yelling back, "I'm using it for a nut cup." At least one woman was able to comment, "God, what an ego," she said laughing.

The lesson I try to make clear to my boys is that protective devices such as condoms and helmets don't protect people from acting irresponsibly. The only person ever to be killed on TRAM was a man wearing a helmet who rode down a winding hill on the wrong side of the road and smashed into an approaching truck. Responsibility doesn't begin with helmets and condoms. It begins with rational actions by each person. And, rational action begins with information that leads to knowledge and wisdom. Knowledge provides facts about yesterday and today. Wisdom provides the power to make sound decisions for tomorrow. "Those ingredients," I tell my boys, "are essential to achieve a higher level of excellence."

TACKLING SINGLE PARENTING

More About Gaining Knowledge And Wisdom

Teaching sexual responsibility is just one of many examples of empowering children to be answerable for their own actions. Teaching children to take responsibility for their own attitudes, actions, and neglects, without blaming others, will help them grow to be productive, prideful adults who live in harmony within their families and communities. Being accountable is an age-old, highly regarded message.

British novelist Aldous Huxley said, "There's only one corner of the universe you can be certain of improving, and that's your own self. So you have to begin there, not outside, not on other people. That comes afterward, when you've worked on your own corner."

This stanza from "Invictus," a poem written by Ernest Henely, was often quoted by the late President John F. Kennedy: "It matters not how straight the gate, how charged with punishments the scroll, I am the master of my fate, I am the captain of my soul."

The message is clear: nobody is responsible for your attitude, actions, or neglects except you. The goal is clear—children need to be taught this lesson of accountability. The road, though, is booby-trapped with diversions and obstacles. Many world leaders, such as Pope John Paul II, have publicly cautioned society about those booby-traps.

When the Pope was in Denver, Colorado during the summer of 1993, he told audiences, "Vast sectors of society are confused about what is right and wrong and are at the mercy of those with the power to create opinion and impose it on others." The Pope was referring to television, movies, news providers, special interest lobbyists, influential role models, politicians, educators, and other large groups who have their own self-serving goals.

For example, most people probably don't see much harm in the beverage commercials that air on television. Nevertheless, the subtle yet persuasive message that comes across to millions of younger viewers is, "Life is for sport, life is for fun." To hell with responsibility. Television and movies glamorize cheap sex and violence in a fashion that appears to be the norm to millions of young, impressionable viewers. News people report on hot issues like abortion, the environment, and gun control with stories slanted by their personal perspectives. Special interest lobbyists spend huge amounts of time and money to win favorable legislation on behalf of the giant corporations they represent. Many influential role models, such as high paid sports stars, send negative messages to millions of youngsters when they mistreat women, use illegal drugs, and publicly express discontent with their grossly inflated salaries. Many politicians vote against their consciences so they can appeal to the majority of voters. Educators decide what issues will be studied in school. They're the ones who teach which side of a conflict was right, which side was wrong, and for what reasons.

With these images and opinions steadily bombarding and influencing my family, I've repeatedly reminded my children to use our three favorite critical thinking questions to help them sort out the facts: What do you mean? Can you give me an example? What do you think of this (or, that)? I remind them that those three questions help boil the images and generalities down to specifics so they can make their own conclusions about what's being done and said. "Be skeptical. Even if you can't ask one of these three questions in person, ask it in your mind. Don't let anybody get away with throwing images or generalities at you without supporting their assertions with evidence that you understand and believe."

Another way of sorting the facts from the non-facts and the generalities from the specifics, I tell my sons, "is to acquire as many different experiences as you can." I've held 13 different jobs in my life, and have benefited from each one of them. I've delivered newspapers and caddied golf clubs, baled hay, rode horses, worked in factories, sold shoes, and been a soldier. I've bartended, worked as a radio announcer, managed a sales team, and run a business. These different jobs, along with a host of other stints—not to mention my community volunteer work and single parenting—has given me that "been around the block" feeling. Personal experience is the world's best teacher.

John Dewey, a U.S. philosopher and innovative educator said, "Education is the sum total of all your experiences." The point I make to my boys is that experience yields knowledge and wisdom and that will help them determine the difference between the message and the messenger.

I've done my best to help my children get those "hands-on" experiences. When they were toddlers, I took them to parades and carnivals so they could get used to crowds, noise, and activity. We took walks in the woods so they could learn to appreciate the beauty and serenity of nature. We often walked to the park to watch baseball games, or to the lake to play in the sand and water.

When the kids were a few years older, they were fascinated with big boats and mansions. One Saturday morning I told the boys, "I know where we can see big boats and a mansion." We drove 150 miles north to Duluth, on the shore of Lake Superior. I can still see the amazed look on their faces the first time they saw a 1,000 foot iron ore freighter move slowly through the shipping canal toward open water. Later, we toured the 39 rooms of the Glensheen Mansion, a turn of the century home built by timber and ore magnate, Chester Congdon. Those adventures never cost us much, but they sure provided a ton of wealth in experience.

A few years later, we drove west into South Dakota to visit Mount Rushmore. Once again, the historical value of a trip like this, with talk of a gold rush, skirmishes between the cavalry and Indians, and a close-up look at four U.S. presidents, was priceless. The trip didn't cost much because we ate from a cooler and spent our two nights in a campground.

When they were 11 and 14, we took a 3,700 mile journey up through the Sault Sainte Marie locks, east across Canada, and down through Niagara Falls. We strolled through downtown Toronto and camped in upper state New York. We visited the Baseball Hall of Fame in Cooperstown and watched the whales near Gloucester, Maine. We ate lobster and toured the Freedom Trail in Boston. We stopped in Cape Cod to swim, and spent a day in New York City to see the Statue of Liberty, Ellis Island, and to walk the streets of Manhattan, taking in the sights, sounds, and smells. We stopped in Philadelphia to see the Liberty Bell and Liberty Hall. Then, onto Washington, D.C. to see the White House, sit in on a session at the House of Representatives, and tour the monuments in and around the Mall. On the way home, we stopped in Chicago, and as my boys say, "We saw everything in downtown Chicago." Most of it was from the top of the Sears building.

It was an awesome trip that lasted 17 days and cost only $1,500. We ate most of our breakfasts and lunches from our cooler and spent many nights in campgrounds. Paul and J.J. not only learned firsthand much about America's history and the world in which we live, they also learned new skills along the way. They improved their ability to read a road map, and became cosmopolitan users of a subway system. They learned how to pitch a tent, take it down, and fold it up the next morning. They learned to keep their dirty clothes separate from the clean clothes, and to keep their possessions organized while we maintained close quarters. As a parent, there were some trying times, but the kids soon got the knack of what needed to be done each day, making the trip more enjoyable for all of us.

Each of our adventures, whether it was a half day at the beach or two weeks on the road, helped create a reservoir of experience for my children. With each new skill they learned and every new tidbit of information they picked up, my boys gained knowledge and wisdom, helping to shape their pride and confidence. I've told my sons that pride and confidence help people feel good about themselves. Research shows that people who possess a healthy self-esteem are less likely to hurt themselves and others. All combined, knowledge and wisdom lead to a higher level of excellence.

There are other ways, besides travel, in which parents can help their children gain knowledge and wisdom through experience. When my boys were preschoolers, I would take them to the library every week for "children's story time." The kids would sit in a semi-circle, and the librarian would read from a favorite children's book. Later, we would choose a book to take home, which I read to the boys during the course of the week.

The early introduction to reading helped increase my boys' vocabulary and gave us cozy, family time together. It also introduced them to new and exciting thoughts and stimulated their imaginations, helping to broaden their understanding of their world. Those are the same benefits they realize by reading as teenagers, and that they'll take into adult life. Reading will help them become wise in making the decisions that will affect them and their families in years to come.

When Joyce left home after the custody decision was made final, she left behind a large box of flash cards that she had used as an elementary teacher before we married. They included spelling and math cards that the boys and I used regularly for years.

TACKLING SINGLE PARENTING

Paul or J.J. and I, would sit at the kitchen table three or four times a week for about 15 minutes. We'd review the questions and answers together the first time through the cards. Later, I'd ask only the questions and let them provide the answers. We started with the easy cards, and worked our way up to the more difficult ones. I always rewarded my kids for their accomplishments with lots of praise, which encouraged them to keep making progress.

The flash card learning style really works. My flash card lessons gave Paul and J.J. a head start going into school, and I continued to use this same style of math and spelling quizzes with them all the way through elementary school. By the time they reached sixth or seventh grade they had mastered the flash card learning style, and could apply it personally without my help.

Knowledge And Wisdom Build Reasoning Skills

To thrive and be happy in a complicated and fast-paced society, a person needs to develop strong reasoning skills. I've told my boys, "Over the course of your life you'll be required to make a lot of decisions, and many of them will be wrong. Your goal should be to make more smart decisions than stupid ones." It's a lesson that Tom Hanks promoted in the movie, *Forrest Gump:* "Stupid is as stupid does." I've helped my kids learn reasoning skills by getting them involved with activities that require them to make smart decisions. Correct decision-making is a learned skill that results from experience. It's a skill that can help a person go a long way towards success.

I remember one of the first hands-on pre-school toys that Paul received as a gift. It was a Playskool work bench. It had a variety of differently shaped holes that the child was to match with differently shaped pegs. Fitting the square peg into the square hole not only helped improve Paul's manual dexterity, it also helped introduce him to the concept of reasoning, through deduction, to make the right decision.

As the boys grew older, I introduced them to a variety of activities that would improve their reasoning skills. Hobbies, like collecting and trading baseball cards and comic books, gave them buying and selling experience. "The goal," I told them, "is to buy low and sell high." Sometimes they'd lose money through poor reasoning, but overall, their experience prevailed and they made more profitable transactions than losing ones. Other entrepreneurial activities, like selling lemonade at the corner, further helped them develop reasoning skills. How much to charge? How much to pour? How to attract customers? Those experiences helped my children raise their level of excellence by learning, through trial and error, how to make correct decisions.

Activities such as team sports and scouting have helped give my boys sound reasoning skills. Those activities require decisions that help children work together as a group, rise in status among their peers, and ultimately reach designated goals. Extracurricular activities at school, such as band, theater, and debate, also help children improve their reasoning skills in similar ways.

A single mother I met at a dance told me that she was teaching her two young sons to do domestic chores like dishes, laundry, cooking, and cleaning. "They should learn to do 'girl' things as well as 'guy' things," she professed. "I agree," I told her, "and girls should be taught how to work with 'guy' things like tools and automobiles." The objective is to teach a wide variety of skills to boys and girls.

Getting involved in their community is another way for my boys to improve their reasoning skills. Edmund Burke, an eighteenth century, Irish born statesman, is often quoted by people who have a need to make a profound statement on the importance of getting involved in one's community:

"The only thing necessary for the triumph of evil is for good men to do nothing." Considering the vernacular of the era, Burke's words obviously included women. I encouraged my boys to get involved by openly discussing both sides of an issue at home. It started when they were in their preschool years, with a topic like race relations. In an easy-to-understand way, I told my kids, "Some people think God created them better than others. Other people think everybody is created equal." Then, to get the conversation flowing, I used one of our family's three favorite critical thinking questions: "What do you think of that?" Discussing social issues is a communication technique which has become more sophisticated as the boys have grown older and more knowledgeable, but the basic format has remained the same. It helps my children improve their reasoning skills so they can make their own decisions and not be led astray by the opinions of others.

TACKLING SINGLE PARENTING

I've worked hard to interest my kids in charitable and community duties. When I attended school board meetings, I shared some of the issues with my kids when I got home. When an election came up, I shared the popular questions of concern with my kids and encouraged their feedback. When I campaigned for a local political candidate in whom I believed, I shared my thoughts about why I supported her. When I volunteered to be a cub scout leader, teach religion, and coach little league sports, I knew that my kids were there watching me. I hope they'll pick up my lead in the future. When I volunteered to help pick up litter at the local park and distribute Christmas groceries to single moms, I encouraged the boys to lend me a hand. When I see one of my boys sitting idly in front of the TV set channel surfing, I'll invariably tell him: "Shut it off and go read the front page story of the newspaper." Later, I'll ask him his opinion about the story.

By encouraging my children to get involved in the popular issues that involve us as a society, they become wiser and smarter. They improve their reasoning skills, and have a better chance of standing firm in their convictions in the face of adversity.

I was rewarded with the fruits of my labor when my sons volunteered to join other teenagers from church to help feed the needy through the Loaves and Fishes program. It's that kind of hands-on experience that helps educate my children about the needs and concerns of our community. I was rewarded with more fruits of my labor when the verdict for the highly publicized and controversial O.J. Simpson murder trial was handed down on October 3, 1995.

The night before the verdict was made public, my kids and I were drawing our own conclusions so that we could make well-reasoned predictions, and then be ready to stand firm in our convictions. After we reviewed the circumstances, each of my boys gave me his prediction about the verdict along with two or three reasons to support his theory. The next day, when the boys came home from school, and the verdict of "not guilty" had been announced, they were both wearing wide smiles. I wholeheartedly congratulated them on making a decision based on their reasoning skills rather than popular opinion. I vigorously shook their hands and gave them each a big hug. "Your decision took a lot of guts, and I'm proud of you. This is a lesson I want you to take through life: When you've seen the evidence presented by all sides, let your experience and wisdom speak for you, and then stick to your beliefs." They understood what I was saying.

Developing People Skills

Over the years, when my children have applied for work at various places, I often reminded them, "The first impression is the most important." Many business owners I spoke to on TRAM told me that more young people should realize the importance of the first impression, but, unfortunately, many don't. "They don't smile or practice common courtesy"; or, "They come across as having bad attitudes." Those are some of the complaints I heard from business owners about many of the kids who interviewed for jobs. Consequently, most of them didn't get hired. Learning to be more considerate might help.

Being considerate of others is an important lesson which I started to teach my boys the first time that I saw them being rude to a playmate. Consideration means to display kind and thoughtful behavior towards others. When people are not considerate, they present a rude and unrefined image that can be hurtful and offensive to others.

Teaching growing boys to be considerate is an on-going battle. Many times I feel strapped for time, energy, and patience. Often, it's easier to let a little rudeness slip by, rather than take the time and effort to correct it. And, there's the ever-present image of people acting rude to others on TV, or in the movies. Contemporary Hollywood exposes young viewers to expressions of "screw you" much more than expressions of "yes ma'am" or "thank you very much." Rudeness is often made to look funny or cool, and is therefore emulated. Even at home I've been less than a sterling example of consideration. I use foul language more than I should, and I occasionally have a confrontational edge to my nature that exposes itself with a chilling effect on some people. Still, there are people skills that I've been able to teach my boys. Those skills help them do well in school, at home, at work, and at play. They'll continue to help them excel with their future families, business, and in society in general. Those skills are helping my boys reach a higher level of excellence.

When I saw one of my boys throw sand at another kid in the sandbox, or at the beach, I corrected him. Instead of simply barking out orders, like "Don't throw sand!" I'd give him a good reason for not doing so, emphasizing the danger of throwing sand in someone's eyes. Reasoning goes a lot further with my kids than a flat out "no" or "don't," or worse yet, "because I said so."

The most effective reasons are the ones that rely on benefits to make the point. Not only benefits for my children, but for others as well. Paul or J.J., unwittingly throwing sand at another, could easily relate to the pain of having sand in his eyes. I would ask, "How would you like it?" They in turn didn't want to inflict that kind of pain on another, which helped restrain them from throwing sand. The golden rule sums up this principle of conduct: "Do unto others, as you would have them do unto you." Learning to say "I'm sorry" for displaying a lack of consideration is another people skill that I've encouraged my children to practice.

Understanding people skills helps my children act considerate and respectable in public. That's why I teach table manners at home. I ask that they sit up straight at the table, without propping their heads up with their hands. No reading at the table, unless they're alone, or the other person doesn't mind. No eating with your hands unless we're eating finger food, like tacos or chicken. I want my boys to ask for food to be passed to them by saying "please," and "thank you" after they've received it. Those are words of courtesy that demonstrate thoughtful behavior toward others. I encourage lively conversation at the table as long as it doesn't interfere with the eating pleasure of others. I want them to savor their meal. If they've enjoyed their food, I want them to compliment the chef.

Many of the same people skills that apply to the dinner table also apply in church and at other social gatherings. I encourage the lively participation of my sons as long as the people around them aren't being intruded upon. I also encourage them to pay attention to the message that others deliver. It's all part of being considerate of others.

Whenever my children received gifts, I made it a rule that they send a follow-up thank you note. When they were pre-schoolers, I helped them write their notes, but they personalized it with their drawings and scribblings. The lesson I teach my children is "if the other person thought enough of you to give you a gift, the least you can do is to be considerate enough to say thank you. As teenagers, they generally write their own thank you notes without prodding. I encouraged that practice by telling them that it made me proud of them, how thankful the person on the other end would be to get their note, and how appreciative they would be to receive a thank you note if they had been the senders instead of the receivers. It's all part of extending thoughtful behavior to others.

I've told my children, "Receiving gifts is easy. There are many times, though, when you have to be the one giving. Giving and receiving gifts is a two-way street." When I was married, I would help my children prepare their Christmas, birthday or Mother's Day gift for their mom. We would select a gift at the store, wrap it, and write a special note on our homemade card. In turn, Joyce would do the same for me with the boys. I still have several cards from Paul and J.J. that say, "To daddy, with love," that were written long before either one of them could write.

In a single parent family, when one spouse is no longer available to prompt the kids to give the other spouse a gift, how do the kids learn to be considerate of mom or dad on special, gift-giving occasions? The answer for my family was that I did the prompting, myself.

As special days, such as Father's Day, Christmas, and my birthday approached, I would make my kids aware of the event well in advance, and remind them to work on giving me a gift. It didn't have to be much, just enough to let me know that some thought went into it. In the early years, it was a thrill to receive a specially colored page torn out from their coloring book or a handmade card with pictures drawn on the cover. In later years, it was fun to receive brightly colored socks, or a paperback book.

When a young man named Julio from the St. Paul Pioneer Press interviewed me for a Father's Day story, I told him about my gift-giving practice. Julio confided that the practice sounded selfish. "Actually," I told him, "it has just the opposite effect." I told Julio that it taught my boys to be considerate of others. It taught them about the joy of giving, and it relieved them of any guilt they may have had later for not having given me gifts out of simple thoughtlessness. "And they've always had fun preparing a gift for me while trying to keep it a secret." I told Julio that it gave them a lot of pleasure.

One of the gifts that my two teenagers gave me for Father's Day was a gift that will keep on giving. I could tell from the way they were acting the night before that they had a surprise they were anxious to share. Sunday morning, before church, they brought it up from the basement. It was big, white, and heavy-duty.

It was a laundry basket.

I was stunned.

My first thought was about mothers of America and how most of them loathe any Mother's Day gift remotely associated with domestic chores. Then, my thoughts switched to my five married brothers, and I wondered how they would react to receiving a laundry basket from their children on Father's Day. How totally unthinkable it would be for their children to buy them such a gift. It would seem so inappropriate.

My boys were waiting for me to say something. I started to laugh. "Well boys," I said. "I never in a 100 years would've guessed a laundry basket. What made you think of getting me a laundry basket?"

"We looked all around the house for ideas," they told me. "We wanted to get you something you could use. Then we remembered how beat up the old laundry basket was and thought a new one would be a good idea."

By this time, I was even more amazed with this unusual gift than I had been earlier. It certainly was something I wasn't about to buy for myself, even though the old one was literally falling apart, in spite of the twine I used to keep it together.

"I absolutely love it," I declared. "It's very considerate of both of you and I really appreciate it. I just want to know how you got it into the house without me seeing it." I asked them if they would sign and date my new basket, which they gladly did with a big, black marker. Now, every washday, I reflect on that day and appreciate the extra effort and thought that my boys put into the gift that made it so very special. "To Pop. Happy Father's Day '95. Love, Paul and J.J."

I've encouraged my children to be givers not only inside the home, but outside the home, as well. I ask that they contribute to the church collection every week. Years ago, it was a dime or a quarter. As they grew older and earned more money, they gave more. Paul has told me, "Giving to others makes me feel good." When the boys and I were in Boston, riding the sight-seeing trolley, I turned to see how Paul was enjoying the tour while we were stopped at an intersection. To my surprise, I saw Paul reach into his pocket, pull out a dollar, and hand it to a scruffy looking, older man who had stuck his hand through the open window.

I later asked Paul why he gave that man a dollar. I said, "He probably stands on that corner every day and hits on tourists." Paul defended his action. "He just looked like he could use it." Those words came from a 14-year-old who I'm quite sure had no more than $5 on him. I told Paul how proud I was of his nonjudgmental and considerate attitude and to "keep up the good work."

I've taught my sons to be considerate of younger children by watching out for their safety; for example: at school, near traffic, and not to hit girls unless it's in self-defense (some rules have indeed changed). When I introduce my boys to strangers, I ask that they smile, extend their hand and shake the other person's hand firmly, looking squarely in the other person's eyes, and saying in a sincere manner, "Nice to meet you." It's a considerate approach to building a friendly rapport and making the first impression a positive one.

Many teenagers—and many adults for that matter—find it unreasonable and out of nature to greet people so openly. Their attitude is, "I'm not a doctor or lawyer. I don't have to act that way." I tell my boys, "It's true, you're not a doctor or a lawyer, but you may be dealing with doctors and lawyers, and that's how they act. You'll make a much more favorable impression on professional and business people if you treat them the way they're accustomed to being treated."

Most of the time, my boys make me proud of the way they act in public. They greet people well, interact easily with their friends and relatives, are courteous to teachers and other adults, and basically, go through life with an upbeat, positive attitude. Occasionally, however, that attitude turns ugly, and many times I'm on the receiving end. And I don't like it.

The problem lies mostly between Paul and me. It started when he was about 15. Sometimes, all it takes is the slightest little spark to set it off. One Saturday morning I allowed Paul to sleep late, but apparently 11 hours of sleep wasn't long enough. When I woke him up at noon to begin chores he roared: "Why didn't you let me sleep?" He was rude to me the rest of the day—sullen, short-tempered, and totally disagreeable. It was as if he went out of his way to be mean to me.

While he was ignoring me, one of his friends called. He instantly broke into his "Mr. Personality Plus" routine. Then, when he was off the phone, he continued to treat me rudely. The indiscriminate, petty reasons for his insolence were typified when he became angry at me for pressing and folding his clothes "the wrong way." Some days, as far as Paul is concerned, I can't do anything right. He makes it very clear that I'm cramping his style. His inconsiderate actions hurt me and make me to wonder what I've done to deserve the nasty treatment. It's extremely unsettling.

Through my observations and research, I've come to realize that the problem that Paul and I have is not unique. It's a concern of parents of teenagers from coast-to-coast. Many parents have more trouble with it than I do, and others hardly notice it. Some parents dismiss it by saying, "He's doing the normal teenage thing of resisting authority"

"It's just a phase"

"It's a quest for independence."

"He's searching for his own identity."

Or, "It's those raging hormones." One parent at a business dinner told me that she was shocked when her 15-year-old son came home from school and told her, "Today we had a speaker who told our class that as our bodies develop, our parents should understand that we'll be hard to live with for the next couple of years, that it's part of growing up." I said, "It sounds to me like the school gave your kid permission to be an asshole." She smiled, nodded, and agreed.

I choose to believe that rude and irresponsible behavior doesn't need to be an acceptable part of growing up, and Paul needs to be more accountable for his actions. I'm making progress on improving his disposition by confronting the situation head-on rather than ignoring it.

One day, Paul's attitude turned so sour towards me that I felt like taking him out to the garage and putting on the boxing gloves. Thankfully, I got past the anger and looked for more practical solutions. I began to rely on communication techniques, discussed earlier.

My first step was to remember that Paul is a BIG BEAR, just like me, and our behavioral styles can easily clash. I noticed that our conversations would sour when I would give him a directive. If I asked him how school was going he was happy to give me an update. However, when I told him to clean up his room, he would get abrupt with me. So, instead of giving him orders, I gave him choices, which is what a BIG BEAR prefers. "Are you going to clean up your room tonight or tomorrow?" That was often met with a much more positive answer than, "Clean up your room!" It was a matter of allowing Paul to exert his independence.

There are other communication techniques that help me deal with Paul's occasional, sour disposition. I use our family's three favorite critical thinking questions: "What do you mean?" "Can you give me an example?" And, "What do you think of this (or, that?)" They help to narrow the generalities down to specifics. For example, Paul says, "You didn't let me sleep long enough." I reply, "Can you give me an example of how long is long enough?" Another communication technique I've used to help define specifics is the "note pad process."★ It helped me confirm my suspicions that Paul's negative attitude was nothing more serious than rudeness. It wasn't problems with friends, drugs, or with school. It wasn't pent up distress about the divorce. It was simply a matter of not making the effort to show more consideration to another family member.

Another technique that improves Paul's sour attitude is to get him involved in a project away from the daily routine, one that serves the welfare of the family. It might be cleaning out the garage, basement, painting the garage doors, washing the car, or cleaning out the gutters. I've even thought about making some phone calls to volunteer my boys' services doing farm work.

Nothing clears the mind and builds a feeling of self-worth quite like manual labor. One time, I had Paul chop down a back yard pine tree that had died of disease. He worked hard all afternoon. He got his arms scratched, he got sweaty, he had to turn down several offers from friends to do other things, but when the job was over and the wood was stacked, I was looking at a proud 16-year-old boy who was anxious to show me the good work he had completed. The job made Paul feel good about himself, because it allowed him to contribute to the

---

★ Detailed in the Communication Chapter.

good of the family in a large, tangible way. When he feels good about himself, he's more apt to treat me with respect.

Paul told me that he wants more space, so I give it to him. I don't start as many conversations with him as I once did. Instead, I let him come to me more. It seems to work. He wants his privacy, and I try to give it to him. Some evenings I make a point of going out, even though I have no particular place to go, just so Paul and J.J. can spend some time at home away from me. It lets them turn up the music, and be teenagers, without the scrutinizing eye of a parent. I surprised them when I told them they could have a few friends over after the homecoming football game, and that I'd spend the night at a hotel.

The boys couldn't believe it. They were thrilled; actually, so was I. I made arrangements for a pleasant night, relaxing in the pool and sauna, elegant dining, and dancing. I discovered later that my teenagers had a few more friends over than I had bargained for, but they were out of the house by the prescribed time of midnight. The next day, I found cigarette butts on the lawn, but, for the most part, the party went well, and served Paul's quest for independence. I wouldn't recommend that all single parents take a chance like that, and some parents might claim that I acted irresponsibly by allowing my 17-year-old son, Paul, to host an unchaperoned party, but I'm glad I did. It helped Paul mature by my showing confidence in him and as he matures, the rudeness seems to be softening.

There are other techniques that I've used successfully to improve Paul's disposition towards me: They're elements of discipline. ANTICIPATION worked when I introduced Paul to the concept of empathy—identifying with the feelings of another person: "I want you to realize that you're not the only one around here who has feelings," I told Paul. "Your rude treatment hurts me. It makes me wonder what I've done to you to deserve the lousy treatment." He got the message.

The element of PERSUASION worked well when I recounted a story to him that helped him see his nasty temperament from an objective viewpoint. I reminded him about the time, when he was 14, that he came home after visiting a friend who had a 17-year-old sister. She had caused the household a lot of trouble with her rudeness. "I can remember your exact words: "Man, was she being a bitch." I told him, "that's how you act around here sometimes. Now, what do you think of that?" He understood.

The element of FEAR worked well. One evening when Paul and I were in a heated argument about his disposition, I warned him, "Paul, it's getting to the point where I can't take your abuse anymore. You'll either have to make a change or I'm going to pull you out of school and send you to live with your mother." As soon as he realized I meant business, his rudeness mellowed out. He loves his mother, but the punishment would mean having to leave his friends, school, work, and sports. It was a threat which I knew had muscle, and it worked.

Later, I relayed this incident to Paul's high school assistant principal during a casual conversation. He advised against using threats of sending children of divorced parents to live with the other parent. "It happens all the time," he cautioned me. "The kids use the absent parent as a port in a storm during a parental dispute." His message was clear—if you threaten to send your teenager to live with the other parent, be prepared for the consequences. It might backfire.

The lesson that I think worked best to help Paul curb his rudeness and act more considerate towards me followed the principle of SHAME. One day, as we drove to the grocery store, Paul's rudeness and sullenness got the best of me. I was fed up with his insolence. "You know how I feel about your rudeness," I told him. Paul said nothing, but he listened. "You get angry with me when I talk too much. You get angry with me when I ask you to do chores. You get angry with me when I don't give you enough space. I think you get angry with me just for being me." I told him a story that I hoped would make sense to him.

"My older brother, Phil, left Minnesota for California in 1968. He landed a job as a parking lot attendant for a popular bar and restaurant in Santa Monica. The owner's name was Al.

"Before long, Phil was promoted from parking lot attendant to bartender, then to part-time night manager, then to part-time day manager, and then to full-time general manager. Phil was enjoying great success. He liked Al, and Al liked Phil. Phil planned to stay there for many years to come.

"Soon, Phil became regional director, as Al expanded his bars throughout California and neighboring states. Phil negotiated for real

TACKLING SINGLE PARENTING

estate, secured liquor licenses, and just about ran the whole show for Al.

"After about 15 years, however, Phil's philosophy of doing business moved away from Al's philosophy. Neither one was right or wrong; they just wanted to move in different directions.

"Finally, when it came down to push and shove, Phil was smart enough to realize that Al would ultimately win the tug of war, because he was the owner. Even though Phil was Al's right hand man, and had served him well for 15 years, it must be understood that Al had also served Phil well all those years. When the rift grew deeper and wider, it was Phil who needed to leave the company, not Al."

I was sure that I had Paul's undivided attention, because he likes and respects Phil, and that was a story he hadn't heard before. "The point I'm making, Paul," I continued, "I've tried my best to treat you fairly, and to make our relationship benefit you just like Al treated Phil all those years. I want you to fully realize, however, that I'm the boss of our home. Not the 50 percent boss, or the 75 percent boss, but the 100 percent boss—just as Al was. You might not like it that way, but that's the way it is. I try to understand the issues and concerns that affect you, and my ultimate goal is to watch out for your welfare. Then, when you're 18, 20, or whenever you're finished with school, you'll leave home and go on to become your own boss. When I come to your home to visit, you'll be the boss, and I'll need to respect that."

Some people might say that I'm a control freak because of my demand to be in charge. I don't agree. I'm putting my years of experience and wisdom in front, to take charge, and steer my family's ship. Indeed, I think that the biggest strides Paul and I have made toward mutual peace, understanding, and consideration for one another since he was 15 have been made since I told him that story. It helped him to appreciate and understand our situation.

As Paul and I go through this learning process together, I've made the decision not to give in. I intend to be firm, and to help him improve his level of excellence. I try not to let his lousy disposition ruin my day or make me angry. Sometimes, I try to laugh it off. If he ignores me, I refuse to play the same game. When two people ignore each other, they certainly have no chance of coming together. Last, but not least, I reaffirm my love and commitment, telling him so. "Paul, even though we are sometimes on different plains in life, I want you to know that I love you and I'm working on behalf of your welfare." I'm quite sure he realizes that to be true.

Paul and I spend many more good days together than bad ones; I try not to be too antagonistic about the issue of rudeness. I realize that a maturing teenager has many other concerns on his mind than thinking about parents and, in all likelihood, his rudeness, just like an extremely long bout with the flu, will disappear of its own accord after it runs its course. At least that's the comforting news I heard from one of the experts.

I had a lengthy phone interview with Dr. Edward Christopherson, Chief of Behavioral Pediatrics at The Children's Mercy Hospital in Kansas City. He's the author of eight books on parenting, 144 parenting publications, has made close to 600 public presentations, and almost 300 TV and radio appearances. Christopherson admitted that his son had a two-year bout with the rudeness bug. "There was nothing I could do or say," this highly respected pediatrician told me. "My 19-year-old son and I have spoken more to each other during his first semester in college than we did during his last two years of high school."

That conversation made me feel better about my occasionally stormy relationship with Paul. It helped me find comfort knowing that my feelings of incompetency and frustration were in good company and that, in all likelihood, the light at the other end of the tunnel isn't a train. Still, knowing that Paul will probably outgrow his rudeness doesn't justify his harshness towards me. I intend to keep a focus on persuading Paul to treat me and other people with courtesy and consideration because those lessons serve children well in later years. It's a delicate balancing act that I need to accomplish to help my sons learn those lessons.

Learning To Stand Tall

Learning to "stand tall," or, adhere to ethical values, is a lesson that I'm teaching my children to help them build pride, contentment, and confidence in their lives. I want them to learn the value of a personal reputation where they're trusted and respected by others. Learning to stand tall is an important lesson in raising my children's level of excellence. It's a lesson that has been written about throughout the centuries.

Nineteenth century poet and abolitionist, John Greenleaf Whittier wrote in *Ichabod,* "When honor dies, the man is dead." Shakespeare wrote in *Othello,* "Good name in man and woman, dear my Lord, is the immediate jewel of their souls: Who steals my purse steals trash, but he that filches from me my good name robs me of that which not enriches him, and makes me poor indeed." As my brothers and I were growing up, my mother taught us the same lesson: "You don't have anything if you don't have your good name."

I'm teaching my sons that there are three elements to standing tall: Integrity, which is being sound and complete in character; Fairness, to be just, un-biased, and equitable; and Honesty, being courageous, upright in dealings, sincere, truthful, and genuine.

INTEGRITY

I tell my boys that I really question the integrity of some people. Especially those who are so quick to blame others for their own short-comings. I'm not passing judgment when I make that statement. I'm simply making an assessment based on my experience and observations, and trying to teach my children important lessons that will benefit them. I don't want them to place the blame for their short-comings on others. A business friend of mine shares the same concern.

Ed is the president of a family-owned company founded in St. Paul in the late nineteenth century. One of Ed's biggest challenges, he confided, is the need to "walk on egg shells" as blossoming nieces and nephews mature within the ranks of the business and ask for promotions. "I try not to hurt any feelings within the family," Ed said, "but at the same time, it's my job to make sure the company stays profitable. I don't want anybody holding down a position they can't handle just because they're part of the family."

A big industry-wide convention was hosted in St. Paul and Ed's 25-year-old niece, Susan, who had worked for the company for six years, asked Ed to be added to the list of speakers. Ed was skeptical about Susan's speaking skills, but felt pressure from the family to add her to the agenda. Susan's speech was a disaster. She was poorly prepared, her presentation was uninteresting, and her delivery was choppy. The next day, Susan and Ed saw each other in the company coffee room. Susan said, "That audience was sure intimidating. I'll bet if I was a man they would've warmed up to me and been more receptive to what I was saying." Ed told me, "I asked Susan to sit down. I was quite emphatic with my message. I told Susan that gender had nothing to do with it. Her speech was unprofessional, and if she wanted to represent us again in a public forum she needed to join a group like Toastmasters International to get professional training." Susan had mistakenly put the blame for her poor speech on the predominantly male audience. Ed helped her discover the real cause of her short-coming. It was her lack of proper training.

Placing one's failings on another person or thing is a mind set that runs deep in society. It shows up regularly in our daily life. For example, one Saturday I was shopping for plumbing at the local hardware store when I overheard a man complaining to the store manager that there wasn't a safety device on the market to prevent his clothes washer from springing a leak and flooding his basement. I interrupted and told the shopper that all he needs to do is turn off the water source after each use. He said he forgets to do that. I asked him if he forgets to turn off the engine of his car after he's done using it. He glared at me and walked away.

Another time I was inside the door of a large supermarket getting money out of the fast cash machine. I was about to slip my card into the machine when a woman came running up. "Can I please get in front of you?" I asked: "What's the hurry?" I expected to hear about an emergency. Instead, she said, "My car is parked in a NO PARKING zone and I want to get out there before I get a ticket." I told her, "Lady, if you parked illegally, you deserve a ticket." Then I took my own sweet time.

I told my boys both of these stories, "Those people were in the habit of using safety nets to protect them from their own failings. Unfortunately, many people have come to expect safety nets to be luxuriously cushy." I told my sons, "placing the blame for your own failings on others is a negative frame of mind that can keep you from making positive strides forward in life." To help build their sense of integrity

TACKLING SINGLE PARENTING

and keep them from placing blame on others there are certain techniques on which I have learned to rely to help get the job done.

When the boys were much younger, even during pre-school years, I gave them jobs for which they were made accountable. One of these was to turn their dirty socks right side out before they went into the wash. I told them that inside out socks are a hassle for me on wash day, and it saves me time if they helped out that way. Teaching the lesson took plenty of persistence on my part, but soon it became clear to Paul and J.J. that I wouldn't allow them to fail in fulfilling their duty. My persistence not only helped to build a sense of integrity in my boys, it also pays me rewards of fewer hassles every wash day. Making an effort to compliment them on their achievement serves as encouragement to keep up the good work.

As my sons grew older, I gave them other duties that they were expected to fulfill. I taught them to wash dishes properly and to rotate the job between each other. I told them that I didn't care if they rotated every day, or every other day. "Just make sure you keep track of whose turn it is because I don't want to get involved. It's your job." I told them that I wanted the clean dishes put away in their correct places so that someone needing a dish or pan wouldn't be inconvenienced by having to look all over the kitchen. I've told my boys, "It's all part of fulfilling your duty, and learning to fulfill duties helps to build integrity."

Other duties include cleaning up their own spills and messes, keeping us stocked with milk from the corner store, keeping their rooms tidy, and doing weekly household chores. Here's a homespun technique for making sure household chores get done properly which works well for us. Every week the boys rotate jobs. For instance, one week Paul will vacuum and clean their bathroom, while J.J. dusts and mops the kitchen floor. The next week the jobs reverse. This system encourages each boy to inspect the work of the other because that's the job they'll be accountable for the following week. It's a great system for encouraging each boy to fulfill his duty without me having to oversee their work each week.

There are other ways that I help my boys learn integrity. I encourage them to fulfill their duty to do well in school. I expect them to achieve at least a B minus average. If they come up short, then they have to study more and play less.

I've tried to teach my kids to accept compliments graciously, saying "thank you" rather than bragging "It was easy."

I think flaunting wealth shows a lack of integrity, and I try to teach that lesson to my boys by helping them learn modesty. For instance, I encourage them to save money, rather than to spend it foolishly. I want them to dress well without needing to parade around in the latest fashions. I believe that extravagance breeds resentment in other people who don't have much money. I demonstrate the benefits of living comfortably in a modest sized house: less maintenance, lower taxes, easier to clean, and less likely to get burglarized. "Learning to be moderate with your money," I tell my boys, "will help you stay out of high personal debt. It can ease the financial pressures that come with starting a family, and help you live in peace and contentment, instead of strife and uneasiness."

Another important lesson in learning integrity affects all of us on the planet Earth. My family practices the three R's: REDUCE, REUSE, and RECYCLE. I want my sons to know that it's a matter of integrity not to buy more consumer products than can genuinely serve them well. "Each item you buy contributes to pollution somewhere—it negatively affects land, air, water or all three. It's inescapable. The less you buy, the less need there is for an item to be manufactured."

Some economists might object to my frugal philosophy by claiming the economy will suffer if consumers stop spending. All I'm telling my boys is not to buy frivolously. "And when you do make purchases, try to buy an item that can be re-used instead of thrown away after a single use." I also encourage them to buy items that can be repaired instead of disposed of when a part goes bad.

My boys and I practice recycling, helping to reduce the continual need for raw materials. We take pride in sorting metal, aluminum, plastic, glass, newspaper, junk mail, and cardboard and leaving the separate bags outside for pick-up. I've also encouraged my boys to help me pick up litter throughout the neighborhood. Our example encourages others to chip in and leaves us with a feeling of accomplishment. Teaching the three R's helps build my boys' integrity by showing respect to Mother Earth, and that's their duty.

One of the most important lessons in integrity that my boys can learn is their duty to be loyal. I urge them to be loyal to their family, friends, community, country, and God. I caution them, "You'll be tempted to be disloyal because loyalty is often the most difficult path to take. However, without the support and devotion that comes from loyalty, families, institutions, and governments crumble."

LOYALTY TO FAMILY

I've encouraged my boys to learn and understand family loyalty. Even though I've occasionally said angry words about my ex-wife, Joyce, I have, for the most part, encouraged my sons to be devoted to her. I've had them write letters, send gifts, update her about school and social activities, and keep her in their family loop. I've told my sons that Joyce is a good mother, and how much she loves them. I nurtured such a strong loyalty between my sons and their mother that as they have grown older I can't say an unkind word about her without me being scolded by one of my boys. I'm proud of that.

I try to build loyalty between my boys and me. When I was involved with the controversial Ladies' Night issue, the kids had to take some heat about it at school. Sometimes it wore them down, and they began to question my integrity on the issue. I told them, "It's your duty to be loyal to me. You might not agree with all the reasons behind everything I do, and that's okay. I just expect you to stand tall and try to understand that I believe in the merits of my actions. You need to respect that. In turn, I'll respect you for the causes you support. I might not agree with them, but as long as you firmly believe that you're right, I'll respect you for your beliefs."

A few years after I began my single parent career, my friend Blanche, who used to baby-sit Paul and J.J., sent us a Christmas card. Inside the card was a poem on which Blanche had written: "This was in our local paper. I thought you would like it."

I love it.

It speaks about the often unsaid adhesive that helps to keep families together, Loyalty.

STEVE HORNER

WHAT IS FAMILY

First, a family is people giving and receiving love.

Second, a family is people talking and listening to each other.

Third, a family is people caring about what happens to each other and letting it show.

Fourth, a family is people getting angry with each other, and then loving again.

Fifth, a family is people loving the differences among them.

Sixth, a family is people laughing and crying without feeling ashamed of it.

Seventh, a family is people reaching out, instead of fencing in.

LOYALTY TO FRIENDS

I helped promote loyalty among my sons and their friends by encouraging them to follow the same principles that a loving family professes for each member. I also helped to point out the features in people who don't make such good friends, such as the desire to be "takers" instead of "givers" and to put people down when it's not popular to be their friend.

LOYALTY TO COUNTRY

To help inspire loyalty to their country, I've taught my sons the principles on which the country was founded. I've taken them to Fourth of July festivities and Memorial Day services since preschool days. Those events instilled in them a sense of pride and appreciation for their country which will help them be loyal and participating citizens. I taught them that the same concept of loyalty applies to the city and state in which we live.

LOYALTY TO GOD

"God is the most important matter in your life," is a vital lesson with which my sons are growing up. "God does not desert His people but sometimes His people desert Him." I've nurtured a sense of loyalty and love for God by introducing my kids to the doctrines of our faith. I keep them involved through church, and we're trying to live our faith from day to day. From my observations, the loyalty they've built with God is a real source of their strength and contentment. I hope they never take God's friendship for granted.

FAIRNESS

I remember watching a television program with J.J. when he was just three or four years old. The show featured a classroom full of kids who were discussing race relations. There was only one African American child. The rest of the kids were Caucasian.

As J.J. and I watched the classroom scene and listened to the dialogue, my son turned to me and innocently asked: "Hey, dad! Which one is the black kid?" I couldn't believe what I was hearing. My son was completely color blind to the issues of race. What a beautiful question: "Which one is the black kid?"

Unfortunately, as many people grow older, they lose the innocence of racial color blindness. They begin to evaluate people as Blacks, Whites, Indians, Asians, Hispanics, Men and Women, instead of as individuals. Character assessments are often made about individuals for the wrong doings that mistakenly become identified with their ethnic, gender, or religious group. Many people think all White men are insensitive to the needs of others who are less fortunate. Some people think all Black people can't be trusted. Others think all Hispanics are lazy.

I try to teach my boys that typecasting another person based on his or her nationality, gender, or religion is unfair. It's not just. Prejudice creates anger and resentment and denies many people their rightful opportunity to happiness and success.

I've helped my children to be unbiased through education. I've encouraged them to read books that deal with prejudice. Books about World War II and Hitler, along with books about the Civil War and Abraham Lincoln have given my boys a realistic look at the serious problems that prejudice can cause.

I've taught my boys to evaluate people according to their qualifications, not on their race, gender, or religion. "If people are called upon to do a job," I tell them, "their credentials should be assessed on their experience, reputation, knowledge, and wisdom, not on their race, gender, or religion."

I've also tried to discourage my sons from labeling others. "Negative labels," I tell them, "unfairly cast people into molds that can become self-fulfilling prophecies." It seems logical that if positive labels such as "wise, conscientious, and courteous," serve to encourage, praise, and build self-esteem, then negative labels must have just the opposite effect, by making people feel less of themselves.

When I visited the Early Childhood Family Education Center to learn more about contemporary policies on discipline, one of the directors labeled a whole group of children. She did it very innocently, and in a manner quite acceptable to society. I heard her tell the group of parents, "The two to five-year-old children test your limits on everything. That's their job," she said in jest.

I wondered: "Who said that's their job?" The comment caused me to recall the labels I heard when I was a child. I remember being saddled with the term "attention getter" in elementary school. I don't remember that negative label dissuading me from looking for attention. In fact, I think I tried to attract more attention because of the label. I wonder how I would've reacted to the more contemporary labels such as Attention Deficit Disorder. And how I'd react to a daily dose of the behavior altering drug, Ritalin, like so many millions of kids today.

Negative labeling works like an automobile owner who designates his car a "lemon" whenever it breaks down. Occasional break-downs are inevitable for any machine—or, person—and the label "lemon" might be a hasty, unjustifiable designation, especially if the car, or person, isn't receiving the right amount of tender loving care needed to keep running smoothly.

J.J. used to have a friend, Mark, who lived down the street from us. Most of the neighborhood parents labeled Mark as "hyper" because he was extremely active and would throw his toys at others. I encouraged my boys to befriend Mark because I thought of him as quite a nice kid who simply had responded negatively to the hyper label.

My boys and I showed Mark expressions of love and understanding, rather than flinging insults at him. He calmed down and became quite a little gentleman. Mark and his family have since moved from the neighborhood, but Mark has occasionally returned to visit. He's a good kid and doesn't seem the least bit hyper.

The boys know another young man, Jerry, who is overweight and keenly interested in technology. His own family regard him as a nerd. I encouraged my boys to focus on Jerry's advanced knowledge of digital equipment and not to negatively label him. I've since overheard Jerry make positive and complimentary comments about my sons to others. It's probably because my boys have accepted Jerry with love and understanding, rather than insulting him with negative labels.

I try to practice what I preach in regard to negative labeling. If my child tells me a lie, I don't label him a liar. If he steals from me, I don't label him a thief. Instead of labeling, which I think would only perpetuate the problem, I try to find a solution to the problem through effective discipline such as ANTICIPATION, PERSUASION, or PUNISHMENT* that will serve as an expression of love. Expressions of love encourage people to feel good about themselves, helping to raise their levels of excellence.

Being fair to others also means to pay them their fair worth in salary and not to take advantage of them. People who feel that they've been ripped off can become angry and resentful. People who feel as though they've been treated justly are more likely to feel satisfied and accomplished. I learned a powerful lesson through business dealings which taught me the importance of treating people fairly.

When I first started my own business, I was anxious to take on work so that I could start earning a living. I hurriedly contracted to do business with a man named Cliff. Entering into the contract, I failed to understand all the work that was needed and soon discovered that I bargained for much more than I could deliver at the agreed upon price. I was angry with myself, but was determined to fulfill my obligation.

Cliff eventually sensed my dissatisfaction with the contract and offered to renegotiate with me at terms which were much more to my liking. I told Cliff how much I appreciated his understanding and that I was much happier with the new contract. I became inspired to work

---

*Covered earlier in Chapter Six

harder than ever for Cliff because of the fair way he treated me. I delivered a superior product, ahead of schedule, and under budget.

The Cliff lesson is one of the important lessons on fairness which I have taught my boys. When Paul marketed his baseball cards on the street corner, I reminded him to deal fairly, especially with the younger kids who might not have known when they were getting a raw deal. I remember several times when Paul came home with a smile on his face and a tale about how he could've ripped off a younger, less sophisticated card trader. Instead, he stood tall and bargained fairly. I told Paul that those dealings make me proud of him. And he earned a good reputation for being fair, an asset that's a lot more valuable than the couple of extra dollars he might have otherwise made.

HONESTY

We all hear slanderous jokes and comments about lawyers. It's as if lawyers are the cause of most of the world's evil. Carl Sandburg wrote, "Why does a hearse horse snicker hauling a lawyer away?" Lawyers are characterized as greedy, self-serving, manipulative and trouble makers. I tell my boys that most lawyers don't fit that nasty image. "Many lawyers thrive because they're needed to straighten out the lies, deceit, and dishonesty that their clients perpetrated or were victims of." Somebody most likely was dishonest, and honesty is the third element of "standing tall."

I tell my boys that cheating, stealing, and lying happen around us every day. It's often glamorized on TV and in movies. The news reports about welfare fraud and white collar crime. We hear reports about church leaders stealing from their congregations. Even staid and reputable organizations like The United Way have been under fire for fraudulent use of funds. Students cheat in class, family members lie to each other, politicians lie to the voters, and taxpayers cheat the government, rationalizing: "unfair tax laws encourage me to cheat." I tell my kids that's the same faulty thinking used by highway speeders who justify their cheating, claiming: "The fools who set the speed limit don't know what they're doing." I point out to my boys how quickly those speeders brake when they see a cop. "All of a sudden the cheaters aren't so bold and righteous. They become cowards when they shrink from accepting the consequences of their cheating, such as a speeding ticket."

"Most cheaters are cowards" is a lesson about honesty that I teach my kids. "Cheating may seem to be the best route for many people because it's often the most convenient. In many cases, though, it turns out to be the most complicated when the cheaters get caught and have to pay a big penalty." The important part of the message is: "Even if you don't get caught speeding and end up with an expensive ticket and increased insurance rate, or aren't kicked out of math class for cheating on a test, or fined by the Internal Revenue Service for filing a fraudulent return, or caught cheating any number of other ways, you'll still pay a penalty. You'll have the personal pain of your dishonesty to contend with and what you think of yourself is a lot more important than what others think of you."

"People who live honorable lives," I tell my kids, "don't ever have to act like cowards and fearfully brake, like the speeders. Honorable people never have to brake for anything. They have courage, pride, and confidence in knowing that their mission is always upright and respectable. Being honorable empowers them in everything they do."

I've taught my boys that stealing—like cheating—is another form of dishonesty. It's a breakdown of character which I've tried to help my kids prevent through communication and discipline. Communication techniques, such as THE THREE WEEK WINNING CALL,★ help me stay in touch with what's going on in my boys' lives. ANTICIPATION, PERSUASION, and PUNISHMENT★★ are discipline techniques that encourage my boys to stay honest and raise their level of excellence.

I think the most effective technique I've used to discourage my boys from stealing has been to set a good example. When we would stay in hotels, I'd tell my kids that guests often feel that they can "take" items from their rooms. Similarly, many grocery shoppers feel that it's acceptable to eat candy or peanuts from bulk bins without paying for them. "We won't take anything that we haven't paid for or

---

★ Referred to earlier in Chapter Two
★★Referred to earlier in Chapter Six

that hasn't been given to us," is the message I've promoted to my boys.

When I'm working in my office and note that a business customer has inadvertently overpaid, I'll point out the situation to my boys: "It would be easy for me to steal," I tell them, "but that's not the honorable thing to do. The problem is that stealing often hurts others by denying them what's rightfully theirs.

I've reminded Paul how hurt he felt after someone stole his bike from outside the movie theater. He knows that's a pain he wouldn't want to inflict on someone else. "Many people justify stealing from large companies or the government by saying, 'They can afford the loss,' or, 'I deserve it.'" I tell my boys that many people have that same self-serving attitude, and that the cumulative losses caused by millions of people stealing hurt others through increased taxes and higher retail prices.

"Damaging other people's property is the same as stealing," is another lesson about being honorable that I teach my boys. I remind J.J. and his friends, who are all avid skateboarders, that "Your skateboards chew up handrails, steps and curbs, all of which take time and money to replace. Don't feel that you're entitled to wreck property 'because it just happens' as a result of what you're doing." Plus, I tell them that they need to get permission to skate from the property owner, and if they don't get it, then they need to move on.

Not lying is another way of helping my kids learn to stand tall. Mark Twain said, "One of the striking differences between a cat and a lie is that a cat has only nine lives." I tell my boys, "once a lie gains life it's hard to put to rest. It becomes a greater burden just to keep up the lie. If you don't tell lies then you don't have to be on guard with what you say. Honest people can be forthright with their message and not have to worry about being caught in contradictions. It's a much more peaceful lifestyle."

I've told my sons that in most cases there's no reason to lie. Paul said that he had been scheduled to work at the grocery store on a Friday night, but that he wanted, instead, to go to a party he had found out about later in the week. He wanted to call in sick. I told him that he had been a good worker with a good attendance record. "Just call your boss and tell him what you want to do. You might be surprised at how understanding he is. He's probably been in the same situation. As a matter of fact, you'll probably gain points with him for being honest." Paul took my advice and got the night off. He enjoyed himself at the party without the pangs of a guilty conscience. The next day he was able to tell his boss about the fun he had without having to hide behind a lie.

I've told my boys that being deceptive, or misleading, is as bad as lying. "If I ask you whether you've done something wrong, and you lie, that is wrong. And if you have done something that you know is wrong, and fail to come forward with the truth, then you're being deceptive."

In the past, when I caught my boys telling a lie or being deceptive I relied on communication and discipline techniques to help keep it from happening again. I've cited an axiom that has made a positive impact on Paul and J.J: "Lying and deception is a violation of trust. If you want me to trust you, and to give you more responsibility as you grow older, I need to be able to trust you. Even if you've done something wrong and you know you'll be punished, I'll feel much better if you come forward with the truth." Here's another point of view: "If you were in business with another person who always lied to you about what he was doing with the business; would you trust him?" I think not.

Real life examples of honest business dealings have been the most persuasive techniques of encouraging my boys to strive for honesty in their lives. Several times I've made business blunders. Instead of hiding my mistakes and not telling my customers, I've come forward and told them about my errors. "Ordinarily," I tell my boys, "my customers have been understanding, we make the corrections, and go on from there." When my boys have come forward with the truth, I may have been stern, but I also tried to reward them with words of appreciation to encourage their future honesty.

Punctuality

I served as a religious education teacher for about five years, mostly when my boys were in elementary grades. Our church needed volunteer teachers, without whom many kids, including my own, might not have had weekly religious training. So, I volunteered.

For the most part, I really enjoyed the work. That old adage about volunteering is true—you receive more than you give. I'll never forget the words of a little third grade girl who came up to me after class. We had been talking about love, peace, and happiness. She took hold of my hand and said, "Today, during class, I felt like I was in heaven." I just about melted.

Most of my students had great support from home. They arrived at my house on time, and were picked up on time. If one of them was going to be absent or late, I would be notified by a parent. Work assignments, which I expected to be done at home, were completed and handed in on time the following week.

Something happened, though, when the kids moved on to high school. That's the year I volunteered to be Paul's first year confirmation teacher. The kids showed up late for class, or didn't come at all. The parents rarely notified me about absences. Projects that I expected to be worked on at home with mom or dad were ignored.

After repeated phone calls and warnings, I sent a stinging letter to the parents telling them that I needed better involvement from them. I sent a copy of my letter to the confirmation coordinator at the church. A few days later, the coordinator phoned me. I thought for sure that she would support me. Instead, she said, "Many of the parents are angry about your letter. It might be a good idea if you took the rest of the year off. It would be okay if you wish to continue with Paul as your only student."

I told her that those parents had been rude to me by not appreciating my time and efforts, and that she "shouldn't let them off the hook just because I called them on their irresponsibility." She disagreed. I signed off and kept working with Paul for the rest of the year.

At the beginning of Paul's second year of confirmation training, which I didn't volunteer to teach, the church had a September orientation for the candidates. Paul and I attended, listened to the orientation, and were introduced to Paul's teacher. Two weeks later, the church sent a letter to all candidates. It stated, "There were 59 candidates who did not come to the orientation and the confirmation team, religious education commission, and myself, don't feel we have gotten off to a good start. We were all disappointed at the large number of candidates who didn't come." The letter was signed by the confirmation coordinator. Those were the same parents with whom I had to cope a year earlier. If the coordinator hadn't caved in when the parents called to complain about my letter, she would probably have had greater parental involvement at the orientation.

There is a truism in salesmanship: "If you allow your clients to dump on you, then you'd better be prepared to be dumped on." People will take advantage of you by throwing more and more demands at you unless you take a resolute stand. Those parents had been my "clients." They had been given permission by the coordinator to continue their dumping by her failure to reprimand them. Had she clarified the rules early, and supported my efforts by telling the parents: "Mr. Horner must have parental support," then she most likely wouldn't have been short 59 candidates at the following year's orientation. They would've had more regard for the rules of punctuality.

"The lesson that's to be learned about being punctual," I tell my kids, "is that you need to be considerate of other people." Each week, I took time out of my busy life to help the children of those parents get through confirmation class. It necessitated an hour or two of preparation, an hour of class time, clean-up, and teacher workshops that were required throughout the year. Yet, most of the parents dismissed my time and effort as irrelevant, by not exercising more discipline with their children, allowing them to be late, absent, or ill-prepared for class.

Through various techniques of discipline such as ANTICIPATION, PERSUASION, and PUNISHMENT, I've encouraged my children to be punctual. I require that they turn in school assignments on time, be at work on time, come home on time, and be at church on time.

Punctuality is a matter of courtesy. Still, there are people who claim to be considerate of others, yet they are habitually late. How does that happen?

When I first met Karen, a women I dated a few times, she cautioned me that she was always late for appointments. I thought about her remark. The next time we got together, I asked her to be more specific. "If you know you're always late," I said, "why don't you do something to correct it?" She told me that she had an obsession to finish whatever she was working on. "I can't leave until it's done or it bothers me until I get back to it."

Karen's answer made me reflect on the time management principles that I've taught my boys. "Give yourself plenty of time," is a lesson I remember hearing since I was a kid, and I've passed it on to my boys. I have repeatedly told my boys, "If you have to be somewhere at noon on Saturday, you had better be up early to work on your chores, because they need to be done before you go anywhere." Those demands have helped my kids learn to manage time well. They learn to allow themselves plenty of time to finish each project before moving on to the next one. "Just as important," I told them, "if you're going to be late, be sure to extend the courtesy of making a phone call. Those calls are appreciated because they let other people know that you value their time."

Those two lessons: appreciation of another person's time, and learning to estimate how much time each project takes, have helped my boys learn punctuality. And that's another step that raises their level of excellence.

Perseverance

Sir Winston Churchill, the wartime prime minister of Great Britain, spoke to a commencement class at Oxford University during the early 1950s. After he was introduced, his large, imposing frame lumbered up to the podium. He looked out across the sea of smiling graduates as he chomped on his huge cigar.

After several moments, he put the cigar aside, but continued to gaze into the eyes of his young, enthusiastic audience. A minute and a half passed, the smiles disappeared, and new expressions of anticipation surfaced.

After what seemed like an eternity, Churchhill declared in a very slow and deliberate manner, "Never, never, never, never, never, never, give up." He put his cigar back in his mouth, turned, and walked off the stage to the sound of thundering applause.

Perseverance means to continue in your endeavor despite opposition. It was that spirit of perseverance that allowed Churchill and the allies to defeat Hitler during World War II. I tell my boys that the same spirit of perseverance will help them accomplish whatever they set out to do in life. "You'll probably experience plenty of failure as you try to

TACKLING SINGLE PARENTING

reach your goals," I tell them. "Keep trying. You can never fully appreciate success until you've suffered failure."

The message to keep trying isn't always an easy one to get across to my kids. I have lots of interference. For example, I knew that Paul was having trouble mastering Spanish in school. I also knew that he wasn't putting in the time or effort needed to get an acceptable grade. I nagged him to bring his Spanish book home, and to ask for extra help from the teacher if he thought he needed it.

One day, Paul came home from school with a printed form titled "pass-no-credit." It said, in part: "This option (pass-no-credit) may encourage students to explore interests in a subject in which they may not be willing to risk getting a low grade." It looked like an escape hatch for students who weren't putting in the effort needed to get a passing grade.

Paul pleaded with me, "Dad, please sign this. I'm not doing well in Spanish, and if I fail, my grade point average will drop. If you sign this," he continued, "it doesn't matter if I fail. I'll just get a no-credit on my report card."

I refer to school policies like pass-no-fail as interference with my lessons of perseverance, because they coddle kids. They spoil students by catering to their whims, not encouraging them to call upon all their resources. I told Paul, "I've been warning you to do more work in Spanish. You're wrong if you think I'm going to allow the school to give you a free ticket out of Spanish just because you haven't put in the time and effort to get a good grade." I made my intentions quite clear. "I'm not signing this ridiculous form, and you'd better get it through your head that either you get an acceptable grade in Spanish or you'll be spending the next semester at home after school doing homework." Paul angrily grabbed the form from my hand, picked up his backpack, and headed to his bedroom. Two weeks later Paul burst through the kitchen door after school wearing a big, wide smile. "Dad! Guess what? I have a B-minus for my mid-term grade in Spanish." I enthusiastically shook Paul's hand and congratulated him for a job well done. "That's really great, Paul," I told him. "You stuck with the job instead of giving up. You found success instead of failure. Way to go! I'm proud of you."

That evening, I heard Paul on the phone tell a friend in a disparaging manner about a mutual friend of theirs who "took the easy way out by handing in a pass-no-credit in Spanish." Paul's hard work and success, due to his perseverance, gave him pride in his accomplishment.

Coddling policies at school, such as the pass-no-credit policy, interfere with the lessons about perseverance that I try to teach at home. It seems to be getting worse every year.

On January 19, 1996 most of the schools in Minnesota, including Minneapolis and St. Paul school districts, closed due to "dangerously cold conditions." I was furious. When I called the superintendent at 8 a.m. to complain about "weather wimps" calling off school, the sky was blue, there was no wind, and my outside temperature gauge read minus 12 degrees, Fahrenheit.

We're talking about January in Minnesota, where it's not unusual for the temperature to drop to minus 20 or more on consecutive days. In fact, on that same date back in 1970, a record low of minus 34 was set. Yet all the schools remained open. Students, teachers, parents, and bus drivers toughed it out.

Why is it different today? One of the reasons offered by school officials is the demand of parents. The day I complained to the superintendent, I was told that the last time we had a stretch of cold weather he received several phone calls from irate parents who complained that the schools remained open in spite of the cold. The superintendent said, "One mother told me, 'how dare you risk the life of my child.' That's what I'm up against," he concluded. It's that coddling attitude taking over.

I know of parents who insist on providing a taxi service for their children. I've been angered by those parents when they've driven my boys home from various events after I told my boys that I wanted them to walk home. Coddling softens kids. I want my boys to be strong, to learn to make their own plans for work, play, and entertainment without involving me. I want them to be able to effectively cope with frustration, and I think that a walk home in a cold drizzle or below zero temperatures, while bundled in appropriate clothing, helps to accomplish that. An accommodating parent who's too quick to come to the rescue when conditions are less than comfortable, works against my efforts.

Many of the women whom I've dated since my divorce had children of their own, and, on occasion, my boys and I went on outings

TACKLING SINGLE PARENTING

with them. My kids usually picked up on whether the woman's kids were spoiled. "Dad, you wouldn't believe it," my sons reported back after several hours at the home of one. "Everytime Chad wanted something, he called for his mom. When he wanted her to bring down snacks to us, he told her to hurry up. When he told her to rent a movie for us, he got really mad about the one she selected. He's really a brat, and the mom does everything he wants."

American kids aren't the only ones being coddled these days. Here's what China is doing to help correct their problem. China has established the Chinese Young Pioneers, a youth organization for 7-14-year-olds. It has become the new trend in summer camps for spoiled Chinese city kids who come from one-child families who need to be taught to fend for themselves.

Far from their coddled lives at home, the kids sleep elbow to elbow on straw mats, sweat through muggy hikes, wash their own clothes by hand, cook meals from scratch, clean their dorm rooms, and regularly work with impoverished farm families.

Young Pioneer officials who run the summer camps say that the camps focus on training children to be strong physically and mentally.

Teaching my children to persevere by effectively coping with frustration, and learning to complete a task despite opposition, has helped them to become strong physically and mentally. That strength has helped keep them from becoming spoiled. I taught those lessons to my boys since they were toddlers. When they were finished playing with their toys, I insisted that they help me pick them up and put them away. When we were done, I'd say, "There, all done. Good work." If one of them didn't feel like helping me pick up the toys, I nonetheless insisted that he help. He couldn't avoid responsibility by running to his room and ignoring my pleas. By means of effective discipline techniques: ANTICIPATION, PERSUASION, and PUNISHMENT*, he would finally do his part.

I used the same process with their bedrooms. As my boys grew to the age of about seven, it was their job to keep their rooms clean without my help. Sometimes, however, the chore was too challenging for the kids, so I chipped in. We sorted crayons and games, and put

---

* Referred to earlier in Chapter Six

things in their proper places. By lending a hand, I kept them from getting discouraged with an often overwhelming job. Finally, after staying with it, the room was cleaned, and I let my sons know they had done an excellent job by telling them and giving them a much deserved hug. An occasional reward of cake and ice cream didn't hurt, either.

As my sons grew older, I encouraged them to accomplish other types of work that taught them to cope with frustration and persist until a job was finished. I remember the New Years Day when my boys and I joined a group of other single-parent families. J.J. was nine years old. The sky was blue and the foot of new snow on the ground made conditions ideal for snowmobiling.

My 1970 Polaris Charger is a rare model that Sears sold for only one year before dropping out of the snowmobile business. I had kept it in immaculate condition and was proud of it.

During the course of the day, I gave the youngsters rides and let the adults take it out on their own. Late in the afternoon, I asked where J.J. was. Someone told me an adult had given J.J. permission to give a friend a ride on the snowmobile. I was frantic, and angry. "J.J. isn't supposed to drive the snowmobile by himself, much less give someone else a ride." Somebody said they spotted the kids and the snowmobile about 300 yards across a cornfield, at the edge of a row of trees. They weren't moving.

As I ran through the snow, I was concerned that the kids might be hurt. My second concern was J.J. disobeying a standing order not to drive the machine alone. My third concern was that my beautiful, cherished snowmobile might be smashed.

As I neared them, it became evident that my third fear had materialized. The kids weren't hurt but they looked plenty scared. J.J. explained that they had attempted to make a turn toward the house, but started to get bogged down in deep snow. When they accelerated they lost control and smashed head-on into a tree. The chrome bumper was mangled, as well as the fiberglass hood covering the engine. It was a mess.

I was so angry I could hardly talk. I said, "J.J. you must know how I feel about this. I want you and your friend to apologize to me for wrecking my machine and start walking back. You and I will talk about this later." I was able to get the machine running again, and I nursed it back to the yard.

On the way home I told J.J. how I felt, and listed the many reasons why he shouldn't have been driving the machine. When we got home, I spanked him and sent him to his room. The next morning, I drew up a plan to make this lesson memorable. We were going to fix the snowmobile together.

For the next several weeks we straightened out the bumper, re-chromed it, and repaired the hood with new fiberglass. J.J. spent many hours sanding the fiberglass until it was smooth, and ready for paint. He didn't complain once. I think he realized he was getting off easy and, besides that, he was enjoying the fruits of his labor. I was proud of the way he stuck with the job until it was finished. He had learned a valuable lesson in perseverance. Paul had his day, too.

For many kids, one of the most intimidating and frustrating chores to tackle is repairing a flat bicycle tire. Especially if it's the back tire on a bike that has lots of gears.

When Paul worked at the grocery store, he relied on his bike for transportation. One day, he got off work early, only to be discouraged by a tire that had gone flat. I told him, "It's up to you to fix the tire, not me, and I'm not going to drive you back and forth to work, either." The next morning he jumped right in.

Repairing a flat tire can be a challenge for anybody because it's a messy job that most people never master since they don't do it very often. You have to use the right sized wrenches, slip the chain off so that you remember how to put it back on, take the wheel off the frame, and then the tire off the wheel. I told Paul to run up to the store and buy a 89¢ tube repair kit and "be sure to follow the directions closely, or the patch won't hold."

A couple of hours later, Paul had found the leak, repaired the tire, and put the wheel back on the bike. I was very proud of him. The next day, the tire was flat again.

Paul was angry and determined to simply buy a new inner tube. I told him that was unacceptable. "You need to take your time, pay attention to the directions on the patch kit, and do the job properly." A couple of hours later, the bike was standing upright again, and Paul was gleaming with pride. The next day the tire was flat again.

"What's going on?" Paul shrieked. I suggested that the problem might be coming from somewhere else. "Maybe something is causing your tire to go flat. Why don't you take the wheel to the repair shop to get their advice?"

Once again, Paul got out the wrenches and proceeded to solve the problem. When he returned from the repair shop he reported, "The guy at the shop told me that the inside wheel band needed to be replaced because the spokes kept puncturing the tube. He also suggested that I tighten up the spokes." This time Paul's repair job held. He had gotten past the anger, his frustration, and persevered until the job was done right. He was really proud. "Let me tell you, Dad," he boasted, "I could fix a flat on that bike blindfolded." Paul felt accomplished, and deservedly so. He had exercised perseverance by finishing what he had started, in spite of agonizing frustration. It had become another lesson in accomplishment that raised Paul's level of excellence.

Maintain Your Focus

My boys can undoubtedly recall the many times I shouted directions from the sidelines while coaching their sports teams. My most common directive was "Focus!" I used the word to remind players to bring the game into their center of interest, being alert to the situation at hand. It makes no difference whether the situation involves school, home, work, or play. When one's focus is blurred, their performance suffers. When my kids are alert, their focus is sharp, and their level of excellence rises.

Before Paul's adolescence, I could tell when he was overly tired and needed to get to bed early. He'd become emotional, and cry easily. The slightest disturbance would set him off—a friend not calling, feeling like he got a raw deal at school, making a bad play during a sports game, or simply having to stay home after supper, after he had played all day. He would lose his focus, become irrational, and cry. The sure cure for him was a good night's sleep. The next morning he would be back to his bright, alert self, ready for action. I tell my boys that getting plenty of rest is a main ingredient for anyone who needs to be alert so that they're able to focus on their center of interest.

There are other ways I help my boys stay sharp and keep their focus. I teach them about the negative effects of tobacco, alcohol, and illegal drugs. I help them get plenty of exercise, encourage them to drink lots of water as health experts advise and stick to a sound diet.

All through my kids schooling I've insisted that they eat a full breakfast, consisting of cereal, fruit, and toast. They don't always pay attention, and sometimes skip out with only half a breakfast under their belts. For the most part, though, they go to school without being hungry, ready to dig into the day.

Many school kids begin their day with not much more than a donut, if anything at all. To compensate for that meager breakfast, some school districts have instituted a mid-morning snack time to help the elementary kids "fuel up" so they can make it to lunch.

I wasn't aware of snack time at the schools until J.J. was in eighth grade. I was thumbing through some of his old scrap books and came to a printed form requesting that parents send a snack to school with the kids each day. "Hey, J.J.! I called from the living room. Why didn't you let me know about snack time? I would've packed a treat for you."

"That's okay," he answered, "I was never hungry at snack time."

"It's probably because you usually had a full breakfast," I gloated; he agreed.

Proper hygiene doesn't come without training, and that training helps my kids maintain their focus. I tell them, "Looking good and smelling good, makes a fella feel good." During the early elementary grades I reminded my kids to put on clean socks and underwear every day. I taught them to brush their teeth properly, to trim their finger and toe nails, and to wash their hands and face with warm water and soap. As they grew older, I reminded them when they needed to use a deodorant. I bought Paul his first razor and shaving cream at 15. He didn't have much more than peach fuzz, but I told him that it looked shabby and needed to be shaved. The self-confidence that comes with proper hygiene definitely helps a person raise his level of excellence.

Last, but certainly not least, is the need for prayer. It helps us maintain our focus about what really matters in life. I've emphasized the value of prayer since my children were old enough to grasp the message. Prayer helps us pause to reflect on our priorities, to catch our breath and to maintain momentum in our daily struggles. It has much the same effect as stopping along the way to enjoy the fragrance of a flower. It can be relaxing, as well as inspiring.

In Conclusion

Dr. Jack Westman, a child psychiatrist and professor at the University of Wisconsin, has written a book to promote the idea of government regulating parenthood through licensing. Westman says he witnesses the results of incompetent parenting on a daily basis. "One of the things that I'm trying to move away from," says Westman, "is the notion that the child is the possession of the parents, that the child is owned by the parents as chattel. We're looking then at parenthood as a responsibility, really as an opportunity and a privilege."

People who oppose the idea, like Michael Warder, the executive vice president of Rockford Institute, a conservative think tank, argue, "The idea that a government agency would determine who is qualified to be a parent is one of the most repugnant ideas that I can imagine."

I agree with Warder in that we don't need parental licensing. Nevertheless, one can't ignore the rising tide of children who develop anti-social life styles, a disproportionate number of whom are children of single parents.

The good news is that single parent families are not doomed to failure simply because of their single parent status. John Richters, the Assistant Chief of The Child and Adolescent Disorders Research Branch at the National Institute of Mental Health in Washington, D.C., and co-author of the "stable and safe" versus "unstable and unsafe" study on families mentioned earlier, had some encouraging words. "Many families don't have a choice about being a single parent family. It happens, and in spite of environmentally challenging situations, they not only survive, but do well." Richter continued, "Human beings are one of the most adaptable species on this planet. Normal operating perspectives are all that's necessary in order for parents to cope with desperate circumstances."

A large part of my family's success is due to striving for a higher level of excellence. I try to accomplish that by teaching my sons The Seven Qualities of a Champion. They learn POWER and BALANCE through information and experience. By developing people skills, my boys learn FLEXIBILITY, and by adhering to ethical values, or, standing tall, they learn POSTURE. Punctuality promotes TIMING, perseverance rewards them with ENDURANCE, and maintaining focus creates QUICKNESS.

Those lessons in excellence have worked well to help my sons learn to be happy and successful in life, just as they have helped me tackle the pursuit of effective and productive single parenting.

Time To Eat

I Made The Decision Not To Sentence My Kids To A Life Of Junk Food

The evening that I left my teenagers home alone to entertain friends after the homecoming game, hoping that it would help satisfy their quest for independence, I went to a dance. While there, I made the rounds, had a beer, and danced several numbers. I was visiting with some people, when a woman approached me, "Hi Steve, remember me?" I drew a blank. "I'm Katherine. You and I dated a couple of times a few years ago." After a moment, I recognized her, but she looked much different. Still, her straightforward manner—which I found appealing—came shining through. "It took you a while to recognize me underneath all this fat. It's a result of work and more work and plenty of junk food. I never cook at home anymore, I just eat junk food, and look at me. It's disgusting."

Katherine's problem is a common one. In this rush-rush world of overtime, pressure cooker schedules, and dozens of daily deadlines, many people choose not to cook when they get home. They, like Katherine, find that ready-to-eat junk food or eating out is more convenient after a hard day on the job. The negative results are apparent—just listen to Katherine: "I'm about 40 pounds overweight, I have high cholesterol, I look and feel like hell."

One of the first parenting decisions I made soon after my divorce was not to sentence my kids to a life of pizza, canned meals, macaroni and cheese, and take-out food. Surprisingly, though, many people commonly believe that those are staple items on a single dad's weekly menu. That's what I discovered when a newspaper journalist asked me some questions about single parenting. When the topic of food came up, she said, "I think it's great that you're taking care of your kids full-time. Who cares if they live on milk shakes, cereal and pizza? At least they have the benefit of a man's presence."

Her naiveté was unexpected. I told her, "From my observations and experiences, my children eat healthier meals than the children of most single moms I know. As a matter of fact," I continued, "I've heard from many women that it's not unusual for men to discover a new interest in cooking after being divorced." I am one of those men.

I didn't cook many meals when I was married. I was good for backyard barbecues and an occasional ranch-style breakfast of eggs, bacon, and hash browns, but Joyce took charge of most of the meals and the grocery shopping. After the divorce I learned to shop, cook, and feed my family out of necessity and from a desire to do a good job. I'm not a dietitian, nutritionist, or accomplished chef. Nevertheless, my kids love my cooking, all three of us are healthy, in good shape, and I'm able to keep my grocery shopping expenses within a strict budget. I'm proud of those accomplishments, but the job isn't over. It's an on-going struggle to find solutions to the difficulties of keeping my family well fed. Grocery shopping, meal preparation, and eating are a significant part of effectively tackling single parenting.

Shopping For Groceries

Shopping for groceries with young children can be a frequent test of your patience. When the kids were young I had no choice but to take them shopping with me. It mostly went well due to my utilizing discipline techniques such as ANTICIPATION, PERSUASION, and PUNISHMENT.★

I exercised ANTICIPATION with my kids when we went shopping by telling them the rules before we even entered the store. I exercised PERSUASION by encouraging their active participation: pushing the cart, gathering food items, and bagging. They enjoyed helping. When they didn't follow the rules, and if my repeated warnings didn't work, then I resorted to PUNISHMENT to gain their cooperation."

★Discussed Earlier in Chapter Six

We've had some funny times grocery shopping, and I must admit to once or twice being guilty of encouraging my boys to join me in mischief. Like throwing a head of lettuce to Paul while he's on a flare-out pattern across the produce section. Or yelling to my kids from the dairy section, while standing in a group of women who were inspecting eggs, "Hey fellas, this carton has 13 in it."

Other times I would pick through the bananas, standing next to other shoppers, then jump back and shout: "Did you see that?" Nearby shoppers would quizzically respond with wide open eyes: "What?" Then, in a calm and innocent tone of voice I'd ask: "What do they call those big, black, furry spiders from South America that are found among bananas?" The feedback was usually hilarious. Quite predictable to my boys who were used to watching the action unfold.

One of our most memorable grocery store pranks happened when I was shopping for morning glory seeds from a rack next to the produce section. A pushy woman grabbed the rack away from me and rummaged through the packets. I asked her what she was looking for as my boys watched. "Morning glories," was her abrupt answer. I told her, "Me too! I use them to attract hummingbirds." That piqued her interest. "Oh, is that right?" She enthusiastically asked. "Yes," I answered. "They're such gorgeous little creatures," she said. "Yes indeed," I agreed. "And they taste good," I assured her. "What?" She shockingly blurted. I told her, "Every morning when the flowers are wide open the little hummingbirds gather to suck out the nectar. I sneak up from behind the trellis armed with a fly-swatter and then I swat them one by one. Later I fry 'em up and eat 'em with French fries. They taste terrific.

"God, that's sickening," the woman said, and she marched off to another aisle. My kids were bursting with laughter.

Those antics aren't funny to everyone. Many people probably find them rude and childish. However, they make sense for us, if you look closely. The wackiness helps me find some pleasure in what is otherwise a tedious, time consuming, and costly necessity. It goes back to the philosophy that "With each passing day, I'm as happy as I set my mind to be." Most people dread going grocery shopping. I try to look at the bright side of shopping by appreciating the huge selection, the packed shelves, and the relatively low prices of high quality food items, compared to many other parts of the world. It's easy to treat grocery shopping as a drudgery. It can just as easily be looked at as a privilege.

When I go grocery shopping, I usually focus on finding my groceries and getting out as quickly as possible. That's why I was horrified when my cozy little local grocery store quadrupled its floor space and turned into a mega-warehouse, literally overnight. I couldn't find anything anymore. I was intimidated by the enormity of the place, and I was mad at the owners for ruining my shopping comfort zone. How dare they?

The boys and I hung in there, and made an effort to learn the new floor plan. In no time, it seemed like the same old place again. Knowing the store's layout helps to expedite my shopping. I can usually go from one end of the store to the other, picking up everything on my list, without needing to return to an aisle. It also speeds up shopping if I organize my shopping list by category. I list fruits and vegetables first, and end with frozen goods and bakery items. I put the heavy items on the bottom of the cart, and the squashables on top. I save dairy and frozen goods for last, to help keep them cold until I get home.

Meal Preparation

One of the first survival tools that I bought after I became a single parent was a cookbook. I wanted a book with basic recipes—nothing too fancy. I found what I needed in Better Homes and Gardens. On the inside cover I wrote this inscription to commemorate the occasion: "To Steve Horner, a great guy on a new adventure in cooking. Best Regards, your best friend, Steve." It was dated April 11, 1984.

I value my cookbook because the recipes are easy to read and offers familiar meals. My book lists weights and measures, defines terms in easy-to-understand language, lists alternate ingredients in case I need to improvise, and provides a nutritional analysis for each recipe. I like how it's made. The cover is plastic-coated, so it cleans easily with a damp rag, and it's bound so that it lays flat, handy for frequently checking an unfamiliar recipe.

A cookbook, like any other instruction manual, takes time, patience, and energy to master. Just making a tuna-noodle casserole was a challenge for me at first. I wasn't sure how to chop the vegetables, or how long they took to cook "until tender," as the recipe prescribed. With each step I had to refer to the book for assurance that I was following the steps in order, and including all the ingredients. I felt awkward and unsure of myself with this new challenge. I labored over each measurement to make it precise. Nothing came easy or as second nature.

After several weeks and a half dozen new recipes I became more comfortable preparing meals. My cooking dexterity improved, I handled a chopping knife with more agility, and my measuring became more confident and went faster. I even began to experiment with different ingredients to suit my family's taste. It was a memorable experience to take that first, bold, unaccompanied pilgrimage away from my trusty cookbook and into the world of innovative cooking. I felt comfortable in adding a little more of this or that, and a little bit less of this or that, to suit our taste, without botching the meal.

I reached another milestone in my new adventure when I learned about the importance of timing in cooking. Now, my motto in the kitchen is: "Timing is everything."

For example, the burgers need to be done at the same time as the French fries. The mashed potatoes need to be done at the same time as the turkey. The rice has to be done at the same time as the pork chops, and the garlic bread has to be hot and ready to serve with the spaghetti.

Timing is also important in knowing when to start a meal so that food can be served at a prescribed time. Serving at a prescribed time came to be more important to my family as the boys got older. They needed to know when supper was going to be ready so they could plan for other activities.

Timing allows me to serve my meals hot, properly prepared, and at a prescribed time. Learning timing was a matter of trial and error, learning how long each item took to prepare. Trial and error taught me another valuable lesson—it pays to be a good kitchen manager.

Kitchen management begins with keeping my work space free of clutter. If I'm making spaghetti sauce, and using several pots and pans, I clean each pan as I go; at least I'll rinse it out and set it aside, out of the way, while I continue. I know cooks who specialize in creating fabulous meals, but when they're done, the kitchen is a disaster area.

TACKLING SINGLE PARENTING

Cleaning while I go not only helps keep a clutter-free work area, but it also reduces the work load for when supper is over.

Good kitchen management requires keeping the pots and pans, dishes, and eating utensils in their proper places for easy access. I keep my knives sharp, so they work well when I need them, by using the grinding wheel built into the back of my 20-year-old electric can opener. It still works great after all these years.

Another important element of efficient kitchen management is safety. I tell my boys to cut away from your body when using knives. Don't cut too fast, and keep your mind on what you're doing when handling knives. Also, I try to concentrate on what I'm doing when I handle large trays of food, such as turkey, and when handling hot trays, dishes, and pans. Common kitchen accidents, like cut fingers, burned hands, spilled food, and broken dishes can be kept to a minimum if I focus on what I'm doing; it's one of the primary lessons in kitchen management that I try to follow, and teach my sons.

Making the most of meal preparation time is another crucial element of kitchen management for busy single parents. Cooking provides an opportunity to wash a couple of loads of clothes, because each chore has periods of time that I call "wait time": when there's not much you can do to help the process along. So, just before I start dinner, I can start the laundry. While the meal cooks, I can put the clothes in the dryer. Later, I can fold them and put 'em away. When the boys were younger, cooking time was also a good bath time for them as long as they were old enough to bathe safely without constant supervision. Even then, I looked in on them regularly. It's part of making the most of your time, and, for dedicated single parents, time is a scarce commodity.

Planning Ahead

A big advantage in having a home office is that there's not much wait time. If my business duties are finished for a while, there are always plenty of domestic chores to do—laundry, mowing the lawn, shopping for groceries, or starting early on supper. If my supper plans are for roast, I'm able to set the frozen meat out in the morning to thaw, and pop it into the oven at about three o'clock. Many single parents don't have the luxury of being home to start supper early, so they make other plans. They plan ahead by taking the frozen roast from the freezer and place it in the lower compartment to thaw gradually. Then, in a day or two, they season the roast and use a slow-cooker, setting it on low and letting it cook all day. It's a great aroma to come home to, and eating a home-cooked supper is just minutes away at day's end, with virtually no hassle.

An important factor with my successful home cooking has been planning ahead. I rely on a menu of maybe a dozen different main courses. When I'm shopping, I make mental notes of the meals I want to serve during the next week. Planning meals requires cross-checking my menu with my family's activity schedule. If I know that the week ahead will be action-packed with commitments, I want to have food on hand that will allow me to whip up some quick, tasty, and nutritious meals.

One way to meet meal preparation challenges of a super busy week is by cooking a large casserole or turkey on Sunday afternoon, when you've got more time. Then you can rely on quick-heated leftovers throughout the week.

After developing a routine, I discovered that I actually enjoy making big meals for my family. The preparation time gives me time to unwind. I find it relaxing as I busy myself with recipe hunting, chopping, dicing, patting, and mixing. It takes my mind off the worries of the day. While cooking, I'll fix myself a cup of coffee and flip on the TV to catch a game or listen to music. Cooking can be a soothing, peaceful time in which I can enjoy my own company, especially if the kids are out of the way. When they were younger, I did my big weekly cooking while they took naps. As they got older, I was usually able to keep them busy with a project, or they played with friends outdoors.

I mentioned earlier that my sons have referred to me as the Caveman. It's because I don't have many modern appliances or gadgets, and that includes a microwave oven. A women with whom I do charitable work has warned me for the last couple of years that sooner or later I'd have to buy one. She's wrong. I get along nicely without a microwave. It takes only 15 minutes to warm food in a conventional oven, and most meals on my weekly menu can be prepared from start to finish in 45 minutes or less. So what's the problem?

TACKLING SINGLE PARENTING

When I serve turkey with all the trimmings on Sunday, the boys and I have plenty of leftovers so we can enjoy a duplicate meal on Monday. On Tuesday, we can have turkey sandwiches, leftover stuffing, and a can of soup. On Wednesday, we can cut up some hunks of turkey, stir it into an easy-to-make cheese sauce, and lay it over a bed of rice. Most people toss out what's left of the turkey at this point—not us. Turkey frame soup is one of our favorite meals. I simmer what's left of the turkey in a dutch oven with three quarts of water, a little salt, and a couple quartered onions. I later discard the bones and add a variety of vegetables, cooking them until tender. The last item I add is the noodles. It's a great meal served with hot garlic bread, and we always have enough for leftovers.

Taking the time to plan meals in advance helps me keep quality meals on the table at the same time helping to reduce the stress in my life. Following a game plan helps me avoid last minute meal preparation chaos, and we have almost eliminated all food waste at our home, helping us to stay within our strict food budget.

Our meals could be classified in three ways. The "freshly cooked meals" are those we prepare and enjoy the same day. "Leftovers" are what we eat the first night or two after a freshly cooked meal. Finally, the third meal classification is "pick-ups," comprised of leftovers from several recent, freshly cooked meals. It takes a little creativity and lots of management to plan and serve pick-ups before the food from the assorted re-sealable containers spoil. The last food that I had to toss out during the past six months was a half-used package of bacon that I neglected to freeze the week we were eating turkey. It had spoiled by the time I got back to it Saturday morning.

What's On The Menu?

When I was 10 years old, I had a neighborhood friend, Bill. Bill was normal in all respects except one—he ate only peanut butter sandwiches. Bill ate peanut butter sandwiches for breakfast, for lunch, and for supper. It's not that he had food allergies, it's just that his parents rarely encouraged him to eat anything else.

One summer afternoon my mom invited Bill and me in for a snack. Bill thought we were going to have peanut butter sandwiches, but he was wrong. We had cold milk and lemon meringue pie waiting for us on the kitchen table. Bill was nervous. "Mrs. Horner," he begged, "I would rather have a peanut butter sandwich, please." My mother was urging Bill to try the pie when a couple of my older brothers came into the room. When they found out that Bill wasn't willing to eat the pie, they started making fun of him. Bill bowed to the pressure. He took a bite, gagged, and ran to the bathroom to vomit. My mother had a peanut butter sandwich waiting for him when he came back to the kitchen.

There was a time in Paul's life when he tended to be a fussy eater, like Bill. I wouldn't allow it. When I noticed that Paul wasn't eating his potatoes, I knew I had to take a stand. Items like potatoes needed to be staple items in our weekly diet. They're nutritious, filling, and inexpensive. I pay about $2 for an eight pound bag, and that goes a long way toward feeding us. With potatoes, I can fry up a pan of American fries, or cut several potatoes into eighths, add seasoning, and lay them on a greased tray in a 400° oven for about 40 minutes to make French fries. I can quarter a half dozen of them, add a variety of other vegetables, pile them into a dutch oven, add a half cup of water, and cook at 375° for about an hour. Served with sour cream, butter, salt and pepper, it makes a delicious accompaniment to fish, or to any kind of meat. The same goes for a big bowl of mashed potatoes and gravy, or scalloped potatoes.

I needed to have Paul enjoy spuds.

I started my strategy by asking Paul about the type of potatoes that he liked best. I listed the options, and he responded, "French fries are my favorite." For awhile I served a lot of homemade French fries. Then, I tried to expand our potato menu to include mashed potatoes. When I served a meal of mashed potatoes and a slice of ham, I got sour looks from both the boys. Paul's dislike of potatoes was rubbing off on J.J. I came up with a solution.

It was all a matter of image.

"I want to tell you boys an important story," I said with a serious tone of voice. "There once was a famous king who was well-loved by everyone in his kingdom. His name was King Tuscaloosa-alabama (how's that for coming up with a great, spur of the moment name?). I then made up a crazy, far-fetched story about how everyone in the kingdom lived fine, happy, healthy lives until a long drought dried up all the crops and made people very hungry." I had the boys' attention, so I continued.

"The king knew that he had to take action to save the lives of all the people in the kingdom. He decided he must get on his horse and search for the golden staff which, as legend stated, would make rain fall so the earth could once again produce food."

My story took the king through all sorts of perils and close calls with dangerous animals and nasty villains. Through it all, the king captured the golden staff that had been hidden in the bedroom closet of an evil witch by a midget sorcerer.

As the story neared the end, I told the boys, "The king held the golden staff high as he proudly rode through the open gates of the wall that surrounded the kingdom. All the people cheered loudly for the king. Suddenly, the sound of thunder boomed and the precious rain fell from the sky to nourish the ground with life-giving moisture. The crops appeared overnight because the rain was magical. A large feast of celebration was planned by the king."

"When all the people of the kingdom were seated at huge picnic tables with King Tuscaloosa-alabama at the head of the biggest table, the meal was served. Dozens of the king's royal chefs brought cart after cart of the celebration meal to the people so they could eat as much as they wanted."

Then I told the boys, "The meal that I've served you tonight is the same meal that the king and his people enjoyed during their special celebration. This is the Meal of Kings, I declared. "And those aren't any old potatoes, those are King Spuds." There was no time wasted. The boys dug right in and ate everything on their plates.

The technique of creating an exciting image of the meal you've prepared has as many versions as your imagination can devise. With a clever story your meal can become: The Meal of Sports Heroes or of Adventurers, Inventors, or Wizards. It helped me persuade my boys to enjoy potatoes, tuna, rice, beans, pasta and other foods for which many kids need to acquire a taste. By the time my young boys caught on and realized that my stories were a scheme to encourage them to eat, they had acquired a taste for my cooking. The stories worked.

Here are some of the foods that a visitor might experience if he lived with us for a month. Breakfasts are usually dry cereal with milk and sugar, fruit and toast. When I do my shopping, I'll buy a medium sized box of sugar sweetened cereal for the boys, but that goes quickly. Then they eat Raisin Bran, Shredded Wheat, Cheerios, Wheaties, Grape-Nuts, or whatever else I bought.

Some mornings I'll make oatmeal, and on weekends it's not unusual to have pancakes, or eggs, bacon, and hash browns.

I don't keep many snacks around the house, other than cookies that I buy from the bakery. I don't bake much. Occasionally, I'll buy potato chips that go so well with sandwiches and pickles during the summer months, or for lunches during the school year. The three of us also crave root beer floats from time-to-time. My boys have grown to love a snack that my mother instituted when she helped us out with child care. She would slice up several carrot sticks and celery stalks, place them in a jar of water, and put it in the refrigerator. They taste great and are cold, crisp, and refreshing on a hot summer day. My kids love 'em. Another idea is to spread peanut butter on a celery stalk. Also, plenty of fresh fruit on hand like apples, oranges, grapes, cherries or bananas work well as snacks. Raisins are another popular snack suggestion. During the summer, we get fresh raspberries from our garden. All three of us love sunflower seeds, and an occasional candy bar.

Summertime meal specialties include potato salad, cold meat trays for making subs, or a bowl of tuna salad that can be used for sandwiches or piled high on a bed of lettuce served with buttered toast and milk. Fresh sweet corn and string beans from the local garden stand are other summer delectables that we enjoy.

Grilled cheese sandwiches are one of our year-round favorites. I butter both sides of the top piece of bread, and the bottom of the other slice. I lay American or medium cheddar cheese between the bread slices, cover, and cook on low until browned, and then flip. Bacon, lettuce and tomato sandwiches served with mayonnaise are another favorite. Hamburgers and tacos also work well for us. Many people might shy away from some of those menu items, fearing the high grease content. I drain the grease and store it in glass jars. When a friend of mine, Kay, saw all the jars of grease under the sink she said scornfully, "All that grease is bad for your health." I clarified the practice for her: "That's the grease we *don't* eat." Then I told her how I dispose of it. "After I accumulate several jars full of grease, I haul them out to the corner of the backyard, dig a hole, spoon the grease out from the jars, and bury it." It couldn't be any more harmful to the ground than a dead animal decomposing. Later, I rinse out the jars and recycle them."

Chicken is another one of our favorites. I usually buy whole chickens and cut them up, instead of buying them pre-cut. I was happy to find that my cookbook had easy to follow cutting instructions, because whole chickens are a lot cheaper. The same holds true for other foods, like vegetables and cheese. Shredded cheddar is $2.20 a pound, while bulk cheese is only 81¢ a pound. That's a big savings in exchange for a little time and effort.

Fried eggs with a slice of turkey ham, or alone with mayonnaise on toast, make delicious sandwiches that my boys love, and coupled with soup or canned corn, is one of many meals that's easy for them to cook by themselves. Homemade chili with cheese slices and buttered toast is another one of our specialties that makes a tasty and healthy meal that also provides leftovers for later in the week.

My kids started enjoying fried fish with French fries ever since I began referring to them as "fish 'n chips." Once again, the image is important. I usually buy pollock or cod because it's only about $2.50 a pound, and has a good taste. Compare that price to walleye that can run as high as $9 a pound, even here in Minnesota, known for walleye-rich lakes. When I saw the exorbitant price on walleye, I asked the meat man if there was a pearl hidden in each one. "There doesn't need to be," he answered, "I sell out even at that price."

"Not to me you won't," I replied.

When my kids fry eggs, American fries or leftovers, I remind them to lay a pat of butter in the skillet and then add enough vegetable oil to lightly coat the bottom, adding taste while allowing the food to cook without burning. I also remind them to keep monitoring the heat. "The object is to cook your food all the way through without burning it."

I earlier suggested menu items such as chicken, pork chops, and fish. There's a seasoning recipe I use when cooking these foods. It adds a taste that my kids love.

Crack an egg or two into a bowl and add a splash of milk. Stir the mixture with a fork until it's smooth, pour it on to a large deep plate or tray, and soak the meat or fish in it. Transfer the food to a dry plate and lightly salt and pepper. Use one of the plastic bread bags that you're re-cycling and pour in about a half cup of flour, then add a tablespoon of garlic powder, a tablespoon of chili powder, and mix. Put the meat or fish in the bag with the seasoning and shake until every piece is lightly coated. Now set the whole bag on a plate and place it in the refrigerator until you're ready to cook. To cook it, lay the pieces of meat or fish on a lightly greased pan and bake at 375° until done. Meat and fish should be turned only once. Fish cooks much quicker than meat because it's less dense, and when done should be white on the inside and easily flaked with a fork. The meat should be cooked throughout, and is best tested by cutting into a piece. Well-cooked chicken and pork will be white, with no signs of pink. Be sure to check your cookbook for exact cooking times and temperatures.

Almost all of our suppers are accompanied by a vegetable salad. My boys have become expert salad makers. Their salads begin with fresh lettuce, and they add whatever we have in the refrigerator. That could be two or three of any of the following: carrots, celery, cucumbers, radishes, broccoli, cauliflower, or tomatoes. Our favorite salad dressings are Italian and ranch style. Another option is to mix equal parts of mayonnaise and ketchup to make a delicious thousand island dressing.

When time, energy, and patience are limited, I rely on my "Great American" meals. They're hot dogs, brats, pizza, canned stew, canned chili, frozen pot pies, fish sticks and a few others. They're fattening and expensive, but they're quick and tasty, and the boys like them. Nevertheless, convenience always comes at a price.

I rationalize my occasional use of Great American meals with the same philosophy that I apply to the rest of my cooking—moderation. Sour cream and butter on potatoes is fattening, and would probably be a poor choice for healthy nutrition if we ate it every night—but we don't. I rotate meals. If we have meat twice in a row, then I cook fish or make cheese sandwiches. If I serve a high fat, Great American meal one night, I counter it with a low fat, home-cooked meal the next night. I think the philosophy of moderation not only keeps a tasty zing into my meal line-up, but helps keep us healthy as well.

The challenge of regular grocery shopping, meal planning, and cooking is a formidable one for single parents. Nevertheless, the practice of eating is a human necessity that goes hand-in-hand with the need to spend money and expend effort: I might as well try to enjoy it and make the most of it. Abraham Lincoln said it best: "I hold that if the Almighty had ever made a set of people that should do all the eating and none of the work, He would have made them with mouths only and no hands; and if He had ever made another class that He intended should do all the work and no eating, He would have made them with hands only, and no mouths."

There is no free lunch.

Where's Your Level of Happiness?

The Best Things In Life Are Free, Aren't They?

What makes you happy? I remember giggling to myself as I got down on my hands and knees, clutching my tape recorder, and slowly crawling towards J.J.'s bedroom. I was hoping to capture the moment on tape without disrupting his gleeful and carefree singing and humming as he packed his suitcase for his Arizona trip to see his mom. I've had a lot of fun being a parent.

I have happy memories of Paul's excitement and pride after he got the game-winning hit during extra innings, and all his teammates cheered and patted him on the back. Those are happy moments that both of us will always remember.

Many things have given me great joy. When I was a child I remember thinking how fantastic life would be if I could have a Superman outfit for Christmas. My mother surprised me by making one for me, and for weeks I was the luckiest kid in the world as I was able to "fly" through the house faster than a speeding bullet. Then my life changed.

I got a job at the horse ranch where I could ride horses every week-end and all summer long.

For a kid who loved horses as much as I did—I couldn't have been happier. And then my life changed.

When I was 17, I couldn't wait to get a car. I thought, "a car will give me independence, elevate my social status, and it will certainly help me do well with the girls." My 1956 Ford was a nine-year-old beater, but that didn't matter to me. Being behind the wheel on my

TACKLING SINGLE PARENTING

maiden outing was one of the most satisfying moments of my young life. That car was my pride and joy. I loved to wash and polish it, and show it off at the drive-in restaurants. Shortly thereafter, I was drafted into the Army, and my life changed again.

J.J. once asked me, "Dad, when were you the most frightened in your whole life?" I told him about the time I was in Vietnam when for three days and nights we fought a heavily fortified battalion of North Vietnamese Regulars in the middle of thick jungle underbrush. At one point, I was laying facedown, while all around me, leaves and branches were shattering from machine gun fire. I needed to be so low to the ground that I unfastened my pistol belt to gain another half inch. I told J.J., "That's how close those bullets came to ripping into me." Then he asked, "When were you the happiest?"

"When the shooting stopped and I hadn't been hit," I answered. That thought still rejuvenates me—I'm glad to be alive.

There have been times of great cheer. I remember stepping out of the shower, getting ready to go to the church to marry Joyce. I caught myself singing out loud as I wiped the steam off the bathroom mirror. I looked at my reflection and thought, "I'm about as happy as a man can possibly be."

There have been many people, things, and events that have given me happiness and satisfaction in my life. Unfortunately, not the least of those things was money. When I got out of the Army, I attended college and worked part time at a variety of jobs. Usually I was broke. For several weeks I had been irritable, dejected, and downright miserable. Suddenly, the glumness did a turnabout. In the mail that memorable Saturday afternoon was a letter from the United States Army, containing a check for $300, owed to me for back pay. The money made a new man out of me. I instantly became friendly with people, excited about life, and happy as could be. Then it occurred to me that my entire level of happiness hinged on a stinking $300—how pathetic.

Beware Of Chicken Little

We all know that lots of money can't buy happiness, right? Why is it, then, that we often tie the two together? Several years after my divorce I had lunch with a group of six business executives. I suggested to them that winning the lottery might infuse a new set of problems into one's life, and wouldn't necessarily bring long term happiness. I was amazed at their response. The whole group, to a person, disagreed. One of them answered my claim, while the others nodded in agreement: "Winning the lottery wouldn't guarantee happiness, but it would sure make living miserably a lot more tolerable."

Chevrolet TV ads imply that money is of the utmost importance to parenting by saying that: "Being a parent means getting the most for your money." To me, being a parent means a lot of things, but getting the most for my money is not on my top ten list of important items—contrary to what Chevrolet would like me to believe.

I'd like to know who started the philosophy of equating successful parenting with the amount of money you have. Many days you can pick up a newspaper and see a distorted story like the one written by St. Paul Pioneer Press writers Nancy Livingston and Linda Owen: "Students at East Consolidated Elementary School on St. Paul's East Side sometimes come to school hungry and cold, and they return home to family lives steeped in the uncertainty that poverty can bring." The article went on to link poverty with low student performance.

Mike Meyers, the national economics correspondent for the Minneapolis Star Tribune, is another notorious doomsday alarmist. He wrote a long, fawning report which ran in conjunction with the 1995 World Conference on Women that was held in China. It was titled: "World's women facing bleak economic reality: Work, life still aren't fair.

Meyers opened his bogus story with: "Women are stuck in a pernicious cycle of poverty," then he fueled his assumptions with scattered pieces of prickly kindling that has been strewn about by other Chicken Littles who cry: "The sky is falling." This "kindling" includes: "Two-thirds of the work done by women is unpaid—caring for children, keeping house, running errands; while only a third of a man's work is unpaid." Meyers quoted the Congressional Budget Office to show that the incomes of women age 27 to 33 have reached 98 percent of the incomes of men. "The catch," cautions Meyers, "the figure applies only to women who have not had children."

"The implication seems clear," claims Meyers, "Women who don't interrupt their education or career to raise children have a shot at being as well off as men in the economic arena. Those who do, risk being left behind. Millions of other women, meanwhile, have no hope. They are teenage mothers who were never married." Meyers' conclusion to all this kindling? "Women + children = poverty."

That last line was the clincher. How could this newspaper employee be so sure of himself about parenting issues? It was such a rash statement: "Women + children = poverty." I had to call Meyers to find out how a financial analyst became an expert on the difficulties of raising children.

"No, I'm not a single parent," was Meyers' answer to my first question, but I've seen the statistics."

That's like a response from the armchair quarterback who has never played a game of football, who would tell the Minnesota Vikings how to improve their winning percentage. When asked by the coach, "How do you know what works and what doesn't?" The prima donna says, matter of factly, "I've seen the statistics." That doesn't help, bub—get lost!

Why do people like Mike Meyers write such disheartening stories? Do they purposely play the role of dissenter to provoke controversy? Are they misinformed about the issues? Do they try to suck up to women as a means of being accepted in an inner circle of fellowship? Are they politically correct kiss-asses trying to hang onto their jobs? What did Meyers mean when he wrote, "Those who do (take time out to raise children) risk being left behind?" To many hard-working single parents, that could be construed as an ominous warning that places the blame for their lack of wealth unfairly on their children.

The men and women who are like Mike Meyers have a message of discontent and hopelessness; they make tackling single parenting more challenging than it already is. They create a losing environment, instead of a winning one. The Meyers message is contrary to the can-do philosophy that helps people hurdle obstacles. If I had raised my kids on that message of hopelessness, that's exactly where we would be today—hopeless.

When did raising children become a money-making proposition for dedicated single parents? Both goals of raising children and making money require time, patience, and energy, and for single parents there's only so much to go around. That's why raising children and making money are conflicting goals for most of us single parents. Baseball Hall of Famer, Harmon Killebrew, told me a story about conflicting goals while we were working on the production of a TV spot. "We had a neighbor when we were kids who used to get angry at my father for allowing us boys to play ball on the yard. My dad would defend his rules by saying, "I'm raising boys here, not grass."

Yet, the Chicken Littles of this world keep fanning the flames of discontent. "Having a baby is the most economically irrational thing you can do," said Shirley Burggraf, an economist at Florida A&M University, in January, 1996 at the annual conference of the American Economic Association in San Francisco. In a paper presented at the conference, Burggraf concluded that financial hardship that's tied to caring for a family is linked to sliding birth rates, a climbing divorce rate, deadbeat parents, and child abandonment and abuse.

It's no wonder that many parents aren't satisfied as parents—they're told by people like Burggraf to appraise their children as debits rather than assets. Both Meyers and Burggraf call on the government to "fix the problem" of raising children by spending more money.

Will more government spending buy happiness for dedicated single parents and their children? The answer might lie in the following excerpt of *The Decline and Fall of the Athenian Republic* written by Alexander Fraser Tyler (1748-1813).

A democracy cannot exist as a permanent form of government. It can only exist until the voters discover that they can vote themselves money from the public treasury. From that moment on the majority always votes for the candidates promising the most benefits from the Public Treasury with the result that a democracy always collapses over loose fiscal policy followed by dictatorship. The average age of the world's greatest civilizations has been 200 years. These nations have progressed through the following sequence:

From bondage to spiritual faith
From spiritual faith to great courage
From courage to liberty
From abundance to selfishness

TACKLING SINGLE PARENTING

From selfishness to complacency
From apathy to dependency
From dependency to back into bondage

I tell my children that if we keep electing government officials on the basis of how much they'll spend on our self-serving needs, then dependency on government will grow until we've slipped back into bondage.

Government spending causes taxes to go up, which causes parents to work longer and harder to make up for the extra tax burden while they must continue to pay their ever-increasing, day-to-day personal living expenses. If the demand for government spending continues to rise, so will the tax burden and the amount of work necessary from each taxpayer to pay the rising debt. At what point will the increasing work load become involuntary servitude? That's what "bondage" means.

As we continue our drift toward bondage, the time that parents and children can spend together drops. In 1965, parents spent about 30 hours a week with their children. By 1995, it was less than half of that. And that's bad news, because, as the National Institute of Mental Health discovered in their 1993 study on families, "At the bottom of our social woes is trouble in the family."*

Slowly, the truth seems to be sinking in that the social suffering in our incredibly prosperous country has little to do with poverty. Roxy Foster, the executive director of the Minnesota Parenting Association, told me in a phone interview, "This country doesn't focus itself around our kids, it focuses itself around economics." That's a major problem for which Foster offers a solution: "We shouldn't value how well we're doing with our children by the material things we're able to provide for them and ourselves; rather, the character we're building and instilling in ourselves and our children. Unfortunately," she concluded, "society doesn't have us pointing in that direction these days."

I tell my sons, "It's up to people like you and me to help point society in the direction we want it to go. Be shepherds, not sheep. Shepherds are leaders and counselors who are selfless, dedicated and

---

*Refer to Responsibility Chapter

involved." I caution them, "We need to counteract sheep like Mike Meyers and Shirley Burggraf who are ever eager to articulate the short-sighted, self-serving needs of a few members of the flock who meander with the wind. The shepherds are doing what they can to slow up the demand for government spending, because they know that's a step towards strengthening families and maintaining their independence, a step away from bondage. The sheep, on the other hand, are being led aimlessly into blind ravines where many will unwittingly get caught in crevices and end up as lunch for the hungry wolves.

Anyone who has been a single parent knows that single parenting is not a "get rich quick proposition." And, in many cases, being a single parent means living with extremely limited funds, but let's face the facts: we're not talking about a mid-nineteenth century, third-world, abandoned underclass who have been left to rot in filthy city slums, giving birth to children who have no comfort or security, and whose only real hope lay in a life of crime. I'm talking about contemporary America where enough social programs are in place to give the vast majority an opportunity to succeed and be happy.

It doesn't matter if the parent is collecting AFDC or has $50 million. How much money is required to make certain that a child has a bowl of cereal, toast, a piece of fruit and is sent to school with hope, smiles, and a kiss? How much money is required for the child to be greeted at the door after school, by the parent or care provider, with cookies and milk, and then told to take an hour to read a book or some other constructive activity? If the parent lacks the desire, all the government money in the world won't make that child successful and happy.

If the schools, state governments, and teacher unions aren't willing to toughen up, enforce rules, and restore basic skills learning to the curriculum, then all the government money in the world won't educate children. If the desire is missing, nothing will happen. When the desire to make it happen is there, enough proof exists that poverty has very little to do with achieving excellence.

Minneapolis school officials reported in March, 1996 that Ericsson Elementary, a K-2 school, made the largest gains in reading test scores in the Minneapolis district during the past three years. Their average reading scores soared from the 25th to the 56th percentile, well above the national norm of the 50th percentile. The school also has above average math scores.

Ericsson has a high poverty level. Of about 450 students, 70 percent qualify for free or reduced price lunches. Ericsson's low scores were addressed several years ago by changing the teaching methods to focus on basic skills in reading. The most effective change appears to be the daily 55-minute period devoted to reading.

Debra Leigh, executive director of the Minnesota Minority Education Partnership said, "When student achievement is low, it's not just a reflection of the student or their family income, but the teachers, what they're teaching and how they're teaching it." When parents, teachers, and other policy makers are shepherds, the children will be shepherds, the Chicken Littles will be ignored, and our quest for liberty and happiness will be strengthened.

Where The Action Is

I jogged up the final hill, slipping and sliding on the early spring mud as I approached Horsehead Tree. It's a name I've given to the giant old oak tree that marks the finish line on my daily run through the woods. I so-named the tree because the top of the trunk has been splintered, probably by lightning, and it resembles the head of a wild, snorting stallion, reared back on its hind legs, thrashing at the air with its outstretched branches. I did some calisthenics and then walked the half mile back to my car to cool down.

Near the end of the soccer field I heard a loud, adult voice from the swing and slide area on the other side of a row of trees. There was an unrestrained silliness in the voice that I felt would embarrass the person had it been known that another adult was listening. I heard spontaneous expressions of all-out joy: "Wheeeee! Yahoo," punctuated with enthusiastic outbursts of laughter. I couldn't wait to see what was going on.

When I got around the trees I saw the merrymaker. He was a 30-something, rather paunchy, bearded man playing on the slide with his young son. Both of them were totally engrossed in their fun and never glanced my way as I continued on.

I was happy for the man and his child. I remembered the times that I spent laughing and playing with my kids at different parks over the years. In almost 25 years of business, I never heard anybody, including myself, laugh with such zeal while receiving a paycheck.

Most single parents have to spend lots of time, working hard, to earn a living. Their reward comes from a feeling of accomplishment and a certain security that comes with bringing home a paycheck. Many a celebration party has been hosted to recognize increased financial success. Drinks and lively conversation are followed by a scrumptious meal; toasts are made to the occasion as the guest of honor enjoys the praise. When the hour of glory is over, everybody goes home, and the next day, everyone returns to the routine. The world of making money is like that—dedicated single parenting isn't. The rewards of parenting are more fulfilling, and are longer lasting.

Watching Paul bring the house down with laughter while he played a female nurse in his high school play made me laugh so hard that I had tears rolling down my cheeks. I'll never forget the time when J.J. came running in the house and said, "Dad, hurry, come outside! I want you to see me do a heel flip on my skateboard." I'm glad I was there to help my kids on to the school bus for their first trip to kindergarten, to watch their first, successful solo bicycle ride after numerous tip-overs, and to inspire them to bring the D in math up to a B.

Special events like birthday parties and sleepovers that involved several kids were plenty challenging. Yet many of them were equally rewarding when my boys and their guests expressed their genuine thanks for a great time. And, as in business, I enjoy the personal satisfaction of those successes, knowing that my planning, organization, and effort have paid off.

The pay-offs make the big difference. I remember one wintry Saturday afternoon when J.J. was grounded. After he did his chores I invited him to join me on some errands. Afterwards, we stopped for an ice cream cone at a place where some of J.J.'s teenage friends had gathered. J.J. walked over to greet them and I followed. One of the boys, Joey, told us, "We were just talking about you, J.J., and how responsible you're going to be as an adult." He was referring to my style of discipline and to J.J.'s grounding. I told his young friend, "I think you're kidding us."

TACKLING SINGLE PARENTING

"No I'm not!" He said, "I'm serious."

Later, J.J. assured me that Joey had indeed been sincere. I was flattered that those words came from one of J.J.'s peers as he sat among his buddies—it was as gratifying as anything I'd ever heard directed at me. Jim Croce said it in *I Got a Name:* "If it gets me nowhere, I go there proud."

There have been an untold number of parents who've never fully experienced the thrills of parenting. Many have spent their time focusing on building, expanding, devouring, risking, spending, and altering. They have spent their parenting years looking for action elsewhere, away from their families.

"A lot of parents are much too busy for their own good," I was told by Reverend Jerry McAfee of the New Salem Baptist Church in North Minneapolis, and former chairman of the National Baptist Convention on Violence. We met for a discussion on social issues at the City Inc. School in Minneapolis, an alternative learning institute for inner city youth and their families. Referring to children of all colors and from families of all income levels, McAfee cautioned, "It's the children who are paying the price."

"Many parents busy themselves with other things and don't play a big enough role in the lives of their children," McAfee said. "Their kids are raised in front of a TV set without any positive parental role models. They see murder, sleazy sex, con jobs, corruption and multi-million dollar athletes. The kids learn a false value system. They end up feeling unloved and insignificant. As a result we have gangs, drugs and crime. And sooner or later, no matter where you live, whether it's in the middle of the city or deep in the suburbs, you will be affected with higher taxes, crime inflicted on you and your family, or the breakdown of your own family. We need to get with it and change our attitudes on raising children."

McAfee said, "Parents need to instill moral values in their children." He was referring to things more precious than money, things like wisdom, knowledge, decency, and pride.

Earning less money and spending more time with the family is an age-old concept, even though, it's still not a popular one. It means fewer goods manufactured, less damage to the natural environment, tighter knit families who place little value on electronic gadgetry and outside entertainment. It's a value system based on simplicity and self-denial over comfort, convenience, and leisure. It's how the Amish have been living since their seventeenth century ancestors founded the group.

We have quite a few Amish in Minnesota. One Sunday afternoon in April, when Paul and J.J. were seven and ten, the three of us, along with Kathy, a friend of ours, took a drive through Southeastern Minnesota. The area is known for its towering river bluffs, eagles, quaint small town life, and its Amish population.

On the way, I told Kathy that I was fascinated by the Amish and their way of life, but I didn't know much about them. My boys overheard and said that they were curious to see what the Amish looked like. Canton, Minnesota, a thriving Amish community, was just a few miles ahead.

Main street Canton was closed for Sunday. I turned south, out of town, into farm country and told everyone to be on the lookout for telltale signs of Amish: horse and tire tracks on the gravel shoulders.

As soon as we passed the first crossroad Paul yelled, "I see 'em."

"Sure enough," I said, "That's what we're looking for." We passed the next three crossroads and kept seeing more sets of tracks. As we approached the fourth crossroad we saw all the tracks lead up to a large, stately farm house on a tree covered hill.

I drove by, stopped, and then backed up to get a better look. I continued on, thinking that we shouldn't be snooping. Once more I stopped and backed up. By this time we had attracted a group of curiosity seekers. More than a dozen Amish children stood looking at us from the top of the driveway which lead to the farm yard. Each of them, from the three-year-olds to the teenagers, were dressed alike with white shirts or blouses, black pants or dresses, and straight rimmed, black hats, or bonnets. The scene glowed with that certain, innocent Americana of Norman Rockwell. It was so striking that I wanted an oil painting of it on my living room wall.

The occasion, we discovered later, was a going-away-party for neighbors who were moving back to Pennsylvania. Friends and well-wishers had gathered from all over the county. I told Kathy, "We're here. There's no sense in denying that we're all curious about their lifestyle. I'd love to visit with them. The worse they can do is to ask us to leave." I saw cautious nods of agreement in response so I made a U-turn on the road, and turned into the driveway.

The Amish children parted to both sides of the driveway as we slowly drove between them. They looked at us not with contempt, but rather, with awe. "I'll go up to the house and ask if the boys can see their horses. That doesn't sound too much like snooping." I stopped the car, got out, and greeted the children who by now had circled the car. I walked up to the front door of the house to speak to the adults. This left Kathy, Paul and J.J. looking wide-eyed at the Amish children, who in return were looking wide-eyed back at them.

I stepped onto a sprawling porch and knocked on the screen door—all that separated me from the living room. Inside, the adults were sitting around, engaged in a lively conversation with lots of laughter. I didn't know what was cooking for supper but it sure smelled good.

Just then, a large, bearded man, dressed in the same fashion as the children, appeared from around the main door. He had a pleasant smile and was getting his coat on as he walked out onto the porch.

I introduced myself, and it must've been his inviting manner, but I skipped right over the part about the horses. I told him, "We're from the Twin Cities, out enjoying a Sunday drive and, to tell you the truth, we're curious about the Amish lifestyle. However, I can see that you're having company so we'll move on." He looked over towards the car. Kathy and J.J. had gotten out and were talking to several of the kids. Several others had invited Paul to join them for a game out on the yard. "What do you want to know?" He asked me as he stepped off the porch and walked towards the horses and buggies.

I motioned for Kathy and J.J. to join us and introduced them to the man, who, as we later discovered, operated the farm with his family. He helped J.J. pet the nose of one of the horses while some of the little girls flirted with J.J. by calling his name from inside the barn and peeking out at him. We thought it was cute. J.J. thought they were teasing him. I told him to take it as a compliment.

A couple other men came out, as did a few women, who were carrying coats for the children to wear in the cool spring air. The adults were pleasant toward us, even though we had intruded on their party. The men rolled cigarettes and they answered my questions about their views on society, government, families, religion, education and farming.

The Amish believe that people need one another more than they need machines, and that many modern conveniences separate people rather than draw them together. A machine that allows one person to do a job that used to require several people may save time, but it prevents a sense of community from developing. Theirs was a community based on values of trust, understanding, love, acceptance, and support, rather than on the value of having a lot of money.

The men concurred: "Crops were good last year, our health and that of our families is good, we have lots of friends, and our children are happy. What else do we need? We're living the Great American Dream."

We didn't want to overstay our welcome, so, after half an hour, Kathy and I thanked them for their hospitality, gathered Paul and J.J., and got back into the car. As we drove away, all the Amish kids, from the smallest to the biggest, stood at the top of the driveway waving good-bye to us—another Norman Rockwell classic.

The Amish believe that establishing and maintaining a strong family community is where the action really is. Not everyone, however, shares that sentiment; many people believe that they're entitled to a lot more.

The Age Of Entitlement

A couple of years after our visit with the Amish, I was in downtown Minneapolis when I saw a mass anti-nuclear power protest staged by apparent anti-establishment anarchists. They chanted anti-government slogans, and many were dressed in skull and crossbone garb to represent their idea of the perils of nuclear power.

I walked by, dressed in a conservative business suit, when one of the protesters who was decked out in leather, chains, ear and nose rings, rebellious insignias, grim, white-chalked face, brightly colored hair and a threatening look about him, called me a capitalistic pig. I stopped and attempted to enlighten him. "For nuclear power to go away, along with all other natural-resource devouring energy sources, we'll all have to reduce our demand for electricity. If you use electricity," I told him, "you're part of the problem."

TACKLING SINGLE PARENTING

He became madder than ever; "Oh yeah, man. Then I get screwed out of the American Dream; Right?" What American Dream was he referring to? It certainly wasn't the Amish version.

The American Dream to which the young protester referred is based on an entitlement mentality. It's as if he filed a claim on "the good life," but now feels threatened that somebody might deny him his rightful ownership. Entitlement is the subject of Robert J. Samuelson's, "The Good Life and Its Discontents: The American Dream in the Age of Entitlement."

Samuelson states that in the early postwar decades, we advanced effortlessly toward this perfect society. Then the process slowed, followed by five recessions, unemployment, inflation, down-sizing, family breakdown, and high crime. Superficially, the problems seemed rooted in slower economic growth—money. There had grown to be too much reliance on government hand-out programs, from corporate welfare and farm subsidies, to food stamps and college grants. On the whole, too much was expected of prosperity to cure social ills. And, even though the theory that more money is needed to help families do well and stay together is finally being scrutinized, the entitlement mentality has taken hold and remains alive and well in America.

Samuelson says in his book, "We are caught between the promises and expectations of the past and the insistent social and economic conditions of the present." The expectations of overpromising has systematically generated a distrust in society that in turn has generated similar reactions of resentment, anger, and confusion that it causes in a family. The results are clearly seen in the hostility of the nuclear power protestor, as well as in many other examples. An inner-city youth felt entitled to kill a man to steal his designer shoes with the rationale that, "If he was able to have nice shoes, then so should I." A woman accidentally spilled hot coffee on her lap at a McDonald's and felt entitled to file a multi-million dollar lawsuit against the restaurant. Armed forces veterans feel entitled to monetary compensation, not for wounds received in battle, but for taking time out of their lives to serve their country. Groups of people feel entitled to affirmative action privileges because of the unfair oppression their peoples endured decades, even hundreds of years earlier. Custodial parents feel entitled to increased child support whenever the income of their ex-spouses rise. Cara Boudreaux of

Texas City, Texas, told Dear Abby that she felt entitled to a little respect for being the mother of two children: "I resent the lack of respect I am shown. I respect those who choose to work outside the home and feel that I deserve the same." Abby agreed with her.

Two-pack-a-day cigarette smokers feel entitled to sue tobacco companies for lung damage. Millions of senior citizens living in commercial retirement homes feel entitled to roll their life's earnings over to their children so they can bilk Medicaid for living expenses. Television advertisers chant, "You deserve something better" or "Do it for yourself because you deserve it." Those ad campaigns play to the insatiable demands of the many Americans who have adopted the attitude of entitlement as a way of life. Just think how ridiculous those American TV ads must appear to people of impoverished countries, like Nicaragua or Somalia: "Those Americans deserve more?"

The attitude towards entitlement that I try to profess to my children is one that my friend Joe and I remind each other of every time we get together. After a few laughs, a couple of beers, and when parting company, I'll say, "And don't forget, Joe." His response, "The world doesn't owe you shit." Right on!

Rise Up And Be Great

People who move to Minnesota for its warm weather are soon disappointed. We're much better known for our cold than for our heat. So when we have a stretch of clear skies and warm temps, Minnesotans love to take advantage of it by flocking to the lakes, the walkways, the ball fields and their backyards. We enjoyed a similar stretch of weather when I made my way to the hospital about noon one early summer Sunday.

I parked my car, jogged up to the front door of the hospital, walked in, bought a magazine, and took the elevator up to the oncology department. I got off the elevator and walked toward the admissions desk when I saw my long time friend, Steve, dressed in pajamas and a robe, slowly and carefully walk out of his room with an I.V. pole at his side. He didn't see me, nor did he know I was coming to visit.

"Poor guy looks skinny as a rail," I thought to myself. We had known each other since high school. Shortly after he turned 21 he was

TACKLING SINGLE PARENTING

diagnosed with Hodgkin's disease, and battled it for the next 26 years. Whenever the disease came out of remission he would spend months in treatment, until he got it back under control. Then he would continue to lead his life for another several years until it was treatment time again.

During this stay Steve was not being hospitalized for typical treatment. He had been diagnosed with pancreatic cancer, a much more lethal illness than Hodgkin's. He gingerly walked toward me. I opened up the magazine, put it in front of my face and stepped over to the side of the hallway directly in his path.

As he walked by, I pulled the magazine down from my face momentarily and non-chalantly said, "Hi Steve," and then quickly raised the magazine again. It was as if this was standard procedure, bumping into each other, on an upper floor of an inner-city hospital on a Sunday afternoon. He couldn't keep a straight face. Normally he could play along when we pulled this kind of silliness on each other, but this time he was feeling pretty beat up. I'm glad I was able to make him laugh.

"It's good to see you, Steve" he said, choking back tears. "What's the matter, buddy?" I asked. "Looks like you're crying."

"I am," he admitted. "This morning I was able to keep my juice and Rice Krispies down."

Can you believe it? Here was a man who had two different killer cancers ravaging his body, tubes stuck up his nose, was so weak he could hardly talk, was missing out on one hell of a nice summer afternoon, and yet, he was overwhelmed with happiness because he didn't throw-up after his puny breakfast. I joined him as he resumed his walking exercise through the hallway.

I wonder if Steve ever gave his juice and Rice Krispies much thought before that day. I wonder if he would have believed that juice and Rice Krispies would have been the source of so much joy in his life. Steve died a year later.

"The Rice Krispies caper," a term in which Steve would certainly have found humor, caused me to pause later that day to reflect on how much we take for granted as we go from one day to another in this life. What's really important, and what isn't? What are the priorities?

John, a sales representative for a major Twin Cities radio station, had been helping me put together an on-air advertising proposal for one of my clients. Suddenly and unexpectedly, I stopped hearing from him. He was nowhere to be seen or heard from. After several days I was frantic because of the approaching deadline. Finally, he called. I said, "Where the hell have you been?" He jumped right back at me, "Listen Horner. I've had a death in the family and I want you to know that none of this shit we've been working on means anything. It's totally insignificant to the things that really matter in life." John was 100 percent correct.

John, and many other people who lost a loved one that day, learned a valuable lesson about priorities: "You can replace a person with whom you make money practically overnight, but a member of your family will never be replaced." That's why I tell my sons that we need to always appreciate each other because there's no telling when tragedy will strike. I try to remind them of the many other things that make life so spectacular.

"Just remember to keep the blinders off," I tell them, "so that you can appreciate the beauty of what's going on around you." Just think how fascinating it is that Earth revolves around a star, known as the sun, along with eight other major planets with their three dozen satellites, as well as hundreds of thousands of asteroids and swarms of meteors, all of which comprise our solar system, located halfway from the center of our galaxy, The Milky Way. Galaxies are so vast that they contain hundreds of billions of stars, hundreds, even millions of light years apart. Millions of galaxies like the Milky Way, each with an untold number of solar systems, make up the universe which is so immense that its limits are unknown.

Of course, we don't have to look up into space to explore the mystery of creation. Fascinating mysteries and miracles continuously happen all around us here on Earth. Seasons change, weather patterns recur, seeds germinate, flowers pollinate, volcanoes erupt, and babies are born.

Tom, an acquaintance of ours, is a student of theology. He told us about his travels through the Middle East. During one stop he sat in on a class on Judaism held in a small, open-air building, with desert heat blowing through. Several times during the narrative, the speaker paused for a sip of water to moisten his lips. Before each sip the instructor said a silent prayer of thanks. He recognized the value of cool water in the desert climate. Tom concluded that more of us should be conscious of the good things we have been given on this earth.

As we go through life I try to impress upon my boys the value of those good things. "Let's appreciate the good things, and not wait until a catastrophe takes them away before we appreciate their worth. Let's try to stay aware of the good things before we need that eye-opening face slap of reality."

I hope that type of grassroots level of happiness will make life more enjoyable for my boys—I know that it has for me. It's not always an easy attitude to come by, for it requires sacrifice. I've heard from dozens of single parents, "I go to work when it's dark and come back home when it's dark. When do I have time for the good things? Where's the time to spend with my children?" I respond that I could easily be walking the same path. I could work for a huge corporation with demanding bosses and long hours. I chose a different route. I could expand my business by hiring dozens of employees who would bring in more business, requiring a pool of secretaries to manage the paperwork, which would increase my costs, requiring that I make even more money, and ultimately spend more time away from my kids. I have chosen not to go that route. I believe that the more you have in excess, the more you need. The less you need, the less you lack. It's a philosophy about materialism and happiness that's worked for me throughout my single parenting years.

I could've chosen to be a heavy drinker and drug user after my divorce. I could've invited hordes of people to my home every weekend to party. I could've ruined my health, gone into debt and worst of all, destroyed my relationship with my children. I chose not to go that route.

I've persevered with a desire and determination that arose from the three main reasons I had children to begin with. They're the same three reasons I explained to the judge during the child custody hearing in 1984:

1. *My children are an extension of myself, I don't ever want to lose them.*

2. *I knew that my children could learn from me, just as I would learn from them.*

3. *I felt that I would be derelict of duty if I didn't raise my children to the best of my ability.*

Like anything else worthwhile, parenting is tough work, and single parenting is tougher yet. It has its ups and downs. I love the ups, while the downs are a challenge. It's like the swing curves of business, or professional sports. Twins star, Kirby Puckett, loves to hit homers, make fantastic fielding plays, and receive his paycheck. He might have felt differently about the game as he lay on the ground during the last home game of the 1995 season with blood gushing from his face after being hit by a Dennis Martinez fastball. Kirby rebounded. The following March, he was back hitting home runs with a .345 spring training batting average. Unfortunately, the day before the regular season opener, he awoke with only half his sight. Kirby told reporters, "I'm not going to let it get me down. There're a lot of people worse off than me. I'll do okay." A couple of weeks later his blurred vision was diagnosed as an early stage of glaucoma, totally unrelated to his injury at the plate the previous year. Still, Kirby remained up-beat: "Don't worry about me. I'll be all right."

Kirby Puckett is an example of success far beyond the millions he makes playing baseball. The dictionary definition of success says nothing about money. Kirby is a success because of his desire, determination, perseverance, and dedication to baseball. He's effective and productive, through the ups and downs. Money is only one of the results. It's those ethics, not money, that make Kirby Puckett, and millions of other successful men and women, great at what they specialize in.

One person who thoroughly clings to that ethic is my business friend, Ernie. He loves his job, is proud of his product and of the service he gives his customers. He's at work every morning at 6 a.m., ready to tackle the challenges of the day. Ernie has acknowledged that there are certain mental techniques he uses to stay strong and to keep moving forward.

"A couple of years ago I thought I just about had it," he told me over lunch. "The internal and external pressures of business were getting me down. I was becoming frustrated and angry. I had lost my enthusiasm, things just weren't fun anymore."

TACKLING SINGLE PARENTING

"Finally, after attending a couple of self-help seminars, and reading the prescribed literature, I was able to come to a successful conclusion—I was the source of my problems." Ernie discovered that most of his problems were self-imposed, a common hang-up for millions of people.

"I allowed the same, old negative tapes to keep running," he went on. "Those old tapes in my head kept telling me that I can't do that, It's not possible, I'm not good enough."

Ernie, himself, was the barrier to his own success. "I had to get out of my own way," he told me. "I changed the tapes to say that "I've got the power over what I'm thinking. I'm strong, and in control. I'm not seeking perfection, I'm seeking improvement. When I began to get rid of the negatives I found myself in a positive mode which became freewheeling."

As a dedicated single parent, I sometimes find myself muddling in those negative tapes. I get wrapped up in those tapes when I've temporarily lost focus of my priorities, when my desire has weakened, when I've felt entitled to more rewards, when I assign value where it doesn't belong, and when my positive attitude crumbles. Sometimes those negative tapes are as constraining as if I'm behind bars.

It's then that I have to be strong, stay in control, and not let myself impose a barrier to my own success. That's when I need to rise up and be great with my single parenting efforts.

Pierre Proudhon, a mid-nineteenth century French libertarian who was probably the most influential force on French working-class radicalism in modern history, developed the theory that the liberation of the workers from the grips of the government must be their own task:

"The great are only great because we are on our knees."

Isn't that similar to dedicated single parenting?

Let us rise.

Where Did My Little Babies Go?

I have a family portrait of the three of us hanging on my bedroom wall. It was taken when J.J. and Paul were about four and seven. Many times, especially when the boys are in Arizona visiting Joyce, I'll study that picture and wonder, "Where did those little babies go?" They were here just a moment ago, asking if they could sleep in my bed, cuddle up with me under a blanket as we watched TV, or asking me to help them put their socks on. I see them waving good-bye and throwing me kisses until out of view, walking to school. Where did those little boys go? The ones who needed me to pour milk for them, who couldn't wait for me to read a bedtime story, and who were overjoyed to spend a full day at the park with me?

Where have they gone? They were here just a moment ago.

Time went by so fast. Did I spend enough time with my children or did I spend too much time stressed out? Did I appreciate enough of our moments together, or did I wish them to hurry up and pass? Did I tell my boys that I loved them often enough? Am I sure now that they know how much I love them, and appreciate them?

When I'm by myself, I often catch myself looking at how other parents spend time with their children. If they appear happy and content, I'll wonder if that's how we appeared to others. When I see parents publicly scold their children, and lose patience with them, I'll wonder if that's the way we appeared to others.

Sometimes I wish I had another chance at raising my children.

There are so many things I would do differently. Maybe that's just how life is. We only get one chance with most things. Experience is the teacher and it has taught me that dedicated single parenting is a difficult challenge. I'm sure I could do it ten times over and it would never get easier. But, maybe I'd learn to value each moment more.

I'm lucky that my boys are still here. These are the days that in five years I'll look back and say; "Where did my teenagers go? I miss them."

The time is now.

Where Wass Ya?

On November 4, 1995, Israeli Prime Minister Yitzhak Rabin was assassinated. A couple of days later, his widow, Leah Rabin, spoke to the thousands who gathered to mark the end of the traditional mourning period for the slain prime minister. "Where wass ya?" She cried out to the crowd in an admonishing tone. In her broken English, she referred

TACKLING SINGLE PARENTING

to the groups of people whom she blamed for Rabin's murder by inciting so much hatred. Yet, there they were, feigning sorrow for his death. "Where wass ya?" She yelled, "when Yitzhak fought against the enemies of peace, but was denounced in public? Where wass ya? They are coming to your grave to cover you with flowers, Yitzhak," she said, "where before they let you fight alone. Now they will hear the voice that is sane, and the silent majority will no longer be silent."

Someday, as time flies by, I'll be called upon to face the final judgment. I'll be asked to explain my efforts during my child-rearing days, answering a question not unlike that from Leah Rabin: "Where wass ya?"

My ultimate goal is to be able to stand tall with pride and honor, while I describe each and every account forthrightly. I want to be able to say, "I was in the front lines, where the action was, making progress and being successful."

My ultimate reward, then, will be at the gates of heaven, with God Almighty, the angels, martyrs, saints, and the rest of the faithful. I want to be there when that screen door to heaven slams and there stand my two boys, discarding their heavy, earthly chains, smiling and yelling to me, "Dad, Dad, We're home!"

Then I'll step out from the crowd to greet them and say—

"I'm right here boys. I'm glad you made it. Now, are you ready for that cake and ice cream I promised?"